Progressivism
in America

Arthur A. Ekirch, Jr.

PROGRESSIVISM

IN AMERICA

*A Study of the Era from
Theodore Roosevelt to
Woodrow Wilson*

NEW VIEWPOINTS · *New York* · *1974*
A Division of Franklin Watts, Inc.

Library of Congress Cataloging in Publication Data

Ekirch, Arthur Alphonse, 1915–
    Progressivism in America.

    Bibliography: p.
    1. Progressivism (United States politics)
2. United States—Politics and government—1901–1909.
3. United States—Politics and government—1909–1913.
4. United States—Politics and government—1913–1921.
I. Title.
E743.E29   1974   320.9′73′091   74-2455
ISBN 0-531-05359-8
ISBN 0-531-05564-7 (pbk.)

To
My STUDENTS *and* COLLEAGUES
in the
State University of New York
at Albany

Contents

Preface

AMERICAN Progressivism had roots deep in the past. As a broad movement for social and political change, Progressivism has also affected much of American history in more recent times. Conventionally regarded as an era of reform, the Progressive period from Theodore Roosevelt to Woodrow Wilson was indeed one of change and ferment. Those who considered themselves Progressives believed that the United States had to find a solution to the series of new problems confronting modern industrial society. As Progressives, many of the new leaders in American politics sympathized with mounting public protests against the established order. In the Progressive Era, accordingly, novel currents of thought as well as concrete programs of social and political reformation began to take hold of the American people. In contrast to other reform periods—the Jacksonian and New Deal eras, for example—Progressive goals were suffused with the strong moral overtones of an evangelistic, religious crusade. The idea of progress, long an article of popular belief in America, seemed to gain fresh support as historic national ideals were again translated into social and political action. At the same time, reformers' demands that democracy organize its forces to meet the challenge of the modern business corporation served to introduce a practical note in Progressive ideology. And, more than at any time since the achievement of American independence, the United States entered into the course of world affairs. European ideas and interests accordingly once more exercised a potent influence upon American thinking and action.

In the following study of American Progressivism, I have outlined similarities in the national affairs of America and Europe. Along with political and social reforms, I have given attention to the ways in which peace and war, foreign and military policies, formed an integral part of American life. A single book cannot do full justice to a movement so broad and diverse as American Progressivism. Thus my emphasis is upon the more important issues, the leading figures in social and political thought, and the major schools of interpretation. I hope, of course, that within those limits the following pages may prove useful to students interested in the interrelations of American political and intellectual history during the Progressive Era.

It is a pleasure to acknowledge help from various sources. A Faculty Fellowship from the State University of New York speeded the research and writing. Professor Arthur S. Link and my colleague Robert F. Wesser each read the manuscript and made a number of pertinent suggestions. Kevin Shanley, my graduate assistant for one year, collected materials and aided me in tracking down periodical files. Shirley Motyl and Kathleen Batting cheerfully assumed the chore of typing successive drafts of the manuscript.

PART

ONE

Introduction

Europe and America

THE Progressive Era, that transparently optimistic label that historians, almost uniformly, have fastened on the first decade and a half of the twentieth century, may also be considered the climax of the nineteenth century. In the United States, as in Europe, that century had come to be accepted as an age of progress. After hundreds of years of varying degrees of physical drudgery and enslavement, the human race had thrown off its chains. Hand in hand with technological and cultural advances went the growth of representative government and democracy. As perhaps never before in his history, man seemed close to governing, not only himself and his institutions, but also the natural world. One could easily conclude, therefore, that the still unlocked mysteries of the universe alone remained to be penetrated by man's scientific ingenuity and intelligence.

On the whole the experience of the United States held out the promise of continued high hopes for the future. No other modern nation, after all, had enjoyed a comparable rate of material expansion. With independence won and security largely assured by its remote geographic position, the new American nation had been able to extend its boundaries to the Pacific and to populate the most fertile and richest portion of the North American Continent. Despite the trauma of four years of a bitter Civil War, the national union had been preserved and democracy strengthened. At the same time, in spite of occasional periods of economic depression, America remained a land of opportunity and an asylum for the oppressed. Yet the millions of immigrants who sought American shores were also a constant reminder that the United States was not divorced from the mainstream of European or Western civilization. And so a century that began with American involvement in the French Revolutionary and Napoleonic conflicts found the United States confronted again after the Spanish–American War by the reality of imperialism and the threat of foreign and colonial struggles.

By the turn of the new century it was clear, at least to close students of public affairs, that the United States faced problems which it had formerly been able to dismiss as concerns solely of the Old World. For example, the announcement by the Census Bureau, following the 1890 returns, that there was no longer a discernible frontier to the West terminated a long period in which Americans had exploited almost at will the natural resources of their vast hinterland. Even if this kind of economic freedom had been more symbolic than real, still the close of the frontier, as interpreted by Frederick Jackson Turner and his disciples in the field of American history, stood as a challenge to the new Progressive generation. Economic tensions associated with the frontier's passing and the rise of an industrialized, urbanized society brought the United States nearer the point in history of the major Western European nations.

Although the course of events in Europe was somewhat less dramatic than the rapid progress of the United States during the nineteenth century, those years in the Old World had also witnessed striking changes. Achievements in science and industry made possible new material comforts and a higher standard of living for the mass of the population, even as compulsory education diminished illiteracy and widened popular intellectual horizons. By the close of the nineteenth century, most of the countries in Central and Western Europe had adopted, or were considering, some form of universal manhood suffrage, thus adding a political revolution to the industrial revolution and ensuring a new age of the common man.

For many European peoples the movement toward democracy and the expanded industrial economy of the nineteenth century became the precursors of an awakened sense of nationalism. National self-determination was frequently thwarted, however, by equally strong efforts on the part of existing nation–states to expand their boundaries and incorporate dissident minorities within their domain. Moreover, for England and Germany, like the United States and the American Negro, there were analogous problems of nationalism and democracy vis-à-vis the respective ethnic or minority groups of Catholic Irish and Jews.

Despite internal domestic tensions, modern integral nationalism, especially when linked with the rise of well-defined political states and the principle of the self-determination of peoples, engendered a strong sense of personal patriotism and of loyalty to a particular form of government. As nationalism in the twentieth century thus became an evermore accepted article of popular belief, it also entered into conflict with the limited role that a liberal society had traditionally assigned to the state. Nationalism and democracy, for example, both emphasized the collective social responsibilities of the political state. Significantly, too, the advance of democracy in the Western World diminished popular fears of strong government and heightened national feelings. Instead of the Jeffersonian ideal of "the least government the best government," Americans in the Progressive Era turned expectantly to political agencies as instruments of change and reform.

Almost everywhere in the Western World by the close of the nineteenth century, as faith in an older liberal individualism seemed to decline, there was an accompanying rise of confidence in man's collective ability to reorder his environment and reshape his destiny. And it was the modern national state to which man now looked for the answers to his social and economic as well as political needs. To the dedicated Progressives of the 1900's, progress, therefore, was less a philosophic creed or act of faith than a concrete reality that might be speeded by man's cooperation and determination. In the words of the youthful Walter Lippmann, looking back over the decade following the turn of the century, the Progressive Era marked the transition from drift to mastery.

For most Americans the years at the beginning of the new century, following the hard times of the 1880's and 1890's, were good years. Industrialism and the close of the frontier had already pushed the sectionalism of the Civil War into the past. By 1900 the country again stood at the threshold of a renewed era of material expansion. It had taken three centuries to people the vast transcontinental area of the United States. But the population, which stood at seventy-five million in 1900, quickly reached one hundred million by World War I. In the first decade of the new century, sixteen million persons were added, and the number living in cities nearly doubled. The enormous growth of urban areas was paralleled by a relative decline in the rural and agricultural regions of the nation. In some of the states in the trans-Mississippi West in the early 1900's, more people left than entered. Still agricultural production grew faster than the population and, despite the Panic of 1893, manufacturing continued to expand.

By the twentieth century, industrial and technological development had become the most significant factor in the measurement of national power. For example, Great Britain, economic mistress of the world in the nineteenth century, was now rivaled by Germany and the United States as a major producer of coal, iron, steel, and textiles. Elaborate European and American railroad networks encouraged the further concentration and centralization of industry, making it feasible to supply the teeming millions clustered in large urban population centers. The rise of the city was in itself an important common characteristic of the major Western nations, which almost doubled their collective population in the forty years from 1870 to 1910. In those years, too, new discoveries and inventions in the general field of electricity inaugurated a revolution in the speed of communication via the telephone, telegraph, and moving picture, while also providing the basis for radio and other electrical appliances and labor-saving devices. Meanwhile, the internal-combustion engine, developed by the late nineteenth century, made possible the automobile and airplane of the twentieth century. Already on the eve of World War I the motor vehicle was becoming in the United States an accepted part of day-to-day life, no longer merely a rich man's toy but an article of popular mass consumption.

The increasingly interdependent nature of the twentieth-century world economy, heightened by the revolution in improved means of communication and transportation, gave a novel international aspect to what had formerly been the local concerns of each country. National decisions regarding trusts or cartels, tariffs or immigration quotas, or even labor and social-welfare legislation, affected foreign as well as domestic policies. The world was shrinking, not only because its outlying parts were being brought closer together in their political and economic relationships, but from the fact that several centuries of geographic expansion were approaching an end. Asia, Africa, and the Americas were no longer easily available outlets for European exploitation and settlement. In the United States, the close of the frontier by the end of the nineteenth century meant that the American people were confronted by the unpleasant realization that the natural resources of the nation might be limited. The richness of its vast hinterland to the West had hitherto given vital support to American feelings of uniqueness and isolation. Now, however, the sense of an automatic economic and geographic security was passing, and a new psychology—more conservation-minded and more concerned over national defense— took hold of the country.

Despite the undoubted progress and prosperity of the United States, certain anxieties remained. Prices, including those of farm products, rose in the 1900's, but real wages declined. Moreover, the nation still struggled to find a solution to the problems of its ethnic minorities, now swelled by the rising tide of immigration from Europe. Since the Civil War, approximately one third of the increase in American population was due to the surge of newcomers from the Old World. By 1900, ten million persons of foreign birth—seven million from Eastern Europe—were living in the United States. An additional twenty-six million Americans—34 percent of the population—were children of foreign-born parents. Nativist attitudes toward the immigrant tended to vary with the oscillations of the business cycle, but racial antagonisms multiplied as the so-called new immigrants from Southern and Eastern Europe congregated in the larger industrial cities of the Northeast. In the words of the historian Harold U. Faulkner, "The new immigration gave rise to a demand for ending it." Since the 1880's Chinese immigrants had been excluded from the United States, and in the 1900's pressure mounted for a similar discriminatory treatment of Japanese immigrants.

Though numerically smaller than the immigrants, black Americans presented an even greater problem of assimilation and adjustment. Disfranchised and deprived of their civil rights in the South, Negroes were beginning to move north only to be confronted again by the fresh discriminations characteristic of the newer urban ghettos. Like Negroes, American Indians were subjected to a process of neglect and discrimination, which was concealed from general view by the governmental policy of isolating the Red Man on federal reservations.

In the eyes of most Americans, the social and economic problems which accompanied the country's urban–industrial growth were a greater cause of anxiety than the condition and treatment of the nation's minorities. Cycles of prosperity and depression in the latter half of the nineteenth century strengthened the concentration of American industry. Competition remained keen, but it was increasingly a struggle between industrial giants for control of the nation's twentieth-century corporate economy. Following the Spanish–American War, the growth of the trusts became a major national problem. The centralization and consolidation of business was paralleled by the rise of a class-conscious labor movement. American workers, disciplined by the wage system and decades of industrial strife, assumed some of the characteristics of Europe's proletariat. Meanwhile the middle class, worried by higher prices and fearful of the power of big business and organized labor, gave its support to the movement for stricter state and federal regulation and control of the nation's economy. Progressivism accordingly moved the United States toward an American version of state capitalism or paternalistic socialism. At the same time, however, individual reformers, though too optimistic about the prospects of utopia, were able to point to the numbers of private and quasi-private organizations which took the lead in the crusade for social and economic justice.

The particular concerns of the United States in the Progressive Era—such problems as the ever-greater concentration and centralization of power in both business and government and the accompanying demands for revolutionary social-welfare measures and political reforms—were also important issues in Europe and the British Commonwealth of Nations. Despite intense national rivalries in the nineteenth century, the growth of industrialization and democracy forced upon almost all nations certain uniform types of political response and organization. Socialism, which achieved its greatest strength in the decade before the first world war, was only the most obvious example of the new internationalism in thought and action. On both sides of the Atlantic there were the now-common characteristics to be found in the programs of American Progressives, English Liberals or Labourites, and German Social Democrats.

Although historians have recognized the influence of the European example upon certain types of social-welfare and reform legislation in the United States, Progressivism has been analyzed almost exclusively in terms of the American domestic scene. This national bias is all the more surprising because it has become commonplace for historians to point out that the Spanish–American War and advent of a new century marked the entrance of the United States into world politics. The internationalism and global interests associated with this interpretation of American foreign policy have not, however, generally been considered important to an understanding of the Progressive domestic mentality and ideology. Yet the Progressive movement in the United States and programs looking toward social democracy in Western Europe and portions of the British Empire were in a number of ways part of a common historical experience.

Americans, it would seem, have been reluctant to discover similarities between the varieties of European socialism and American progressive movements. Undoubtedly there are important differences in the character of American Progressivism and its European equivalents. But "if one looks at the record instead of the rhetoric," as historian George Mowry remarks, "one finds, surprisingly, an almost simultaneous development of social democracy in the United States and Europe despite the differences in material conditions, relations between the social classes, and political traditions." Moreover, to American political Progressivism distant Australia contributed the secret ballot, and the Swiss cantons such devices of direct democracy as the initiative, referendum, and recall. In point of time, the Progressives' years were also the ones of the Lloyd George reforms in England and of the rise of the Fabian Socialists and the Labour party there, while on the Continent, Bismarck's state socialism failed to still radical and labor agitation. Both Germany and Great Britain adopted comprehensive programs of social-insurance legislation, the former as early as the 1880's, and the latter in a series of laws culminating in the National Insurance Act of 1911. By 1914, Western Europe generally had accepted the principle of social-welfare legislation with programs that included workmen's compensation for industrial accidents, health and unemployment insurance, and old-age pensions. Much of Europe thus seemed to be moving toward greater social and economic as well as political democracy.

If some scholars have conventionally adopted a narrow-minded, parochial interpretation of the 1900's, certain contemporary American Progressives were less reluctant to avow their indebtedness to Europe. Programs for social-welfare legislation and vague hopes of a coming farmer–labor party in the United States looked toward a more cosmopolitan sort of social democracy. But the influence of European ideas was perhaps most clearly evident among those intellectuals who turned enthusiastically to political and social reform in the early 1900's. Allied with liberal professors in the universities, and clergymen who espoused a Social Gospel of Christian Concern for liberal reform efforts, were a number of middle-class socialists and humanitarians who were widely familiar with the crosscurrents in European and American thought. In terms of ideology and intellectual history, one may conclude that no rigid walls separated the concepts of Progressivism in the United States and social democracy or state socialism in Europe.

A number of observers of the political climate of the early years of the twentieth century agreed that an era of progressive social democracy was destined to supplant the individualism and old-fashioned liberalism of the past. For many it was clear that the new socialist tendencies were internationalist in scope, and they accordingly found much to admire in examples of social democracy in other parts of the world. Conservative critics, on the other hand, deplored the trend toward state socialism and raised the question of whether the United States was being socialized in the name of Progressivism. Theodore Roosevelt's political successes in the Progressive period can be explained in part by his ability to exploit these two discordant strands of thought. Uniting old-fashioned denunciations of socialism and radicalism with a modern advocacy of democracy and reform, and constantly stressing his own personal faith in Americanism, Roosevelt was able to use the traditional language of patriotism to hasten the United States along the revolutionary road toward the New Nationalism.

The very words "progress" and "progressivism" imply, of course, a forward-looking philosophy and break with the past. At the same time, many Americans in the 1900's undoubtedly continued to think of reform as a means of recapturing a mythical golden age. This paradox, reflected in the Progressives' tendency to discard history and still look back with nostalgia to the American heritage, suggests still another possibility: a common European and American experience. By the Progressive Era, the fond assumption of American uniqueness, nourished along with the advancing frontier of the nineteenth century, no longer held true. Frederick Jackson Turner's argument, carried to the next step, indicated that with the new century the old American dream of a distinctive role in history was gone. And with its passing America was once again to be an integral part of a common world experience and future.

On a number of occasions in the past, Americans had turned hopefully to the government for a measure of economic aid via cheap lands, protective tariffs, or internal improvements. They had also accepted a modest amount of taxation and government regulation. But it was not until the initial decade of the twentieth century that they took the first major steps toward the modern, all-powerful, social-welfare state. Following or paralleling similar developments in Western Europe, the United States turned from the individualistic democracy of the past to the institutionalized, social democracy of the future.

In contrast to the classical laissez-faire school of thought which considered liberalism largely in negative terms, the Progressive generation espoused a positive conception of liberalism in which the state consciously intervened to direct the future well-being of the citizenry. The widely held belief in the collective, social nature of the new democracy, and the growing acceptance of its nationalistic overtones, was reinforced for many Americans by direct observation of the course of twentieth-century reform in Europe. There was no doubt, decided George Harvey, the conservative editor and publisher, that "we are face to face with a condition such as confronted Germany twenty years ago and is surely making headway to-day even in conservative England." "In Germany, perhaps more than anywhere else," the reform-minded Jane Addams wrote approvingly, "the government has come to concern itself with the primitive essential needs of its working people. . . . Shall a democracy," she asked, "be slower . . . to protect its humblest citizens, and shall it see them slowly deteriorating because, according to democratic theory, they do not need protection?"

Progressives were not visionaries seeking a millenium, Benjamin Parke De Witt, a contemporary historian of the movement, noted in 1915. "What they do propose," he wrote, "is to bring the United States abreast of Germany and other European countries in the matter of remedial legislation . . . to strike at poverty, crime, and disease; to do everything that government can do to make our country better, nobler, purer, and life more worth living."

With all their rich and diverse contributions to American life and thought, what is perhaps most striking about many of the American Progressive ideals—though this has received comparatively little attention from historians—is the extent to which they borrowed from the political and social thinking in Western Europe in the late nineteenth and early twentieth centuries. Interesting parallels in the parameters of ideas do not by themselves establish proof of international cultural influences, but the interrelations of Progressivism in the United States with nationalistic social and political movements in Europe are too close to be ignored. If the significance of Progressivism as an ideology owes much to its association with European thought, it is important to remember, too, that some of the more notable instances of practical American reforms mirrored transatlantic crosscurrents in political action and organization. American Progressivism and European social democracy were thus parts of a common and broader experience in the world's movement toward a truly global civilization.

The
Pressure for
Reform

CHAPTER 2

Insurgent Intellectuals

PROGRESSIVISM as a broad general movement for reform was most visible in terms of specific measures for social change and a more direct democracy. But Progressivism in the United States was also an intellectual movement and an ideology. Novel ways of thinking, as well as changing material forces, encouraged the impulse toward reform. And in the larger context of what Morton White has called "the revolt against formalism," the new political and economic ideas of the late nineteenth century were an integral part of a whole worldwide revolution in patterns of social thought. In philosophy and law, in economics and history, there was a growing protest against traditional principles, against the kind of abstract formal logic that had characterized the life of the mind throughout much of the early nineteenth century.

To describe the new climate of opinion in Western civilization, Jacques Barzun, after surveying the historical scene in

modern Europe, offered the title "Darwin, Marx, Wagner."
Although Richard Wagner, the virtuoso in music and a bi-
zarre political thinker, had little seeming influence on American thought, Darwin's concept of evolution and Marx's economic interpretation of history were each of far-reaching
importance to the Progressive Era. And even Wagner, in the
way that he became a symbol of German romantic nationalism and statism, could be said to have enjoyed an American
counterpart in the person of Theodore Roosevelt and his political philosophy of a New Nationalism.

One can assert with some confidence that one of the main
roots of Progressivist ideology was the broad concept of Darwinian evolution, applying to man's social needs and institutions the whole spectrum of new ideas or hypotheses in the
natural and biological sciences. Darwin, even more than
Marx, was the seminal figure in nineteenth-century thought,
and his *Origin of Species* was, perhaps, the most significant
general scientific work since Adam Smith's *Wealth of Nations.*

Evolution in the sense of gradual change was, of course,
not a new theory. At least as old as the ancient Greek civilization, it was also susceptible of a wide range of diverse interpretation and meaning. Early in the nineteenth century,
geologists led by Sir Charles Lyell in England had worked out
an evolutionary conception of the age and gradual development of the physical universe. At the same time biologists like
Erasmus Darwin, the grandfather of Charles, began to ac-
cumulate evidence that animals and plants had evolved by
gradual, continuous change from earlier and simpler forms
of life. To the work of his predecessors, Darwin, after twenty
years of research, presented in 1859 his own rich and revolutionary findings in *Origin of Species.* In this and his later work,
The Descent of Man (1871), Darwin emphasized the concept of
the favorable variation and survival of individuals within the
species through adaptation to their environment—the sur-

vival of the fittest by natural selection. Since those individuals and species able to adapt and survive transmitted their superior characteristics to their offspring, and since others became extinct, natural selection demonstrated that all life was a process of evolution and not the result of a fixed supernatural creation. Man himself was simply the most advanced creature of his species.

At odds with traditional biblical, and the then prevailing scientific accounts of the creation of man and the universe, Darwinian evolution made possible a revolution in the social as well as the natural sciences. Encouraged by the example of Herbert Spencer, who enjoyed something of a vogue in America in the generation after the Civil War, scholars turned to the doctrine of organic evolution to enlarge their understanding in such fields as political science, economics, and sociology. Darwinian evolution helped to explain the world of the late nineteenth century, including social, economic, and political changes. While old-fashioned, aristocratic, genteel men of letters deplored the ugliness of modern industrial society, a new generation of intellectuals, more attuned to the advances in science, emphasized the importance of material values, economic competition, and the struggle for life. To Spencer and his followers in the business and academic communities in the United States, the concept of Social Darwinism seemed to correspond to the facts of an industrial civilization.

As the social sciences, like the natural sciences, gained freedom from the restraints of a fixed classification or absolute intellectual order, they too became evolutionary, empirical, and experimental. Moreover, a better knowledge of the so-called laws or processes of evolution seemed to indicate that man might influence change as well as being forced to adapt passively to his environment. Indeed, human progress could be interpreted as the story of man's conquest and control of his natural or physical habitat. Thus evolution provided a basis for optimism and an alternative to a mechanistic, deterministic philosophy. It could serve as a foundation for human effort and social control. Darwinism, in other words, could be Reform Darwinism as well as the Social Darwinism of Spencer and his foremost American disciple, William Graham Sumner. Instead of accepting natural or biological evolution in terms of hands-off or laissez faire, men might cooperate to shape the environment to meet their social needs.

For English and American readers, the ethical, reformist aspects of Darwinism were publicized in such works as Henry Drummond's *The Ascent of Man* (1894), an obvious rejoinder to Darwin's *The Descent of Man,* and Prince Peter Kropotkin's *Mutual Aid* (1902). Cooperation not competition, Kropotkin urged, was the lesson to be drawn from nature. Except in unusual circumstances, in both the animal world and mankind, advances were secured through cooperation and mutual aid and by the elimination of competition.

> "Don't compete!—competition is always injurious to the species, and you have plenty of resources to avoid it!" That is the *tendency* of nature, not always realized in full, but always present. That is the watchword which comes to us from the bush, the forest, the river, the ocean. "Therefore combine—practise mutual aid! That is the surest means for giving to each and to all the greatest safety, the best guarantee of existence and progress, bodily, intellectual, moral." That is what Nature teaches us.

Another neo-Darwinian book, one that became a sensation in the Anglo-American literary world, was Benjamin Kidd's *Social Evolution,* published in 1894. Kidd, hitherto an obscure British civil servant, contended that progress via evolution and natural selection was not rational—at least not in the sense of its being in the interest of most individuals. On the contrary, progress, to be effective, needed an authoritarian, socialist, ethical, or religious support. Such support, he was confident, would be forthcoming via a New Democracy for, he claimed, "The fact of our time which overshadows all others is the animal of Democracy."

Particularly influential in the reinterpretation of Darwinian theory to buttress plans for social reform were a number of social scientists who took an optimistic view of the lessons to be drawn from the natural world. A key figure was Lester F. Ward, like Kidd a government employee before he finally secured a full-time university appointment and came to rival Sumner as a social theorist. Ward's *Dynamic Sociology,* issued in 1883, was the first comprehensive treatise on the subject published in the United States. In this and other works, particularly his *Psychic Factors of Civilization* (1893), Ward offered his concept of a dynamic, applied sociology in opposition to the pure or static sociology of Herbert Spencer. Although Ward utilized the philosophical methods and approach of the Social Darwinists like Spencer and Sumner, he rejected their conclusions. A staunch critic of competition and laissez faire and an early exponent of a rationally planned collectivistic society, Ward separated the purposeless, physical animal evolution from a human evolution modified and shaped by social control and purposive action. The method of nature was too slow, and man therefore must try to speed progress by turning to the collective agency of government. "The individual has reigned long enough," he wrote. "The day has come for society to take its affairs into its own hands and shape its own destinies."

For the Progressive generation, Ward's social theories were given greater precision in works like Charles H. Cooley's *Human Nature and the Social Order* (1902) and Edward A. Ross's *Social Control* (1901). Cooley at the University of Michigan, and Ross at Stanford, Nebraska, and the University of Wisconsin, taught that the individual could be understood only in a social environment. Cooperation and sympathy, rather than competition, were the dynamic forces ruling human society. Ross's *Social Control,* dedicated to Ward and admired by Theodore Roosevelt, called for the modification of the Darwinian struggle for survival through orderly reform and organization. Laissez faire, he maintained in his later work *Sin and Society* (1907), was obsolete in the modern interdependent world. New conditions of life demanded a new morality and an intelligent reordering of society. Progressives, who did not accept the mechanistic determinism of Darwin's evolutionary system or Marx's economics, sought to control progress and sustain human values. But evil had first to be revealed by education and reform before it could be corrected.

By turning evolutionary ideas in the social sciences away from Social Darwinism and in the direction of Reform Darwinism, sociologists like Ward and Ross gave important intellectual encouragement to Progressivist ideals. At the same time, the emphasis on organization and control, as opposed to laissez faire, received additional support from the attacks leveled by economists and historians upon the existing social structure. Borrowing from Marx and the German historical or institutional school of economics, American theorists, often fresh from their studies abroad, questioned the traditional rules and formal abstractions underlying the political and economic structure.

Through much of the nineteenth century, before American universities began to grant the Ph.D. degree, large numbers of college students from the United States matriculated at the well-known German universities to carry on their graduate work. Unlike the heavy classical and religious emphasis of many American colleges, the German universities stressed an historical, empirical approach in their curriculum of philosophical and political studies. Richard T. Ely, long-term professor of economics at the University of Wisconsin, in recalling his student days in Germany, remembered how the sense of intellectual freedom there, "the idea of relativity as opposed to absolutism and the insistence upon exact and positive knowledge produced a profound influence upon my thought. . . . In Germany, I had seen that they developed their economics out of German life, and the German professors were part of this life. Many of them occupied public administrative positions and contributed in this way to the German Empire. My experience in Germany," he concluded, "had first brought to my attention the importance of linking book knowledge and practical experience."

In contrast to American individualism, the German training gave an increased respect for institutions and for the role of the state in encouraging and effecting social reforms. Hegel, in his philosophy of history, argued that ideals were formulated by a conflict in antagonistic ideas and interests—thesis, antithesis, and synthesis. It was his view, in turn, that the national state—though it was not a complete manifestation of the divine spirit—nevertheless represented the highest ideal of which mankind and the individual were capable. Already in the 1870's and 1880's, serious American graduate students in Germany like John W. Burgess, Ely, and Albion W. Small were devoted Hegelians, believers in the idea that among all institutions the state was least likely to do wrong. German professors, it was noted, accepted civic duties as a part of their official responsibilities and status, and disciplines like economics were intimately related to public administration.

For many Americans, the study of economics or political economy seemed particularly appropriate to the needs of the Progressive Era. Led by Ely, Simon N. Patten, Henry C. Adams, and John Bates Clark, an influential group of American social scientists became acquainted with the later German historical school. Although suspicious of some of the grandiose generalizations identified with Hegel and the German philosophers, these American scholars were receptive to German economic theory with its assumption that society was an organism and that man's natural mode of action was collective rather than individual. "Unlike the classical economists," Jurgen Herbst writes, "the Germans emphasized the potentialities of individuals and institutions and argued that men and society could best be understood in the context of their historical development."

Back home in the United States, with the prestige of their German Ph.D. degrees, many of the new American professors eagerly put their experience and ideas to work. To help in the organization and institutionalization of scholarship, new and more specialized professional associations were founded: for example, the American Historical Association in 1884 and the American Economic Association the following year. Spurred on by Ely and some of his friends, the latter association included in its constitution the famous statement of principles beginning: "We regard the state as an agency whose positive assistance is one of the indispensable conditions of human progress."

More than any of his colleagues, Ely in popular works, including several textbooks, familiarized a whole generation with the accomplishments of social democracy in Europe. His book *French and German Socialism,* published in 1883, was a pioneer effort that won the praise of both European and American Socialists. Though attacked later at the University of Wisconsin for his supposed socialist politics, Ely personally espoused a middle way, neither socialist nor individualist. This was illustrated in the support that he gave to the Christian Socialist and Progressive movements. By the 1890's, he believed that the United States possessed the kind of opportunity that Germany had enjoyed twenty years earlier. It could choose between real social democracy or a Bismarckian version of state socialism. Although social democracy stressed the fraternal side of government, Ely warned that a certain measure of paternalism was necessary for true reform. "There is no self-help for the masses," he noted in 1898, "like state action—using the state in its broad generic sense as inclusive of all subdivisions of the state. . . . The state, and the state alone," he added, "stands for all of us."

Like Ely a German-trained scholar, Simon N. Patten, professor at the University of Pennsylvania, rivaled William Graham Sumner as a popular college teacher of economics. Patten, however, was closer to Lester F. Ward in his emphasis upon the psychic factors in progress and on the need for positive social and economic planning. In his books *Heredity and Social Progress, The New Basis of Civilization,* and *The Theory of Prosperity,* all published in the early 1900's, Patten argued that nature was all right if man did not bungle it. But civilization inevitably depleted the world's resources. Accordingly, it was necessary that man, artificially and by his own efforts, take steps to counteract the law of nature's diminishing returns and apply himself to the creation of a social surplus. In America there were still abundant natural resources, but the era of economic individualism had led to exploitation, waste, poverty, and periods of depression. Now, however, Patten maintained: "The final victory of man's machinery over nature's materials is the next logical process in evolution. . . . Machinery, science, and intelligence moving on the face of the earth may well affect it as the elements do, upbuilding, obliterating, and creating; but they are man's forces and will be used to hasten his dominion over nature."

The evolutionary precepts adopted enthusiastically by economists and sociologists like Patten and Ward also proved useful in revamping American ideas of government and juris-

prudence. Classical theories of the state as a deliberate creation by divine act or by Rousseau's social contract, long
under attack from the historical school of Edmund Burke,
now had also to be modified in the light of German theories
treating the state as an organism. The doctrine of a fixed natural law was replaced by the concept of political institutions as
a slow growth. The unusual and striking title and thesis of the
English scholar Walter Bagehot's *Physics and Politics* (1873),
with its treatment of politics as a group struggle to break
down older customs—the "Cakes of Custom"—impressed
such distinguished youthful students of American government as Woodrow Wilson and Walter Lippmann. Wilson, for
example, adopted the evolutionary approach as a central
theme in his textbook *The State* (1889). And in his *Constitutional Government in the United States,* published in 1908 on the
eve of his entrance into politics, the future President pointed
out that the older Whig theories were unacceptable because
in reality "government is not a machine, but a living thing. It
falls, not under the theory of the universe, but under the
theory of organic life. It is accountable to Darwin, not to Newton. . . . Government is not a body of blind forces; it is a
body of men. . . . Living political constitutions must be Darwinian in structure and in practice."

Political scientists in the Progressive Era readily accepted
the new theories and applied them to the practice of American government. Arthur F. Bentley's important *Process of
Government* (1908) described politics thus: a result of the activities of organized pressure groups in society. "The interest
groups create the government and work through it," Bentley
noted. "We often hear of 'the control of government by the
people,' " But, he pointed out: "The whole process is control.
Government is control. Or, in other words, it is the organization of forces, of pressures." Earlier the Russian scholar Moi-
sei Ostrogorski described American political parties in these

terms. In his famous work, *Democracy and the Organization of Political Parties* (1902), he contended that they had on the whole become a corrupting influence upon democratic government. Ostrogorski's solution of a new party system, divorced from machine politics and representing voluntary citizen groups coming together to meet on single ad hoc issues, was a notion popular with many Progressives, and one they tried to put into effect in 1912.

Political corruption, or at least inefficiency in government and a failure to put democratic theory into practice, was an important issue in Progressive politics. Thorstein Veblen's attack at the turn of the century upon the capitalists as not the most fit or able leaders of the economy was matched by similar critiques of American political institutions. The Veblenian distinction between production for use and production for profit—the kind of showy display exemplified in the capitalists' conspicuous consumption and conspicuous leisure—seemed to have a parallel in the symbolism or folklore attached to American law, the Constitution, and the Supreme Court. By the Progressive Era, Darwinian thinking was helping to undermine this traditional American faith in a fixed law and stable Constitution, interpreted and protected by the Supreme Court. With increasing confidence therefore, Progressives turned to Oliver Wendell Holmes's famous assertion: "The life of the law has not been its logic; it has been experience." Further reinforcement for the idea of the law and the courts as instruments of social change and justice came in the detailed studies of liberal academic figures like J. Allen Smith and Charles Beard.

Smith, a professor at the University of Washington, had personal roots in the Populist movement as well as formal training in political science, economics, and law. His book *The Spirit of American Government,* emphasizing its undemocratic features, attracted the attention of both Theodore Roosevelt and Robert M. La Follette, the Wisconsin Progressive senator, following its publication in 1907. Conventionally Progressive in its call for increasing government intervention in the national economy, Smith's study also anticipated Beard's better-known, more factual and scholarly analysis of the class origins of the Constitution. Beard's celebrated *An Economic Interpretation of the Constitution* (1913) was a useful, if unintentional, reform document, and both his and Smith's books, it seemed, strengthened the Progressives' demand for constitutional changes and weakened the case for conservatives' devotion to the sanctity of the Constitution.

The economic interpretation of history and evolutionary theory were each important as weapons of social and political criticism. Abstract ideas, hitherto conceived as absolutes, could now be considered as relative and changing. Moreover, the contention that ideas represented certain economic interests or interest groups provided a basis for pointing out the degree to which selfishness and self-interest influenced both politics and business. In a world constantly evolving and changing, the eternal truths of one generation became the falsehoods of the next. Historical interpretation, like history itself, was subject to change and human pressures. Such arguments, pointing to the relativistic nature of truth and to its continual evolution under the impact of economic forces, were summed up in the philosophy of pragmatism and popularized in the writings and teachings of William James and John Dewey.

James and Dewey, the most influential exponents of pragmatism, brought philosophy, hitherto the least practical of academic disciplines, down to earth. In place of its traditional linkage with the comfortable leisured class, they proposed that it serve the general interest of society. At the same time, they tied philosophy to Darwinism and the scientific revolution of the nineteenth century. In the new laboratory psychology, already well developed in Europe, the human mind was not considered a fixed creation but merely the furthest stage of intellectual development. Ideas and patterns of thought, too, it was now apparent, might be treated as evolutionary and changing.

In his little book *Pragmatism,* published in 1907, James popularized the term that his friend Charles S. Peirce, the founder of modern pragmatism and relativism, had first used. Peirce believed that scientific laws were statements of probabilities only, constantly subject in themselves to evolutionary change. He tried therefore to work out a pragmatic criterion of meaning and truth that could be tested experimentally. The answer to his question "How to make our ideas clear?" he avowed was through results and action rather than in any acceptance of a priori reasoning or absolute truth. Although Peirce himself was too skeptical and cynical to be a good pragmatist, James, repelled by the determinism and lack of free will that he found in German and British philosophy, turned eagerly to some of Peirce's ideas. Ever a staunch advocate of freedom of will and choice in his psychology, James sought a philosophy that would be both empirical and experimental, combining practical experience and laboratory study. Central to philosophy was the human desire to achieve a better life, but philosophy, he argued, must also recognize that life itself was a continual search for truths that in any final or absolute sense could not be discovered.

Personally a nineteenth- rather than a twentieth-century liberal, James was also a traditionalist in his emphasis on religious feeling and the "great-man" theory of history. But his conception of "the unfinished universe" and his pluralistic view that all theories were experimental ranged him firmly on the side of the pragmatists. Already in his masterpiece, *The Principles of Psychology* (1890), and in his *Talks to Teachers* (1899), James had carried psychology and philosophy into the classroom and applied it to everyday problems. As his influence grew in the early 1900's, James was joined by Dewey in making pragmatism the reigning tenet of the Progressive movement.

Dewey's philosophy, like that of James, was broad in scope. Along with the related disciplines of education and psychology, it included both the individual and society. Living on for more than half a century after James's death in 1910, Dewey's reputation reached its peak in the decades between the two world wars. But the general contours of his philosophy, already well outlined in the previous generation, were basic to the ideology of Progressivism. Philosophy, which Dewey defined as the intellectual expression of a conflict in culture, had as its most vital function the task of helping mankind to understand social change. The creative intelligence and potentialities for growth of the human mind accordingly were more significant than any static conception of the mind as a mental storehouse of past knowledge. The very process of reconstructing society, involving as it did continual experimentation, was as important as the ends that such a reconstruction sought to achieve. Indeed, Dewey contended, means could determine ends. Thus democracy in the political process was vital to the goal of a democratic society.

For Dewey, whose application of pragmatism to education became known as instrumentalism, the mind of the individual pupil was an instrument played upon and shaped by the school. The educational process, in turn, was itself the greatest force in changing society and in redirecting it toward democratic ends. Dewey, as an opponent of both laissez faire and the Herbert Spencer school of automatic evolution, stood squarely with the social scientists and the Progressives in their belief that conscious and collective human effort was necessary now, in the twentieth century, to achieve the kind of democracy and progress that had seemed to be largely inevitable in the age of Thomas Jefferson and the American frontier. Though aware of the tyranny of authority and the dangers in a Hegelian reverence for the national state, Dewey nevertheless believed that the individual could realize his full potentialities only by cooperation within the community. His pragmatism therefore assumed the desirability, as well as the necessity, of group action through a positive national state.

Although the pragmatists did not lose sight of individual needs, the overriding emphasis in their philosophy was upon society and the environment. Like the liberal philosophers of the eighteenth-century Enlightenment, the pragmatists believed that human nature was plastic and changing. It could be improved therefore by beneficial changes in the environment. Progressive reformers, too, stressed environmental factors in social change and minimized the conservative's traditional emphasis on an individual's heredity pattern. Man's inner nature was not fixed and unyielding. His capacity for good or ill was largely determined by society. Progress, if not inevitable, as the eighteenth-century utopian thinkers had imagined, was still possible and, given modern man's heightened intelligence and scientific ingenuity, it was also indeed highly probable. Joined together by the new scientific and experimental approach now characteristic of their respective disciplines, the insurgent intellectuals at the turn of the century were able to make their social thought the foundation of the developing ideology of the Progressive movement.

CHAPTER 3

Populists and Socialists

PROGRESSIVISM in its political ideas and reform program gradually turned the Populist and Socialist ideals of the 1890's into an American version of state socialism or social democracy. Neither the Populist nor the Socialist party ever came close to winning a nationwide election in the United States, but both were important in encouraging progressive reforms in the twentieth century. While the Populists held more tightly to older American traditions in their particular demands and ideology, Socialist goals called attention specifically to certain common features in American Progressivism and European social democracy. Ultimately, however, the Progressives, with a broader general program and wider popular appeal than either their Populist predecessors or Socialist contemporaries, were more successful in affecting the character of American reform politics. But Populism and Socialism nevertheless were vital forces in encouraging the impulse toward reform.

The exact role of Populists and Socialists—the two polar left-wing political pressure groups in late nineteenth-century America—in relation to the Progressive movement has continued to divide historians. Both parties reached the peak of their influence in elections preceding American participation in war—the Populists in 1896 on the eve of the Spanish–American War, and the Socialists in 1912 before the first world war. Yet neither party saw much of its program adopted until it had ceased to be an effective political organization. The radical pressure for reform, therefore, was more indirect than immediate or direct.

The Populist movement, from which a national political party emerged in 1892, had its origins in the problems and discontent of American farmers in the decades following the Civil War. Passage of the Homestead Act, construction of the transcontinental railroads, and opening up the Great Plains of the trans-Mississippi West did not bring the hoped-for permanent prosperity to a new generation of postwar settlers. Instead prices for American wheat and other farm crops declined as new and improved means of transportation and production made it possible for Australia, Canada, and Russia to compete successfully with the United States for a major share of the Western European market. At home American farmers complained that they were the innocent victims of Republican practices that discriminated against agricultural interests in favor of industry and the railroads. For example, the post-Civil War return to the gold standard and hard-money policies, plus the virtual demonetization of silver, contributed to a deflationary decline in farm prices without a corresponding reduction in interest rates on farm mortgages or in freight charges.

In despair over world economic forces that they could not control, the farmers demanded political action by the states and Congress. In the 1870's farmers' groups known as the

Granges took the lead in securing state regulation of the railroads, and in 1880 the short-lived Greenback movement called for monetary inflation to raise farm prices. By the close of that decade, a series of devastating droughts and unusually cold winters gave a new urgency to agrarian protests and resulted in the establishment of what became the farmers' Alliances of the West and South. In a series of angry meetings culminating in a national convention at Omaha, Nebraska, in 1892, representatives of the Alliances and other farm organizations formed the People's, or Populist, party with General James B. Weaver, the Greenbacker's nominee in 1880, as its candidate for President. At the same time, in their platform adopted at Omaha, the Populists demanded such measures as reform in the currency and banking structure of the country—especially the free coinage of silver—cooperation with labor to secure social justice, and governmental ownership of the railroads and telegraph and telephone lines.

Although the Populists were the first national party in the United States to call for governmental ownership of such public utilities as the railroads, they were not really socialists. Instead they looked backward to the agrarian democracy of the early nineteenth century. Thus they wanted to break down the monopolies and privileged industrial interests which they claimed were responsible for the unfortunate plight of the country's farmers and workingmen. Like the Jacksonians in the 1830's, they thought of American capitalism in terms of the artisan and the small independent farmer or producer. Those who used their own hands and skills, they believed, deserved the fruits of their toil. If the Populists shared an illusion that was delusive in its simplicity, they nevertheless proclaimed a cause and listed a set of grievances that could not be ignored, and that later historians have interpreted as a turning point in American history.

Rather ironically, better times after 1896 and the war with

Spain two years later did much to relieve the American farmers' economic problems without their resorting to some form of radical agrarian revolution. The contemporary comment by Tom Watson, Populist standard-bearer in the South, that the war with Spain ruined the prospect of real reform in the United States was, accordingly, too pessimistic. As Watson himself recognized, the fusion of the Populists and Democrats in the Bryan campaign of 1896 had already damaged the radical-reform cause. But the sudden rise and fall of Populism, or the People's party, did contribute to a cataclysmic interpretation by later historians. Thus John D. Hicks, author of *The Populist Revolt,* the major work on the movement, called Populism "the last phase of a long and perhaps a losing struggle—the struggle to save agricultural America from the devouring jaws of industrial America." John Chamberlain in his history of the Progressive mind, to which he gave the title *Farewell to Reform,* began with the statement: "The nineties saw the last full-throated attempt of the American dirt farmer to seize a government he had not wholly owned since Jackson's day, and had not owned at all since the Civil War had ended." And Louis Hacker, in his popular text *The United States Since the Civil War,* writing like Chamberlain and Hicks from the vantage point of the 1930's, saw Populism as "the last united stand of the country's agricultural interest . . . the final attempt of the farmers of the land to beat back an industrial civilization whose forces had all but vanquished them already."

Populism, according to the foregoing views, was largely a nostalgic movement, a final crusade to restore America to the purity and innocence of its Jeffersonian–Jacksonian heritage. The People's party's demands for free silver and a graduated income tax, for legislation to control wealth and to protect the rights of labor, and for governmental ownership of the railroads and the remaining natural resources of the West were mainly negative concepts in the antimonopolistic tradition of equal rights for all, special privileges to none. Like the disciples of Henry George, the Populists espoused a limited degree of socialism in order to preserve America as a land of opportunity for the workingman, the dirt farmer, and the small businessman. Populists and Georgeites, in this sense, were collectivists only as a means to a truer, more realistic individualism. As the novelist Hamlin Garland, one of George's early followers, pointed out in an exposition and defense of the single-tax position:

> We are individualists mainly. Let that be understood at the start. We stand unalterably opposed to the paternal idea in government. We believe in fewer laws and juster interpretation thereof. We believe in less interference with individual liberty, less protection of the rapacious demands of the few and more freedom of action on the part of the many.

In similar fashion, Benjamin O. Flower in his reform magazine, *The Arena,* derided the fears that Populism was a forerunner of socialism. Populism, he asserted, was a newer application of the individualism of Thomas Jefferson and Henry George. "It is a revolt of the millions against the assumption of paternal authority on the part of the general government, and the prostitution of this authority or power for the enriching of a favored few."

The idea of reform by a return to an older America was further illustrated in the Jeffersonian leanings of William Jennings Bryan, a western Democrat who as presidential candidate in 1896 united the Populists and agrarian Democrats. Though not a Populist, Bryan was the most Populist-minded among the prominent Democratic politicians in the Progressive Era. Although a visit to Europe in 1903 intensified his interest in governmental ownership of key public utilities,

Bryan was more impressed by the German practice of state rather than federal operation of railway transit. Less a radical than a leader of the loyal opposition to Republican party Progressivism, Bryan was perhaps most significant as the embodiment and last political representative of the Jeffersonian version of liberal reform. His attachment to, and reiteration of, Jeffersonian principles reflected a kind of blind but noble loyalty to a lost cause. While Progressivism moved toward new goals, Bryan went down to defeat three times in his effort to win the presidency and gain control of the forces of reform in twentieth-century America.

Although contemporary foes were often inclined to lump together Populists, Socialists, and Progressives, none was as extreme as its conservative opposition imagined, and each entertained certain distinctive ideas. Unsympathetic modern critics have identified Populist leaders and writers like Ignatius Donnelly, author of *Caesar's Column,* with anti-Semitism in their obsessive concern with Wall Street and the capitalist money power. Moreover, the emotional nature of its supporters in the campaigns from 1892 to 1896 seemed to make Populism a forerunner of the intolerant and illiberal mass movements of the Radical Right in the 1930's and 1950's. Less extreme is Richard Hofstadter's view that the Populists were overwhelmed by the changing conditions of rural America and the improved status enjoyed by the large-scale commercial farmer. Agrarian myths simply did not square with the new economic realities as the return of prosperity by the late nineties enabled American agriculture to enter a new golden age and regain its former parity with industrial price levels.

Most positive among recent historians in asserting the role of the Populists as a major radical influence upon American reform is Norman Pollack, who states: "Had Populism succeeded, it could have fundamentally altered American society in a socialist direction. Clearly Populism was a progressive social force." Populism and Marxism, in Pollack's view, attacked some of the same features of capitalism in America and Europe, and this affinity, he concludes, "might well challenge a basic proposition in historical writing—the uniqueness of America." Yet Populism as an agrarian movement, strongest in the South and West, was unable to win significant support from industrial labor, social reformers, and intellectuals. Its platform had few planks which touched the interests of urban labor. And higher prices for the farmer meant an increase in the cost of living for the city dweller. When the Populists, for example, sought a political coalition with labor—the longstanding dream of radical reformers—they ran up against the generally conservative course of the American Federation of Labor and its leader, Samuel Gompers. Gompers was an effective opponent of the idea of a special labor party or of labor's involvement with existing political parties.

While Populism had its roots in the American agrarian tradition, socialism was European in origin. Utopian socialist communities in mid-nineteenth-century America applied the radical ideas of Robert Owen, the English cotton manufacturer, and of Charles Fourier, an unconventional French businessman. After the Civil War, Marxist socialism was carried across the Atlantic, and the offices of the First International, a radical European workingman's association, were even located on an emergency basis in New York City. Early in the 1890's there was some interchange and hope of cooperation between the Populists and Socialists in the United States. This was especially true of the American Fabians, Christian Socialists, and Edward Bellamy Nationalists, discussed later. But the Populist leaders, looking expectantly to victory in 1896, joined the Democrats, thus disheartening such radicals as Henry Demarest Lloyd, who had sought to swing the Populist party behind the possible candidacy of a leader like Eugene Debs, the workingman's hero in the 1894 Pullman strike.

During the period of the Progressive Era, the bulk of American Socialists moved in a conservative direction, although orthodox Marxist socialism, it is true, remained alive in the United States in the form of the Socialist Labor party led by Daniel De Leon, its rigid and rather academic theoretician. The initial popularization and Americanization of socialism, at least in its utopian format, was the work of Edward Bellamy and his followers in the Nationalist movement. Bellamy's famous book *Looking Backward,* published in 1888, inaugurated a vogue for utopian novels over the next decade. Although none of the others, including William Dean Howells' *A Traveller from Altruria* (1894), approached Bellamy's sales of some one million copies, all expressed the sense of social upheaval and injustice characteristic of the nineties. Bellamy predicted a highly regimented type of future society in which a strong national state, by effecting an economic and scientific revolution, would abolish the profit system and control production. The resulting militaristic, equalitarian society that Bellamy preferred to call Nationalism rather than Socialism would, he believed, lead to a truer individuality. Readers of *Looking Backward* promptly organized some 150 Nationalist Clubs and began the *Nationalist Monthly Magazine.* Bellamy and fellow enthusiasts lectured in support of his ideas, but McKinley's election, returning prosperity, the Spanish–American War, and Bellamy's own death killed the movement. Even earlier, however, Populists and Socialists had taken away most of its mass support. More popular among religious mystics, army officers, and intellectuals than among working-class people, the Nationalists' appeal was essentially to the middle class.

The Nationalist movement, before its demise, helped to make socialist doctrines and ideas respectable in the United

States. Though not intellectually as prestigious or significant as the British Fabian Society, founded earlier in the 1880's by Sidney Webb and George Bernard Shaw, the Nationalists, like the Fabians, spread the notion that the transition from competitive capitalism to a cooperative collectivism or socialism could be effected gradually and peacefully through a political evolution. The object of the Fabian Society, an 1896 report on its mission stated, "is to persuade the English people to make their political constitution thoroughly democratic and so to socialize their industries as to make the livelihood of the people entirely independent of private Capitalism." Moreover, like the Fabians, the Nationalists were patriotic and even chauvinistic, thus introducing a non-Marxist, noninternationalist outlook into the process of Americanizing socialism. The British left was generally critical of American capitalism, which they equated with a harsh and brutal treatment of the workingman. But such prominent Fabians as Sidney Webb, Shaw, and H. G. Wells were impressed even more by the weaknesses of the American administrative state and the need to strengthen the machinery of government in the United States.

By the Progressive Era, America no longer seemed the promised land that the early nineteenth-century European utopian socialists had looked to so expectantly. Although Karl Marx and Friedrich Engels had hoped that the United States as a young country would prove receptive to socialism, later Marxists rejected the promise of America. Despite the fact that each year hundreds of thousands of European workingmen sought America's shores, radical socialists now believed that capitalism in the New World was becoming more ruthless. On the other hand, they considered the possibility that this exploitation of the worker, heightened by the growth of the trusts in the United States, might bring both America and Europe to the brink of a socialist revolution. The Marxist notion that a coming crisis in American capitalism promised to stimulate the sluggish historical forces impelling Europe to socialism was interesting, but it left unanswered the perplexing question of why the socialist movement itself was so weak in the United States. As the more moderate European socialists and critics of Marx sometimes recognized, however, America, if not a worker's paradise, was nevertheless not a land of unrelieved misery. Nor did it seem likely to become the focal point for an approaching socialist revolution. Thus the revisionist socialists, not wedded to orthodox Marxist views, grew more willing to see socialism in Europe and America alike as the culmination of a slow, evolutionary process for which Progressivism and social democracy were necessary first steps.

In the United States, socialism emerged as a more significant movement and influence upon Progressivism when a majority of the existing small socialist groups put aside their doctrinal differences and united in July 1901 to form the Socialist Party of America. Three years earlier Eugene Debs, Victor Berger, and their followers in the Midwest had organized the Social Democratic party and ran Debs for President in 1900. Now, in addition to the Social Democrats, the new Socialist party included dissident Social Laborites, New York City trade unionists led by Morris Hillquit, and former Populists and Nationalists of the 1890's. Anticapitalist, though not always Marxist in their outlook, the delegates to the party's first convention in 1901 were militantly enthusiastic about the prospect of winning American votes for an authentic socialist program. Debs's Social Democratic platform in 1900 had called mildly for social insurance and a more direct democracy along with government ownership of the trusts. Socialism, it seemed, could be progressive as well as Marxist in its agenda, and as Debs explained, it "does not propose the collective ownership of property, but of capital. . . ."

The founding of the Socialist Party of America in 1901 occurred at a time when socialism as an ideology, or expression of left-wing progressivism, was becoming in the United States, as already in Europe, a live social and political issue. In 1900, British trade unionist leaders took the important step of creating their own political party by establishing the Labour Representation Committee, which by the 1906 general election became known as the Labour party. Meanwhile, although American conservatives often declared modern socialism a graver, more radical threat to capitalist institutions than Populism, the merging of smaller splinter groups into the new Socialist party indicated that the socialists' traditional labor base was being broadened by the inclusion of the interests of the intellectuals and the middle classes. Like the Labour party in Great Britain, the Socialist Party of America reflected the increasingly moderate, nonrevolutionary position of those radicals and reformers who, in each country, espoused what was variously called a social democratic, prolabor, or progressive political stance.

American Socialists, despite the growing appeal of their program, faced a dilemma in regard to such problems as immigrant labor competition and the role of the Negro in American society. Officially the Socialists paid little attention to the needs of the Negro, while the black man in trying to improve his status under American capitalism was not anxious to add the stigma of radicalism to his already heavy burden of discrimination and prejudice. In the case of the immigrant, Socialists remained divided by their basic tenet of the international solidarity of the working class and the fears of American union men over the labor competition offered by new arrivals from Europe. Moreover, the typical American conservative's stereotype of the immigrant as an anarchistic, bomb-throwing radical was reinforced by the considerable numbers who enrolled in the foreign-language federations affiliated with the Socialist party. Although most immigrants remained politically indifferent or joined one of the two major parties, those who had been members of left-wing parties in Europe were not always willing to leave their socialism in the homeland. Thus American Socialists, in their concern to maintain the new popular national image of the party, took a compromise position between no restriction of immigration and a frank discrimination on ethnic grounds. Opposed naturally to the mass importation of contract labor for the purpose of undermining American wage standards, the party, however, reaffirmed its stand against racism and demanded that "the United States be at all times maintained as a free asylum for all men and women persecuted by the governments of their countries on account of their politics, religion or race."

Sparked by the rising tide of immigration, the question of world socialism became a popular subject of discussion in American periodicals of the 1900's. Commenting on "the growth of socialism," which he saw aided by the migration of persons and ideas from Europe, Oswald Garrison Villard wrote in *The Nation:* "The experiments in England, Germany, France, Italy and Australia are cited for our guidance by the very schoolboys." An editorial on "Liberal Socialism" in *The Independent* pointed out that the word "socialism" had an unpleasant sound largely because people feared the element of coercion involved. But the increasing extent of public ownership and economic equality, the writer believed, was bringing socialism to the United States, however it might be called. William Jennings Bryan, Democratic party standard-bearer, in a discussion of "individualism versus socialism," contended that the words, so far as America was concerned, defined tendencies rather than concrete systems. In addition to public acceptance of municipally owned utilities like gas and waterworks, Bryan noted the intense moral fervor extended to

socialism by men like John Ruskin, the English reformer and
art critic, and by Christian ideals. Political economist Robert F.
Hoxie, in an article "The Rising Tide of Socialism," distinguished between a "broad, liberal, opportunistic, moderate
type of socialism, of comparatively slow and solid growth," as
in Wisconsin and other states of the Middle and Far West,
and a more class-conscious type of socialism. The latter rested
"very largely on the support of men with European blood in
their veins."

For *World's Work,* Professor Samuel P. Orth, in a detailed
series on "The Worldwide Sweep of Socialism," concluded
that the Socialist party was gaining strength and respectability
in the United States because it was the only party to offer a
concrete program of social justice. It was a question now of
economic more than political freedom. There was a wide gulf
in the United States, Orth admitted, between the mild socialism of the Christian reformers and the radicalism of the labor
unions joined together in Industrial Workers of the World.
But there was nevertheless the danger that the United States
was becoming Europeanized. "Proletariat and bourgeois,
lower class and middle class, are the unwelcome words in our
new political vocabulary. We are fostering a European
'remedy'—socialism—class cleavage. But," Orth added, "this
socialism may be Americanized. . . . At any rate, I fail to
see," he concluded, "how, in a democracy, the people can
shirk the responsibility for allowing things as they are to be as
they are."

American socialist writers, not surprisingly, saw progressivist tendencies toward a stronger social democracy as part of
a coming full-scale socialist society of the future. Most systematic in expressing such a view was Edmond Kelly, an American lawyer resident for years in Paris, whose studies in the
theory of government led him from a strong bias in favor of
Spencerian evolution to an eventual espousal of collectivism

and socialism. Europe, he wrote in 1901, was moving in a socialist direction, and America was not far behind. While the
former was better prepared politically, "commercially the
United States is riper for collectivism than Europe." The
trusts, demonstrating the waste and folly of capitalism, would
teach, Kelly was confident, that "what a few promoters have
done for their own benefit the whole community can do for
the benefit of all."

William English Walling, another socialist intellectual, in
his book *Progressivism—and After* (1914), contended that the
course of evolution could be speeded by conscious human effort. Social scientists, he argued, must hasten the process of
evolutionary thought by "projecting on the present a series of
scientific hypotheses based upon what seem to be the probable future stages of social evolution." Collectivism, to which
the Germans had given the most practical backing, was simply
the further extension of the traditional economic function of
the government. Noting that the labor parties in Europe were
thoroughly nationalistic by 1914, Walling expressed the belief
that the internationalism of the working class, like nineteenth-century laissez faire, was a relic of capitalism. The future pointed, he asserted, not toward international socialist
solidarity, but toward a state capitalism and an eventual state
socialism which, in turn, "will bring a new nationalism. . . ."

To some independent American radicals who were not
sentimental about the political state, socialism's new nationalistic appeal and popular recognition threatened its sincerity
as a challenge to capitalism. Under what he called in America
"Our Benevolent Feudalism" of monopolistic combinations,
W. J. Ghent complained: "The State becomes stronger in its
relation to the propertyless citizen, weaker in its relation to the
man of capital." Neither labor-reform legislation, nor regulatory administrative commissions, in Ghent's opinion, reversed
increasing farm tenancy or urban poverty. Despite progres-

sive ideals, man was still pitted against man in a struggle to earn a decent living and overcome prevailing economic obstacles. According to Henry Demarest Lloyd, author of the celebrated book *Wealth Against Commonwealth,* attacking the Standard Oil monopoly, the large corporations were able to control or adapt legislation to suit their own needs. Outraged also by the Populists' single-minded devotion to the shibboleth of free silver, Lloyd turned late in life to the hope that a democratic socialism might preserve true individuality in America. Government, however, was only a means to an end, and governmental ownership or socialism must be more than mere statism. After all, he pointed out: "The least democratic countries in the world have state coal mines and state railroads, but they have no ownership by the people. The socialism of a kingly state is kingly still; of a plutocratic state, plutocratic."

The fears of men like Lloyd and Ghent notwithstanding, American socialist and progressivist thought accepted a more powerful national state buttressed by new regulatory legislation and administrative commissions. In the midst of the Theodore Roosevelt, Republican version of Progressivism, Socialists were able to win increasing approval from American voters. Roosevelt himself stated that "the growth of the socialist party in this country was far more ominous than any populist or similar movement in time past." Economic grievances laid at the door of the trusts and big business, plus revelations of corruption in American political life, gave support to the contention that only countries with a strong socialist movement would be able to secure passage of the social and labor legislation necessary for genuine democracy. According to Morris Hillquit, party leader and theoretician, "In those countries of Europe in which the socialist movement has attained such political strength as to cause alarm to the parties of the dominant classes, the latter regularly shape their policies with special reference to their probable effect on the socialist vote, and the 'stealing of the socialist thunder' is one of their favorite maneuvers, especially in time of approaching electoral campaigns."

For the Socialist party, the test of its conscious Americanization came with the campaign of 1912 and the outbreak of the first world war. Meanwhile, the country was in the process of adapting itself to a kind of democratic state socialism in the guise of Progressivism.

CHAPTER 4

Urban Evangelists: The Social Gospel and the Muckrakers

 THE Populists and Socialists were able to stir the mass of the people in a more direct way than the insurgent intellectuals in the colleges and universities. But the pressure for reform coming from each of these groups touched only a minority. The great bulk of the citizenry, after all, did not wish to accept Progressivism in terms of a radical ideology or academic argument. More appealing, especially to urban, middle-class America, was the message of the Social Gospel and the sensational, muckraking literature published in the popular magazines of the Progressive Era.

Much of the original impulse toward reform in the United States had been governed by the ideal of an agrarian, small-capitalist society of self-sufficient farmers and independent producers. Although the hold of such an ideal remained strong as late as the 1890's, it was also apparent that the United States, like most of the countries of Western Europe, was becoming a nation of cities, characterized by growing urban–industrial centers of great population density. Instances of poverty, unemployment, ill health, and intemperance that had formerly been considered individual or family matters now became pressing social issues. Since frontier America was no longer capable of absorbing the increasing tide of new arrivals from Europe—reaching figures of over one million persons a year in the early 1900's—the most recent immigrants found themselves squeezed at the bottom of a mounting urban population. At the same time, the individual lost the comparative social security of the family-type, subsistence farm. The complex, interdependent, modern capitalistic economy was itself both cause and victim of the fluctuations of the business cycle. Fewer persons now were able to withstand prolonged periods of economic depression, while the resultant class conflict, industrial violence, and widespread poverty—demonstrated so forcibly in the 1890's—called national attention to the growing demands for social justice.

By the turn of the century, groups of liberal-minded clergymen, preaching what was known as the Social Gospel or Christian Socialism, were able to broaden the horizon of the American churches and bring to the attention of their middle-class parishioners a new concept of Christian nurture. With help from the colleges and reform-minded writers in the mass-circulation magazines, the clergy assumed the role of urban evangelists calling for progressive reforms. Concern for one's fellowman was, of course, one of the earliest and most important tenets of Christianity. But in an agrarian society, not yet divided by extremes of wealth and poverty, this sense of Christian charity and noblesse oblige was confined largely to a small minority of dedicated humanitarian reformers. For the main body of orthodox believers, religion meant a frank supernaturalism and the hope of personal salvation.

Organized religion, measured by church affiliation, continued to grow, increasing faster than the population in the Progressive Era. From 1900 to 1914, membership rose from 36 to 52 million persons. Larger than any single major Protestant denomination were the Roman Catholics who numbered some 13.5 million by 1914, an increase of more than 60 percent since 1900. Urbanization, in contrast to the low population density of rural areas, brought people closer to neighborhood churches, and the heavy influx of immigrants also helped to swell the total of memberships, especially in the Catholic Church.

For the many American Protestant denominations that had ministered chiefly to the needs and desires of middle-class and country congregations, the strange face of the city was a novel and serious challenge. Confronted by the example of the Catholic Church, which was flourishing in the larger American cities, American Protestantism, especially, had to modify its rural ideals and older techniques if it was to meet the demands of labor and a changing immigrant population. The major Protestant theological seminaries accordingly adjusted their curricula to include courses in applied social Christianity, while the more advanced Protestant clergymen adapted their theology to the theory of Darwinian evolution and the new literature of biblical criticism emanating from Europe.

Darwinism, accepted wholeheartedly in liberal theological circles by the 1890's, suggested to numbers of more thoughtful Christians a new concept of world unity, in which God's overall purpose was gradually unfolded in the progressive achievement of his kingdom here on earth. Evolution, in other words, helped turn religion from its concentration on a fixed dogma and absolutist theology to an ethics of social justice. God and the church became active agents in reform, and evolution and progress part of a divine plan. Thus the religious rationalization contributed to a corollary belief in progress and a willingness on the part of the churches to take the lead in programs of social change.

A further challenge to the church was the socialist movement in its varied manifestations in both England and America. Great Britain, where industrial–urban problems resembled those of the United States but in more accentuated form, exerted a pioneering influence on the Social Gospel. Liberal reforming clergy carried on in the spirit of the Chartist movement of the 1840's and its working-class demands for social justice. Charles Kingsley, the clergyman–novelist, and his fellow Christian Socialists, the poet William Morris, and the art critic John Ruskin, found a receptive American audience for their criticisms of British working-class conditions. At the same time, the British Fabians, with their gradualistic program of pragmatic reform, also contributed to the development of Christian Socialism, winning support among the more radical American exponents of the Social Gospel.

American churches, however conservative in their theology, could not ignore the problems of the new urban–industrial age. Many of the clergy in the course of their pastoral work were familiar with the plight of the poor and deeply troubled over their churches' lack of direct contact with the average workingman. In particular, they sensed the unreality of much of the talk of Christian morality in the unchristianlike environment of city slums. The great wealth of industrial America, some of which found its way in contributions to the churches, seemed controverted by the paradox that Henry George had depicted in *Progress and Poverty*. The clergy, moreover, could hardly fail to be impressed by such works as Jacob Riis's *How the Other Half Lives*, Helen Campbell's *Prisoners of Poverty*, or the English journalist W. T. Stead's striking polemic *If Christ Came to Chicago*. In a similar vein, an American clergyman, Charles M. Sheldon, wrote an all-time best seller, *In His Steps,* in which he posed the question of what Jesus would do if he faced the conditions of modern American life.

Almost as popular, and more influential intellectually than Sheldon's tract, were the works of the Reverend Josiah Strong, secretary of the Congregational Home Missionary Society. In 1885 his book *Our Country* created a sensation with its imperialistic and racist plea for spreading Anglo-Saxon institutions by planting missionary outposts around the world. Strong, however, was also alarmed by the perils that faced the United States at home, and his later books, *The New Era* and *The Twentieth Century City,* contrasted an ideal society based on the teachings of Jesus with the materialism of modern civilization and the corruption of American cities. Though his writings could claim significance as pioneer efforts in religious sociology, Strong's conclusions restated the essentially conservative message that "the world can never be saved from misery until it is saved from sin, and never ought to be."

More forthright than Strong as exponents of the Social Gospel were men like Washington Gladden, William Dwight Porter Bliss, and Walter Rauschenbusch, whose careers exemplified the force that liberal or radical Christianity was able to exert on the Progressive movement. Gladden, pastor for almost forty years of the First Congregational Church in Columbus, Ohio, was a practical rather than philosophical expositor of the Social Gospel. Opposed to socialism, though not to governmental ownership of public utilities, he urged Christian unity as a middle way to salvation between the extremes of individualism and statism. Generally conciliatory and moderate in the lectures and sermons that he was invited to deliver in colleges throughout the country, Gladden, however, also aroused much controversy by his attacks on "the ethics of luxurious expenditures" and the evils of "tainted money." As an example, he questioned whether Rockefeller Standard Oil funds should be solicited for foreign missions, and he declared that church officials "must not invite gifts from persons who are conspicuous enemies of society." Increasingly sympathetic to the needs of workingmen, Gladden feared their further alienation if the Christian church was identified with predatory wealth and remained indifferent to social reform. Gladden also helped to challenge the fundamentalist literal interpretation of the Scriptures and to popularize liberal theology in such books as *Applied Christianity* and *Who Wrote the Bible?*

Among the more radical advocates of the Social Gospel by the 1890's, no one was more impressive in his efforts to develop an American Christian Socialism than William Dwight Porter Bliss, who established his Mission of the Carpenter, a church for the working people of Boston, and the Society of Christian Socialists. Bliss also founded the Episcopal Church Association for the Advancement of the Interests of Labor and joined the Knights of Labor. Many of his reform activities were modeled after those of the Christian Socialists and Fabians in England, and he united with Edward Bellamy in encouraging the latter's Nationalist clubs. In 1895 Bliss carried socialism a step further with the formation of the American Fabian Society. Although he complained that Bellamy's Nationalism was too nebulous and passive a version of socialism, his own variety did not go much beyond Fabian concepts of municipal ownership of public utilities. Most of Bliss's associates in the Social Gospel movement, moreover, were not ready to affiliate with the Socialist party. And though he himself struggled hard against great odds, Bliss proved unable to keep alive the American Fabian Society or his Social Reform Union.

In American Social Christianity the towering intellectual figure of the Progressive Era was undoubtedly Walter Rauschenbusch, a Baptist clergyman of German background whose first pastorate was in a slum area of New York City. Although ever an ardent churchman who conceived of salvation in moral and religious terms, Rauschenbusch nevertheless believed that the Kingdom of God demanded a public as well as private ethic. He accordingly was severely critical of the church's traditionally conservative role in relationship to wealth, labor, and social reform. While not a socialist in a Marxist, scientific sense, nor a member of the Socialist party, Rauschenbusch contended that a nation could never be Christian until it reorganized its entire economic life on a democratic, cooperative basis. This, he expected, would come only with the advent of a nonviolent, but still revolutionary, socialist movement. After his health broke down, he became a professor at the Rochester Theological Seminary and wrote his series of influential books: *Christianity and the Social Crisis* (1907), *Christianizing the Social Order* (1912), and *A Theology for the Social Gospel* (1917). Christians, he warned, must unite to form the Kingdom of God on earth or face the bleak alternative of increasing social chaos and national decline as minorities preempt the spoils and the majority loses the energy to produce and live on.

By their preaching and writing, Rauschenbusch, Bliss, and Gladden carried the Social Gospel, and the more radical Christian Socialism, to American Progressives. William Jennings Bryan, Jane Addams, Theodore Roosevelt, and Woodrow Wilson, as well as the Ohio reform mayors Tom Johnson of Cleveland and "Golden Rule" Sam Jones of Toledo, all thought of reform in moral, and even religious, terms. Benjamin O. Flower, the crusading journalist who anticipated the muckrakers, believed that the fundamental error of socialism in Europe and America was in not tying the movement to Christianity—not the Christianity of the churches, but of Christ. Richard T. Ely, probably the foremost popular and academic economist of the Progressive Era, lent unceasing support to the Christian Socialist program by his identification of ethics and economics. The economists' desire to achieve a production and distribution of goods that would best serve the interests of all members of society, Ely asserted, was in harmony with Christian ideals.

For the middle classes, to whom so much of its appeal was directed, the Social Gospel was an inspiration and incentive as well as an answer to the guilt feelings that sometimes plagued the consciences of sincere believers. Beset by economic and social pressures from both the new rich and the poor, the middle class was willing to listen to the kind of urban evangelism exemplified in the Social Gospel movement. Moreover, for many of the clergy—the most conspicuous losers among the professional and aristocratic class in nineteenth-century America—the Social Gospel offered an opportunity to gain a new social status through meaningful protest and reform. From their own difficulties in contending with a business plutocracy, clergymen were able to sympathize with other depressed and disinherited groups. The Social Gospel also made it possible for the clergy to compete intellectually with the rising political and university elites and thus to rehabilitate its reputation and standing in American thought.

The Social Gospel was often unrealistic and naïve in its evaluation of the deeper ills affecting society. Thus it failed in its efforts to convert the urban immigrant masses to its reformist doctrines. At the same time, conservatives as well as fundamentalists refused to accept the optimistic theology of the Social Gospel, even though Billy Sunday and his fellow evangelists adopted some of its radical preaching techniques to the needs of their own rigid dogma. If the Social Gospel accordingly achieved no drastic reforms or changes in society, it nevertheless modified the older conservative theology and narrow institutional bias of the church. And, finally, it supplied the bridge by which Progressivism, as an almost religious faith, and Christianity, as a movement for social reform, were able to join hands and march in unison.

As the Social Gospel movement demonstrated, Progressivism was heavily dependent on the efforts of humanitarian reformers to arouse the conscience of the American people. It was apparent, too, that many of the muckraking journalists and realistic writers, who contributed so effectively to the general enlightenment in the Progressive Era, shared some of the Social Gospel's evangelistic fervor. In an age that had lost the unity of the small town and lacked the instant communication later offered by radio, the journalists, perhaps better than any other group, performed a necessary function of mass education. They were able to reach "everyman" with greater facility than the schools or the churches, thus helping to preserve democracy as a realistic political possibility. At the same time, the muckraking reform literature reflected a new optimism and a reaction against the pessimism that had crept into American literature from the European naturalistic school of writing.

By the 1890's, the more serious American novelists were being affected by naturalism in the arts and literature. Naturalism, which arose in response to the new currents of thought in science, and especially Darwinian evolution, assumed a pessimistic determinism in which personal free will was a delusion, and in which the environment and economic factors, rather than the individual, effected social change. In the United States, the post-Civil War industrial–urban civilization had passed beyond a romantic attitude toward life, and in such an age, calling not for dreams or wishful thinking, idealism and romanticism tended to fade. During this time a number of American writers, like so many clergymen, were intellectuals in revolt. Novels of social protest by the more realistic authors expressed a dislike for the businessman as a type. Even William Dean Howells in his sympathetic portraits depicted the millionaire industrialists as crude and uneducated, uncomfortable in intellectual circles, or in polite society, because of their lack of culture and refinement.

Most American writers, however, including those of the naturalistic school, were not consistent in a fatalistic view of man and society. Despite their doubts, and often in spite of themselves, they continued to yearn and work for various schemes of human betterment. They were not yet overwhelmed by the relativism and despair that characterized the post-World War I years. Thus the pessimism of the nineties was transformed by the Progressive Era into what the critics Granville Hicks and Van Wyck Brooks later called "The Years of Hope" or "The Age of Confidence." Meanwhile, American writers, many of them the so-called muckrackers, diverted American literature into the more practical paths of Progressive efforts at reform. Hopeful still that the individual might exercise some free choice, the muckrackers proposed to help make him make the right choices.

Muckracking as a term was somewhat unfairly applied to the popular reform literature of the 1900's after President Roosevelt likened its more extreme writers to the character in *Pilgrim's Progress* "who could look no way but downward with the muckrake in his hands." In itself the practice of sensational literary exposure of corruption and evil was not a new phenomenon. Henry Demarest Lloyd's *Wealth Against Commonwealth,* published in 1894, and Benjamin O. Flower's *Arena* magazine anticipated many of the techniques, but not the great popular success, of the muckrakers. What was new and significant in the muckraking literature of the Progressive Era was its achievement of a mass circulation and nationwide appeal.

Muckraking was also a dramatic illustration of the important changes taking place in American journalism at the turn of the century. In both newspaper and magazine publishing, technological improvements, involving new special features and higher costs, added immensely to the problems of owners and editors. Even more important, as Richard Hofstadter has pointed out in his *Age of Reform,* the twentieth-century newspaper was being called upon to play a novel role. The immigrants and uprooted farmers who filled American cities were frequently torn from the familiar institutions of home, family, church, and neighborhood. In the unfriendly atmosphere of the large city, the newspaper offered a sense of personal contact with a strange environment. Human-interest stories, personal interviews, and the exposure of crime and corruption all provided a substitute for village gossip and local politicking. At the same time, the emphasis on good reporting reduced the importance of editorial writing and the editorial page. The star reporter, rather than the great nineteenth-century editors—Greeley, Bennett, and Dana—now captured the public eye. Newspapers also became less identified with a particular political party and tried to appeal to the broadest possible social and class interests.

Significantly, as the burden of financing a newspaper or magazine increased, the volume of advertising and number of readers became all-important. The day had passed when a major newspaper could be purchased for a few thousand dollars, and instead the nineties saw the beginnings of the great journalistic empires of William Randolph Hearst, Joseph Pulitzer, and Frank Munsey. In the continuous search for ever-larger circulation, newspapers outdid each other in sensationalism. In 1898, Hearst and Pulitzer were even willing to help stir up a war over Cuba as a by-product of their competitive struggle for more sales in New York City. But some publishers also used the great influence of their papers to support worthwhile Progressive reforms.

Although the muckraking type of article appeared in the popular magazines rather than the newspapers, it utilized the new techniques in American journalism. The particular vogue for the muckraker's product began with the publication in *McClure's* in the fall of 1902 of Ida Tarbell's and Lincoln Steffens' famous series dealing with the Standard Oil monopoly and the corruption of American city government. While the articles seem not to have been the result of any set policy, the ensuing increase in circulation indicated public interest, and other magazines soon followed *McClure's* lead.

No important institution or aspect of American society escaped the muckrakers' attention. David Graham Phillips, the political reporter and popular novelist, seized upon the United States Senate—the "millionaires' club." In his famous 1906 series in *The Cosmopolitan,* which provoked Roosevelt's muckraking epithet, and which achieved what critics have variously regarded as the nadir or the high point in muckraking, Phillips attacked the self-serving instincts of the leading senators whom he depicted as corrupt machine politicians and minions of big business. Charles Edward Russell, after a trip around the world, published in *Everybody's* magazine a popular series describing the Rochdale cooperatives in England, public ownership in Germany, and direct democracy in Switzerland. *Everybody's* also undertook George Kibbe Turner's important articles on the impact of the commission form of municipal government and allied reforms on Galveston and other cities in 1906 and 1907. A number of writers analyzed the trusts and the corporate structure of high finance as revealed in the operations of the New York City banks and insurance companies. And Samuel Hopkins Adams and Upton Sinclair, by exposing laxity and filth in the drug and meat-packing industries, helped speed the passage of the Meat Inspection and Pure Food and Drug Acts.

A large number of the muckraking articles dealt with government–business relations. While Americans were outraged by the revelations of privilege and corruption, the knowledge of evil exposed was also gratifying to the so-called better elements in society. At the same time, articles on problems affecting the lower echelons of the American population—labor, immigrants, and Negroes—seemed to have less reader appeal. American Negroes, for example, still overwhelmingly concentrated in the rural South, were far removed from the Progressives' concern with the city and industrial society. Ray Stannard Baker's series, "Following the Colour Line," reported objectively the continuing extent of race prejudice and discrimination in both the North and South in the 1900's. Also noteworthy was an article by William E. Walling, the socialist writer, who, in describing "The Race War in the North," stimulated the founding of the National Association for the Advancement of Colored People. But the muckrakers generally were not able to arouse widespread public interest in the Negro or the race question.

Some of the muckraking pieces were admittedly trivial or sensational, seeking merely to shock the reader. But as Louis Filler, historian of the movement has shown, a good proportion dealt in a constructive way with important problems; many like Steffens's group on American cities were collected and published as books. The technique of exposure, indeed, permeated different modes of publishing and writing. Novelists and historians, for example, in their works debunking the past, often contributed to the Progressive mentality. Many of the muckrakers, coming from comfortable, middle-class backgrounds, had something of the old-fashioned indignation and liberal philosophy of the civil-service reformers, but the journalists were able to expand enormously the audience for the mugwump type of reform. More than any group, the muckrakers—including the social novelists Frank Norris, Jack London, and Upton Sinclair—infused Progressivism with a certain zest and enthusiasm—a last demonstration, perhaps, of what Alfred Kazin calls the gusto of American life. Although distrustful of big business, the muckrakers recognized the need for organization and efficiency if democracy and reform were to be made to work. They also broadened the impulse toward reform and encouraged the crusade for social justice.

THREE

The

Organization of

Democracy

CHAPTER 5

The Crusade
for Social
Justice

PROGRESSIVISM, in its efforts to reorganize the course of American democracy, added new dimensions to man's search for social justice. The formulas of protest and reform worked out by the insurgent intellectuals and radical thinkers of the late nineteenth century expressed a deep, underlying dissatisfaction with the inequalities and injustices of much of modern American life. In the older preindustrial, preurban America, Christian charity, private benevolence, and public poor relief might have been sufficient to ameliorate the condition of the less fortunate classes. But now those efforts were viewed by many American Progressives as mere palliatives, no longer adequate to achieve substantial social justice or long-lasting, fundamental reforms. They turned accordingly to federal and state legislation and to regulatory measures by administrative commissions and governmental departments. At the same time, the demands for the better management of nonofficial or private reform efforts resulted in the settlement-house movement and in the new profession of the social worker. Thus the crusade for social and economic justice moved forward on two fronts. On the one side there was the traditional American faith in private philanthropy; on the other side the new Progressive concepts of the need for public power and governmental planning.

In the growing industrial society of the post-Civil War generation, the millionaire emerged as a novel American phenomenon. Andrew Carnegie and John D. Rockefeller, with their large private fortunes from steel and oil refining, were, of course, the most conspicuous and successful exemplars of the new rich. Carnegie, more articulate and reflective than most of his fellow millionaires, suggested that men of wealth had a social responsibility that went beyond the old-fashioned almsgiving and Christian charity. His magazine article "The Gospel of Wealth," published in the *North American Review* in 1889 and later expanded into a book with the same title, defended the businessman and his philosophy of individualism, hard work, and competition. But Carnegie also recognized that the increasing concentration and consolidation of small enterprises into larger business units was arousing the fear and envy of great numbers of Americans. Philanthropy by the wealthier classes was necessary, therefore, in order to ward off the dangers of socialism and possible revolution. Only by giving away significant portions of their accumulation could the rich preserve American individualism and acquit themselves of their duty to society.

"As an end, the acquisition of wealth," Carnegie wrote, "is ignoble in the extreme; I assume that you save and long for wealth only as a means of enabling you the better to do some good in your day and generation." The Gospel of Wealth made it possible for Americans to continue to believe in the doctrine of the self-made man and in the ethic of individualism in a corporate age. During the hard times and bitter class conflict of the late eighties and early nineties, it also helped to lessen the hostility of the poor toward the rich. Thus the Gospel of Wealth was a new version of an old idea— an updated, practical example of Christian stewardship and humanitarian reformism.

Through his generous gifts for education, especially in the form of money to build public libraries, Carnegie tried to adhere to his philosophy of self-help and self-culture. But the large amounts that Carnegie and Rockefeller sought to bestow—ultimately almost a billion dollars—made it necessary for them to forego their predilections for an individualistic approach to philanthropy. In a corporate technological age, it was not surprising that philanthropy, too, should become scientific and businesslike. Rockefeller, for example, hired Frederick T. Gates, a Baptist clergyman, to interview applicants and advise him in his grants, and both Carnegie and Rockefeller found it expedient to organize their philanthropies by creating the large foundations that bear their names.

The philanthropic foundation or endowment, which first became important in the Progressive Era, was part of the institutionalization and more efficient administration of social reform. By this time, too, the churches in their application of the Social Gospel were turning more and more to cooperative, interdenominational reform. Such religious organizations as the Salvation Army and the Young Men's Christian Association, originally brought to America from England, became more businesslike in seeking funds and in carrying on their work. The major religious denominations also established reform committees or special branches of the church charged specifically with promoting the cause of labor and social justice. The Federal Council of Churches, organized in 1908 to act as a clearing house for Protestant interdenominational activity, though limited in its functions, did attempt to encourage the individual churches in their social concerns. A manifesto, "The Church and Modern Industry," adopted at the Council's first meeting, ranged official Protestantism on the side of basic reforms in capitalist society through social-welfare legislation and stronger labor unions.

During the nineteenth century leaders of church and charity organizations were aware of European national precedents for a benevolent system of reformation stressing investigation, coordination, and personal service. But as Roy Lubove, author of *The Professional Altruist,* points out, "they considered the systematic implementation of such principles in dozens of cities a genuine innovation." In the larger urban centers in the United States by the turn of the century, the Charity Organization Societies, or Associated Charities movement, begun in England in 1869, had established itself as an answer to the complex needs of the modern industrial community.

The united, citywide charities associations encouraged cooperation and higher standards of efficiency among the already existing societies for dispensing poor relief and welfare. They themselves did not extend direct aid, but they emphasized that if private philanthropy was to be efficient it must purge itself of its old sentimentality and organize its forces more effectively. The new "scientific" philanthropy also meant a shift toward paid workers in addition to trained volunteers—a professional cadre of reformers better able to judge the needs of the poor and to raise supporting funds in a systematic way. By the Progressive Era another profession, that of the social worker, thereby became a familiar part of the reform scene.

An important feature of the businesslike, professional organization of social work was the publication of data surveying the economic conditions and general status of the poor.

Sober factual reports, muckraking journalistic accounts, stories by novelists with an eye for realism or local color, and graphic portraiture by urban artists, dubbed the "Ashcan School," together helped to arouse the American conscience and pave the way for action. Most sensational was the social worker Robert Hunter's assertion that some ten million persons in the United States lived in poverty. His book, simply titled *Poverty* (1904), was based on an analysis of the available data, plus Hunter's personal experiences in settlement-house living among the less fortunate classes of society. Though his estimate of ten million poor seemed exaggerated, it was no doubt a shock to the sensibilities of the comfortable upper and middle classes to be confronted with the possibility that large numbers of fellow Americans were barely able to survive in a country blessed with unparalleled natural resources. Hunter, moreover, spoke for his fellow reformers when he declared that twentieth-century poverty was due to "certain social evils which must be remedied and certain social wrongs which must be put right."

The popular notion that the average American workingman was better off than his counterpart in Europe was undoubtedly true of the country as a whole, but in the larger American cities slum conditions equaled, if they did not surpass, the ghettos of the Old World. Studies carried out by public as well as private agencies confirmed the widespread complaint that wages, measured in terms of prices, were falling behind the high cost of living. Labor spokesmen contended that the average workingman was not receiving his proper share of the total wealth of the country. To back their view, they could point to the federal government's Commission on Industrial Relations, which in its *Final Report,* published in 1915, indicated that the nation's wealth had risen almost 200 percent, or from $65 to $187 billion between 1890 and 1912. Yet the aggregate income of wage earners in industry had risen only 95 percent in the same period. The commission also reported that a large part of America's industrial population, "at least one-third and possibly one-half of the families of wage earners employed in manufacturing and mining earn in the course of the year less than enough to support them in anything like a comfortable and decent condition." Other economic authorities agreed that there was a slight decline in the purchasing power of the dollar during the Progressive Era. The improved status that labor was able to attain after 1900 came, therefore, more from full employment than from wage rates.

The facts and figures assembled by official agencies were further substantiated by the less formal findings of private groups. The organized charities movement sponsored investigations of living conditions among the poor in a number of American cities, and in 1907 the Russell Sage Foundation supported a famous study of Pittsburgh carried out by a distinguished staff of economists and social workers headed by Paul U. Kellogg, editor of *Charities*, the country's leading journal of social work. The so-called Pittsburgh Survey, the most important social investigation in the years before World War I, "put the steel district under a microscope, and the facts revealed were far from pleasant." As Robert Bremner points out in his book on the discovery of poverty in the United States, *From the Depths*, overwork in the form of the twelve-hour day and seven-day week, wages insufficient to support families, and generally bad working conditions in the mills added up to a total picture of appalling human waste. In Pittsburgh it was steel, and not the lives of the men, that was the all-important consideration.

Vital to the search for social justice was the idea of wholeness—the concept that reform should be comprehensive and continuous rather than piecemeal and spasmodic. It should attempt, in other words, to serve the full needs of the individual and society. "Pauperism," wrote Robert Treat Paine, head of the Associated Charities of Boston, in 1893, "cannot be wisely considered alone, but the problem of how to uplift the general level of life must be studied as *one whole problem.*" The churches, for example, by applying the message of the Social Gospel, tried to give greater realism to the argument that Christian teaching could not prevail in an unchristianlike atmosphere of city slums, child labor, and impoverished or broken homes. Not merely food and a roof over one's head, but wholesome recreation, social activity, and physical well-being were important to an individual's health and integrity. Thus the YMCA, boys and girls clubs, nature hikes, summer camps, and the Scouting movement could all be included in the broad reaches of the campaign for social justice.

One of the most practical ways of educating the community to the need for reform was the neighborhood settlement house located in the slum districts of the city. The settlement-house idea appealed to the conscience of those middle- and upper-class persons whose humanitarian reform impulses were seeking a constructive outlet. It also attracted the attention of young men and women eager to translate the idealism of their college years into some practical form of altruism or social service. Given wide publicity in the writings of Jane Addams, its leading spirit, the idea of the settlements captivated the imagination of the Progressive generation and became perhaps its most characteristic reform venture. Not supported by tax funds and free of the narrow sectarian goals of the churches' home missions, the settlements best exemplified the broad reaches of the crusade for social justice.

In England in the nineteenth century, there was already a strong tradition of upper-class concern for the poor dating from Robert Owen's utopian socialist ideals and his practical efforts to provide higher wages for workingmen in his mills at

New Lanark, Scotland, in the 1820's. Later the Christian Socialists, led by Charles Kingsley, an Anglican clergyman, founded clubs for workingmen, and at Oxford University, John Ruskin, the influential art critic and social reformer, contributed to plans for a Working Men's College. Central to those efforts was a belief in the essential unity of life and a desire to preserve spiritual and humane values in a world increasingly dominated by the drab materialism and harsh realities of English factory towns. In 1883 a group of upper-class young men from the universities at Oxford and Cambridge were advised by their friend Canon Samuel A. Barnett, an Anglican minister, to put their education and ideals to use by doing something for the less fortunate classes. "The men might hire a house," Barnett wrote, "where they could come for short or long periods and, living in an industrial quarter, learn to sup sorrow with the poor." In July 1884 accordingly, the University Settlement Association, acting in behalf of Oxford and Cambridge universities, purchased property in the slum district of East End London. Called Toynbee Hall in memory of Arnold Toynbee, a brilliant member of the group who had died the previous year, the new venture launched the idea of the settlement house. Relays of young men from the universities arrived each year hopeful that by living among the poor they might brighten their lives. The motivating purpose was not to extend charity in the form of financial aid, but to provide education, cultural enlightenment, and, above all, sympathetic help and understanding.

The English settlement idea inspired a number of Americans, including Stanton Coit, an Amherst graduate, who in the course of further study in Europe spent three months at Toynbee Hall in 1886. Excited over the possibilities of such a neighborhood organization, Coit, upon his return home in the summer of that year, moved to the Lower East Side of New York City and invited a workingmen's club to meet at his apartment. Coit and a few friends then organized Neighborhool Guild—later University Settlement—as the first settlement in America. Although Coit moved to England in 1887, others carried along his pioneer effort. In Chicago, Jane Addams, who had also visited Toynbee Hall, was determined to do something concrete to promote social justice. Together with her Rockford College classmate Ellen Gates Starr, Miss Addams in 1889 moved into an old Chicago mansion and began what became the most famous social settlement in America. Meanwhile, in the fall of 1889, a group of Smith College graduates led by Vida Scudder, a young instructor at Wellesley, rented a tenement house not far from Neighborhood Guild which they called College Settlement. And four years later Lillian Wald, acting upon her desire to work among the poor, founded Henry Street House, next to Hull House probably the best-known American settlement. A branch of the Henry Street Settlement, established for Negroes, led in 1911 to the Lincoln Settlement House in New York City.

Unsure at first as to how to begin, or what exactly to do, the leaders of the original settlements also knew little of each other's endeavors. Motivated, however, by a common idealism, they were ready to devote their lives to an informal and unofficial effort to achieve social justice. Youthful, well-educated, and mainly from middle-class families, they sought to bridge the growing gulf between the rich and the poor and to ameliorate the social and human problems so characteristic of an urban–industrial society. In the words of Jane Addams: "Insanitary housing, poisonous sewage, contaminated water, infant mortality, the spread of contagion, adulterated food, impure milk, smoke-laden air, ill-ventilated factories, dangerous occupations, juvenile crime, unwholesome crowding, prostitution, and drunkenness are the enemies which the modern city must face and overcome would it survive."

In 1891 there were only six settlements. By 1900 the number had grown to over one hundred, and ten years later there were more than four hundred. As the settlements spread, their work and influence also widened. Many of the residents in the settlement houses had been trained as teachers, and almost every settlement house had its lecture series, amateur theatricals, musicals, vocational classes, kindergartens, and nursery schools for working mothers. The neighborhood needs for nursing care, playgrounds, and parks involved the settlements in problems of public health, housing, and city planning. Since the settlements were surrounded by immigrants, and sometimes Negroes, they were concerned with the particular needs of different ethnic groups. The initial suspicions and resentment of many of the workingmen and labor leaders were overcome by the settlement's willingness to defend labor unions. More hostile were the local political bosses whose paternalistic control over their districts was threatened by the settlement movement's attempts to further good government in cooperation with the Progressives' municipal-reform leagues.

Inevitably the settlement workers found that they could not transform their own neighborhoods without becoming involved in some of the broader issues of city and state politics. The settlements themselves probably reached the peak of their influence in the two decades before the first world war. In the long run, however, the kind of voluntary effort that they exemplified proved inadequate to meet the ever-widening demands for a greater variety of social services and economic welfare measures. To satisfy such needs the reformers were compelled to appeal to the state legislatures and the federal government and to cooperate with labor in a fusion of economic and social Progressivism.

Throughout the country the social-justice movement of the early 1900's, reaching beyond the traditional concepts of private charity and humanitarian reform, began to achieve some of its more important goals. Crowded tenement houses, child labor, long hours for women, public health measures, and workmen's compensation for industrial accidents were major issues that now engaged the attention of the more advanced Progressives and social reformers. Generally speaking, the conditions imposed by modern industrial civilization were responsible for man's mounting social problems. For example, child labor and women's long hours of work, when they were transferred from the farm and household to the factory, became a more apparent menace. In the same way, inferior housing, when it was extended over dozens of densely populated city blocks, was more visible than when it was confined to the fringe of a small rural town.

Already in the 1890's ministers of the Social Gospel, settlement workers, and journalists with a reform bent had been able to focus public attention upon the wretched living and working conditions suffered by the poor. Jacob Riis, an enterprising Danish immigrant and a perceptive police-court reporter, created a sensation with his book *How the Other Half Lives* (1890), a realistic account describing the Lower East Side of New York City. Riis did not discover the tenement house or immigrant problem, but no other reformer was able so successfully to capture the public's imagination and affection. His many books, which served as a catalog of the causes of social discontent, included: *The Children of the Poor* (1892); *The Making of an American* (1901); *The Battle with the Slum* (1902); and *Children of the Tenements* (1903). With Riis, his "main prop and comfort," as a guide, Theodore Roosevelt in his capacity as Police Commissioner of New York from 1895 to 1897 toured the city streets to observe firsthand the crowded tenements with their inevitable results in poverty, crime, disease, and filth. The social consequences of such conditions contradicted Roosevelt's finer instincts and notions of American progress. He could agree therefore with those reformers who argued that better housing was a key to the improved health, well-being, and social stability of the hundreds of thousands of new city dwellers in the United States.

As governor of New York in 1900, T.R. gave his support to legislation outlawing construction of the notorious dumbbell tenements. These buildings were most efficient in terms of utilizing the limited land space of city lots approximately ninety feet by twenty feet. A narrow indentation at the middle of the structure so that it resembled a dumbbell provided an airspace or alley only about five feet in width. On each floor of the tenements, attached on either side to their neighbors and lining the slum streets, it was possible to lay out four four-room apartments, only two of which had light other than from the dumbbell airshaft. The 1900 law, which also created the New York Tenement House Commission, required that all multiple-dwelling apartment houses must henceforth provide private bathrooms, better fire protection, and rooms with outside windows fronting on the street or on interior courts significantly larger than the constricted space afforded by the dumbbell tenements.

The New York measure touched off a nationwide better-housing movement with similar reform legislation in a number of cities and states. In New York itself the action against the old-law tenements was due largely to the efforts of Lawrence Veiller, whom Roosevelt appointed as the first secretary of the Tenement House Commission. In contrast to better-known humanitarian reformers and journalists like Riis, Veiller was a behind-the-scenes social worker and housing expert. At the same time, he became one of the most important municipal reformers in the Progressive Era. A practical-minded liberal who spurned radical innovations in social and economic affairs, Veiller was content to advocate restrictive legislation under the police powers to curb the worst forms of social injustice. After the first world war, Veiller urged a limited program of municipal slum clearance, but he opposed the kind of government-built, -owned, or -subsidized housing already underway in Western Europe. Germany, for example, offered government loans to building societies and cooperatives. Moreover, a number of German cities well before 1914 were already building and operating low-income housing projects, while England's Housing of the Working Class Act of 1890 similarly encouraged the construction of municipal tenements.

The wretched housing of the poor in slum tenements and rural hovels blighted particularly the lives of the women and children. Even worse perhaps were the long hours that they might be forced to work in mill or factory. While middle-class America found it difficult to accept the idea that able-bodied men should need the help of the community, the plight of the women and children was regarded as different. More often than not they were accepted as the innocent victims of society or of male improvidence. Thus the appeal inherent in the title of John Spargo's book *The Bitter Cry of the Children* (1906) found a ready response in the Progressive Era.

The campaign to limit or prohibit child labor was part of a broader movement for the recognition of children's rights. Though nineteenth-century industrialism aggravated the problem of child labor, it was also true that modern, in contrast to ancient, civilization placed a high value upon the lives of its children. Greater overall wealth and smaller families made it possible for society to give more attention to the needs of the individual child. Of first concern was the infant mortality rate in the United States, much higher than in most of the countries in Europe, and especially bad in the slum areas of American cities. In certain states in 1900 as many as 160 infants died out of every thousand and the death rate for children under five was one in every twenty. To meet this challenge the cities looked to advances in medical knowledge to improve the state of public health. They also took preventive measures to ensure a proper supply of milk under clean and sanitary conditions. A number of municipalities supported nursing aid, day-care centers, mother's pensions, and children's playgrounds. In urban America, the outdoor recreational movement now also began to gain significant support. Summer camps were sponsored for underprivileged children, and by World War I the Boy Scouts, founded in England in 1908, became the preeminent boys' organization in the United States. For youths in trouble, juvenile courts were instituted. Judge Ben B. Lindsey, himself the judge of the Denver juvenile court, was chiefly responsible for the passage of the Colorado law of 1901.

Child labor of different sorts had existed from the earliest times in colonial America. It did not become a major problem, however, until the later decades of the nineteenth century when increasing numbers of children began to be employed in the expanding factory system. Although a majority of the children labored on farms, the worst conditions prevailed in manufacturing, and at the turn of the century perhaps as many as two million children were engaged in some form of gainful occupation. In the South child labor was the usual practice in the textile industry. In the North some of the older industrial states like Massachusetts and New York limited the hours or ages of child labor. But neither northern nor southern states had done much by 1900 to eradicate the evil. Then, sparked by the growing interest of reform groups, the movement for restrictive child-labor legislation gained momentum. In 1904 the National Child Labor Committee was formed to coordinate and encourage the efforts of state and local bodies. Alabama, in the meantime, in a 1903 law, assumed the leadership among southern states in setting a higher standard for limiting child labor. Four years later, two-thirds of the states had either initiated or improved protective legislation. At the same time, Congress appropriated funds for investigation and in 1912 created the Children's Bureau in the Department of Commerce and Labor.

In Washington, Albert J. Beveridge, the Progressive senator from Indiana, took the initiative in sponsoring restrictive legislation, introducing the first federal bill in 1906. Public sentiment, including some liberal opinion, was divided, however, on the desirability of a national law. Many shared Woodrow Wilson's view, stated in his *Constitutional Government* (1908), that the proposed federal legislation afforded another striking example of the abuse of congressional power. "If the power to regulate commerce between the states can be stretched to include regulation of labor in mills and factories," Wilson concluded, "it can be made to embrace every particular of the industrial organization and action of the country." Southerners, moreover, were resentful of what they felt were northern efforts to overcome the competitive labor advantage of southern industries. It was not until 1916, therefore, when Wilson—with his earlier opposition now muted—was President, that Congress finally passed the Keating–Own bill excluding the products of child labor from interstate commerce. Although the act was declared unconstitutional in 1918, most of the states by that time had fixed a minimum age and maximum hours for all working children. A majority also insisted on adequate schooling and literacy before a child could be put to work. But the states refused to follow the Progressives' lead and abolish child labor everywhere in the nation by a constitutional amendment.

The partial success in restricting child labor paralleled educational advances in the Progressive Era. The schools were perhaps the most important of all environmental influences in training the child. Under the leadership of John Dewey and other Progressive educators, the traditional curriculum was revamped in terms of the child's social as well as personal needs. The public school was looked upon as the means, not only of imparting formal academic knowledge, but as the chief remedy for the ills of society. From 1898 to 1914, the number of children in elementary schools increased from sixteen to more than twenty million, while the registrations in high schools and colleges more than doubled. School terms were lengthened and efforts were made to raise the qualifications for teaching. By the turn of the century, a significant feature of the expanding American educational system was a growing concern with the efficient, the practical, and the vocational. Though some professors complained that education was not a business, nor the school a factory, educational administration now became a part of the new cult of business efficiency that was satirized so effectively in the writings of Thorstein Veblen. In direct contrast to Veblen, Andrew Carnegie, in his book *Empire of Business* (1902), criticized the nonvocational, classical curriculum in the colleges. At Harvard, President Charles W. Eliot's elective system helped find a place for more science courses in the curriculum.

The specialization and professionalization of the nation's schools and colleges in the Progressive Era, though welcomed by many educators, interfered with some of the historic goals of public education in a democratic society. Specialized training with different courses of study and bureaucratic control by professionals became a barrier to the traditional role of the public school as a social force and center of community life. There was the paradox accordingly that the demands of "progressive reformers for differentiated studies and for

'meeting individual needs' had resulted in the schools per-
petuating social class lines and schooling people into their
social places."

In the South especially, education was hard put to meet
the challenge of the Progressives' concept of social justice. Illiteracy remained an intellectual blight. In 1900 among southern whites it amounted to 12 percent. Among Negroes in the
South, illiteracy, though declining from the 50 percent of
1900, was still about 30 percent a decade later. Although the
South thus lagged badly behind the educational progress of
the rest of the country, such private foundations as the Pea-
body Fund, the Rockefeller General Education Board, and
the Southern Education Board made helpful grants for
teacher training and for the general improvement of education among the poorer classes without regard to
race. Unhappily, the spirit in which educational philanthropy
was administered in the South—while helpful to poor
whites—tended to widen the gulf between the races. Louis
Harlan, assessing the role of the Southern Education Board
in his book *Separate and Unequal,* concludes that the educational expansion in the South, within the context of racial
segregation and discrimination, was of little benefit to black
children and had almost no effect on Negro schools. Northern philanthropy provided funds for an education of accommodation which meant accepting the race arrangements of
the South.

The discriminatory patterns in education tended to be
characteristic of other areas important to the movement for
social justice. Rural communities, especially in the South, as
well as the ethnic minorities of Negroes, Indians, and certain
immigrant groups, although often most in need of help, were
likely to be the very regions and social groups most easily ne-
glected. While blacks and Indians faced poverty and discrimination in the agricultural South and West, newly arrived im-

migrants were crowded into the urban slums of cities like New York and Boston. There they suffered the kind of desperate living conditions so well described by Jacob Riis. In addition to their poverty, many of the immigrants, who had been coming in ever greater numbers from Southern and Eastern Europe since the 1880's, were subjected to social prejudice on the grounds of their Jewish race or religion. With the return of economic prosperity by the late 1890's, some of the hostility to the new-type immigrants temporarily diminished, while their numbers reached an all-time peak, averaging approximately one million arrivals each year between the Spanish–American and first world wars. But racist feeling, fear of radicalism, and the pressure of organized labor all contributed to the growing demand that Congress adopt a literacy test as a means of restriction. "By the end of the century," Oscar Handlin writes, "the pattern of racist practices and ideas seemed fully developed: the Orientals were to be totally excluded; the Negroes were to live in a segregated enclave; the Indians were to be confined to reservations as permanent wards of the nation; and all whites were expected to assimilate as rapidly as possible to a common standard."

In the case of the Negro, although a few militant leaders, notably W. E. B. Du Bois, called for full social and political equality with an end to all discrimination, most Progressives continued to accept the gradualistic policy of vocational education and hard work prescribed by Booker T. Washington. The Progressive Era accordingly brought little change in the southern pattern of discrimination and segregation, and the years 1900 and 1901 were characterized by a holocaust of lynchings and race riots. In 1900 the last of the southern Negro Republicans from Reconstruction days was defeated, and a black man was not elected again to Congress until 1928. Yet the beginning of the twentieth century was not without hope. The number of skilled laborers, operating farmers, and black homeowners all increased at a greater rate than the population. Lynchings gradually declined, although no year before World War I had fewer than forty-nine such crimes. In the new areas of concentrated black population such as New York City, Progressives united with religious groups to sponsor a wide variety of charitable organizations concerned with the Negroes' social welfare. Scholarly studies of black society on the pattern of Du Bois's *Philadelphia Negro* (1899) were undertaken for other large cities. Settlement houses, churches, and missions cooperated to find better job opportunities and living accommodations for blacks who were already becoming segregated in such urban ghettos as New York City's Harlem. In 1909 the National Association for the Advancement of Colored People was founded by a distinguished group of reformers. Du Bois became an officer of the association, while Oswald Garrison Villard, the grandson of William Lloyd Garrison, the abolitionist, wrote the first appeal for support in which he said: "We call upon all believers in democracy to join in a National conference for the discussion of present evils, the voicing of protests, and the revival of the struggle for civil and political liberty."

Largest of all underprivileged groups, at least in their own eyes, were American women—one half the population, as they liked to point out. Although women had played an important role in the abolitionists' crusade against slavery, in the Progressive Era feminists disassociated their own campaign for equality from Negro rights. In a broad sense Negroes and suffragists both appealed to the American democratic tradition. But suffragist support for the Negro's right to vote would have destroyed their own cause in the South and weakened it in the North. Much of the women's reform energies was devoted to politics and gaining the right to vote for themselves, but such organizations as the Consumers'

Leagues and Women's Trade Union League gave staunch leadership to the movement for better working conditions for their sex. Since the Civil War, the numbers of gainfully employed women, married as well as single, had been steadily rising, and by 1910 a fifth of all nonagricultural workers were women. Black women employed as domestic servants were particularly subject to economic exploitation. In factories and offices women's long hours and low wages were a threat, not only to their own health, but also to the general well-being of their homes and families. If special protective legislation favoring women involved a type of paternalistic or preferential treatment, it was no less a fact that women customarily received lower pay than men for equal work.

First of the states to act in their behalf were New York in 1896 and Massachusetts in 1900, with legislation limiting the work week for women to sixty hours. Once the Supreme Court accepted such laws as constitutional, most of the other states followed suit. The Progressive attorney Louis D. Brandeis, in a brief replete with sociological evidence demonstrating the adverse effect of long hours, played a key role in convincing the court, in *Muller* v. *Oregon* (1908), to rule in favor of the maximum-hour laws. Less successful, in contrast to this achievement, was the women's campaign for minimum-wage legislation. Australia and Great Britain offered models of such statutes with their laws enacted from 1896 to 1909, but by the first world war only nine American states had approved minimum-wage laws for women.

The economic conditions under which women worked were often considered more a matter of social justice than a labor problem. In the same way, the advocates of financial compensation for workingmen involved in industrial accidents identified their cause with issues broader than labor's rights. The voluntary benefit funds provided for workers at the end of the nineteenth century, in such dangerous industries as mining and the railroads, served as a precedent for a more comprehensive type of workmen's compensation. Already such compensation was widespread in Europe, but the United States, where the death toll was much greater, remained the last important industrial nation to accept the principle that responsibility for accidents on the job should rest with the employer rather than the employee. In Germany workmen's compensation was financed through a compulsory insurance system of wage-related benefits and contributions with little or no governmental support. The British system, in contrast, provided flat rates of scheduled benefits with a governmental contribution.

Despite labor enthusiasm for these programs in Europe, American labor was slow to back workmen's compensation in the form of compulsory insurance. If they favored any system, labor groups preferred the British scheme. Organized labor in the United States, particularly the leaders of the American Federation of Labor, feared that compensation, whether by welfare capitalism or governmental insurance, might undermine labor's independence and subject it to the paternalism of business or the state. On the other hand, the National Association of Manufacturers was a leading advocate of workmen's compensation on the German model. Such a plan, it believed, would decrease industrial accidents and cut costs. Workmen's compensation would also relieve employers of the need for liability insurance and resultant court cases. For this reason, the NAM opposed the British system, which permitted the laborer first to sue for damages and then, if the suit failed, to seek compensation.

American states moved slowly to establish employer's legal liability for accidents suffered on the job. Even after the first laws were passed in the early 1900's, the employer still had to be sued for the compensation. Once these ineffective laws were redrawn and judicial opposition overcome, the federal government in 1908, and some twenty-five states over the next several years, passed measures establishing an employer's liability for some form of accident insurance or workmen's compensation. The results, nevertheless, were disappointing. Benefits were much too low, and with the first world war the movement faltered even though the United States Supreme Court ruled in 1917 that the state police powers were an adequate basis for all types of workmen's compensation laws.

Other causes beginning to win state approval in the prewar years were pensions for dependent or destitute mothers and laws for the inspection of factories in order to improve working conditions and reduce the dangers of fire and industrial accidents. On New York's East Side, the Triangle Shirtwaist Factory fire in 1911, in which 148 female employees lost their lives, led to the appointment of an investigating committee and revisions in the building code.

Disasters like the Triangle fire stirred Americans to action. But the United States, with no comprehensive social security or welfare program until the New Deal laws of the 1930's, lagged far behind Europe and some of the British Commonwealth nations. New Zealand, for example, as the reformer Henry Demarest Lloyd pointed out to American readers of his popular books on state democracy in New Zealand and Australia, had compulsory arbitration of labor disputes and old-age pensions. Each country had also instituted a broad program of land reforms modeled in part on the ideas of Henry George. Yet the crusade for social justice in the Progressive Era was not a failure in the United States. Child labor was much less a problem by 1918, the settlements and stricter housing laws alleviated some of the worst conditions in the slums, and women had gained greater respect and job protection. Most of all, the Progressives were able to win support from the country for their view that America's rich resources should be shared more equally. There was also now a greater confidence that the social evils linked with modern industrial progress could be conquered and permanent reforms achieved.

CHAPTER 6

Forces of Urban Liberalism

THE crusade for social justice was largely an urban phenomenon, related particularly to the needs of labor and the millions of immigrants and older Americans who were clustered in the emerging metropolitan centers of the East and Midwest. Following the Civil War, and certainly by the 1880's and 1890's, the central focus of American life shifted from the small towns in rural regions to the larger urban areas. The city accordingly bore the brunt of the revolutionary changes that were components of the new industrialism. The difficult problem of governing American cities was often, in turn, simply a result of the speed with which they were growing in the late nineteenth century. Despite the popular and scholarly attention to the settlement of the last frontiers to the West, most of the increasing American population, swelled by the tide of European immigrants, was finding its way to the cities. There the forces of urban liberalism, responding to the demands of both political and social Progressivism, combined to advance the cause of reform and good government.

In the early 1900's almost one half the American population found itself living in cities or towns of over 2,500 people. Already by 1900 one-third of the population lived in places of more than 8,000 inhabitants—the Census Bureau's original definition of a city—and in the decade from 1890 to 1900 the rate of urban growth was almost double that of the entire population. Most of the increase in the cities' population came from European immigration, but the internal migration of discontented Americans leaving impoverished rural areas was also important. Southern Negroes, for example, were drifting to northern cities at the rate of fifty thousand persons a year by the early 1900's. Urban problems meanwhile were aggravated by the surge of newcomers, and in the larger cities of the Northeast and Midwest, factories and slums developed together, creating the need for additional, expensive governmental services.

Though united in their overriding desire to improve political and social conditions in American cities, the municipal reformers of the Progressive Era were less certain of the best means of attaining their goals. Older liberals of the Grover Cleveland, mugwump school of civil-service reform emphasized simple honesty in government and the overthrow of the Tammany Hall type of political bosses. Advanced political Progressives and Socialists stressed efficiency and organization with municipal ownership of key public utilities—the so-called gas-and-water socialism of European cities. Like many of the Socialists, labor and the multiplying ethnic groups in the cities looked to a more positive kind of urban liberalism characterized by social-welfare legislation. In contrast to the upper-class, mugwump type of reformers, labor leaders were comparatively indifferent to simple political, as distinct from social and economic, reforms.

Progressive-reform elements recognized that the American city, lacking the European tradition of a municipal socialism and urban autonomy dating back to the feudal era, was all too often merely "a place in which to make money. It was also a place out of which to make money. . . ." By lax or corrupt procedures in granting franchises and contracts for public utilities, politicians were able to exact fees and bribes from the equally corrupt businessmen who gladly paid large sums in return for privileged profits. Corruption was frequently less a moral issue than a result of the desire to gain political control and power. Or, as Frederic C. Howe, an assistant to Tom Johnson, the reform mayor of Cleveland, explained: "It is privilege, not wealth; franchises, not business; the few, not the many, that have overthrown our cities within the past few years." "The greatest movement in the world today," Johnson himself wrote retrospectively in 1911, "may be characterized as the struggle of the people against Privilege."

The noted muckraker Lincoln Steffens discovered in his tour of American cities and states in 1902 and 1903 that it was often the best people who were most involved in the sorry story of corruption and bribery. *The Shame of the Cities* (1904), his influential account of the seamier side of politics in New York, Philadelphia, St. Louis, and other cities, documented what most Americans already knew or suspected. But Steffens and his fellow journalists reinforced the point that the "respectable businessman" was the worst enemy of reform. He was too eager to protect his own interest and too busy to exercise his responsibilities as a citizen. The popular evangelist of the Social Gospel, the Reverend Josiah Strong, in his book *The Twentieth Century City*, blamed its problems on the materialism and irreligion of modern American life. But he also complained that the "so-called 'good citizens,' who are so mindful of their own business . . . are singularly indifferent as to the administration of their own city government. They are lacking in civic patriotism." Steffens, like Strong, indicted the American people for neglecting their civic duties. Yet he believed that his magazine articles, appearing originally in *McClure's* in 1902, demonstrated that Americans could stand the truth.

It was apparent that the rise of the city resulted all too frequently in a decline in those older American standards of civic virtue that had characterized small-town life. In the process of losing much of its original political dominance, the old-stock, native American population often manifested indifference, if not hostility, to the newer immigrant and his problems. Unconsciously, perhaps, older Americans reflected their Protestant, rural mores and the country life of their youth. Sharing the liberal intellectuals' traditional fear and dislike of the city, they accepted the classical Jeffersonian agrarian prejudices. America, Jefferson had warned, would remain virtuous only "as long as agriculture is our principal object. . . . When we get piled upon one another in large cities, as in Europe, we shall become corrupt as in Europe and go to eating one another as they do there."

Although perhaps a majority of the Progressive leaders, like other Americans in the twentieth century, came to the city fresh from rural backgrounds, they were also the first generation of reformers willing to deal seriously with municipal problems. They responded accordingly to urban demands for broad social and economic reforms as well as for sound and honest government. As Progressives motivated by humanitarian sentiments, they also forsook the laissez-faire individualism of the older liberal reformers in favor of the more community-minded outlook of the new social democracy.

Some of the assumptions of the Progressive reformers were related, at least in a general way, to what Richard Hofstadter has called a status revolution in American life and thought. As representatives of the upper classes, who were impelled less by financial necessity than by their own inner dissatisfactions with the society of which they were a part, many of the Progressives turned to reform to fulfill what seemed a deep psychic need. Large numbers of the Progressives of the 1900's resembled the abolitionist sons and daughters of the New England clergy, who, in the mid-nineteenth century, no longer held the prestigious position that they had enjoyed in colonial America. Like their Yankee forebears, these children of the old liberal aristocracy—reaching maturity in the 1890's, but in grave danger of being displaced by the rising post-Civil War, nouveau-riche business class—aspired to retrieve their status by becoming the nucleus of a new political elite.

Hofstadter's thesis, supported by George Mowry's study of California Progressives—native-born Protestant Republicans of the upper middle class, transplanted from New England via the Middle West—and Alfred Chandler's statistical study of "The Origins of Progressive Leadership," has been both challenged and defended in a number of monographs and articles on particular cities and states. The Hofstadter typology of the average Progressive was perhaps least characteristic of the reform leadership in great urban immigrant and labor centers like New York and Boston. There first-generation Americans and members of religious and ethnic minorities, Democrats rather than Republicans, were often the driving force behind political and social reforms. But it was also true that Progressivism in the cities and states across the nation owed much to the leadership of what could be called a patrician class of civic-minded reformers. Whether or not this class was driven to reform by its own anxieties and declining social status was more doubtful than the fact that prominent business and professional men seemed, in any case, to be the most active leaders of practicing municipal-reform movements. "Available evidence," Samuel Hays writes in his article "The Politics of Reform in Municipal Government in the Progressive Era," "indicates that the source of support for reform in municipal government did not come from the lower or middle classes, but from the upper class."

Nevertheless, in the Progressive Era, the patrician class and the city political machines sometimes found themselves in strange alliance. As Oscar Handlin has pointed out in his study of immigrant acculturation, *The Uprooted,* both the boss and the do-gooder were forced to consider anew the needs of the urban immigrants. The party machines by the close of the nineteenth century had worked out a system for managing the vote by providing favors to the large numbers of politically ignorant immigrants who made up the bulk of the cities' new populations. The machine, from its ward heelers to its party chieftains, opened to the immigrants the prospect that government might be the means through which they could gain the beginnings of social and economic security. Certainly American government was not the despotic monster that the average immigrant had learned to fear in the Old World. At the same time, many of the Progressive advocates of good government accepted the desirability of combining political reforms with greater responsibility for the social and economic welfare of the urban masses. Thus the city was becoming what Fred Howe called "the hope of democracy," a place where, according to J. Allen Smith, democracy was "likely to win its first victories."

A simple or direct popular democracy, keeping government close to the people, was a traditional part of the American dream. "The smaller the area, the stronger the pressure of public opinion," Charles B. Spahr, author of a pioneering essay on the distribution of wealth, asserted. "As a rule, the middle class can control the legislation enacted under their eyes by those whom they know, but only the wealthier classes can act unitedly and effectively upon legislation at the national capital." In the complex modern world, however, the time-honored slogan "Let the People Rule" did not always work to ensure effective government. The reorganization of democracy accordingly seemed necessary to protect the people's rights. "The ideas of government organization which we have borrowed from an earlier period, and which have worked great good as applied to our state and federal governments, are no longer applicable to the conditions that prevail in our cities," declared Leo S. Rowe in a scholarly article on "The Relation of Municipal Government to American Democratic Ideals."

On the national scene, President Roosevelt in his first annual message to Congress in 1901 called "the betterment of social conditions, moral and physical, in large cities . . . the most vital problem with which this country, and for that matter the whole civilized world, has to deal. . . ." Soon thereafter, following a visit to the United States some twenty-five years after his first trip here, James Bryce, author of *The American Commonwealth* (1888), revised his famous indictment of American municipal government as "the one conspicuous failure of the United States." American cities, Bryce now wrote, seemed better governed. In any case, he pointed out, "before long the United States will be like England, and, one must almost add, like Germany also, a land in which the urban type of mind and life will predominate. The change may be regrettable. Jefferson would have regretted it. But it is inevitable."

In America, as in Europe, it was apparent that specific instances of the growth of governmental activity in the twentieth century would be most likely to affect the average citizen in his capacity as a city dweller. Much of Europe, for example, had already achieved a practical working system of municipal administration. Albert Shaw, a pioneer student of comparative public administration, believed that common problems justified United States consideration of this European experience. Moreover, traditional American individualism could best be reconciled with socialism on the municipal level. "In the theory and art of modern city-making," he declared, "we must frankly acknowledge, collectivism has a large and growing place." The rapid growth of European towns and cities in the late nineteenth century emphasized the need for municipal planning. "A general familiarity with their attempts and achievements," Shaw observed, "might save our American cities from some mistakes, and might stimulate them to adopt broader and more generous municipal programs." Shaw pointed out that the German city was a "far more positive factor in the life of the family or individual than in America." This, he believed, stemmed from "the German conception of the municipality as a social organism. . . . There are, in the German conception of city government, no limits whatever to municipal functions. It is the business of the municipality to promote in every feasible way its own welfare and the welfare of its citizens."

Shaw and Fred Howe, both former graduate students of Richard T. Ely at Johns Hopkins University, published detailed accounts of how British municipal government operated. Although Howe believed the city to be the most democratic institution in Great Britain, he was critical of its failure to go beyond the elimination of corruption in order to deal more constructively with the problems of poverty. "The life of the people, their standard of existence, the condition of their homes, their health, education and happiness is a matter of something more than honesty and efficiency," he wrote in his book *The British City: The Beginnings of Democracy* (1907).

In Britain a major area of interest to Howe and American reformers were the industrial towns where municipal socialism had a strong hold. There the key to success was home rule as well as public ownership. In America, in contrast, charters voted by rural state legislatures did not provide adequately for democratic self-government or home rule. Moreover, when the voter had to choose among a bewildering number of minor officials, it seemed that democracy might be better served if only the most important and responsible offices were made elective. James Bryce, for example, though he found much to praise in American presidential elections, complained that in local contests the "elective offices are so numerous that ordinary citizens cannot watch them, and cease to care who gets them."

By the late 1890's the notorious defects of American city governments were bringing about the beginnings of a strong reform movement. Since the days of Boss Tweed in the 1870's, Tammany Hall, with its nefarious machinations in New York City, had been an object of concerned attention. In the early nineties, Charles H. Parkhurst, a Presbyterian clergyman of stern moral views, and president of the Society for Prevention of Crime, instigated the influential Lexow Committee investigation, which resulted in the temporary ouster of the Tammany regime in 1894. Several years later Seth Low, president of Columbia University, elected as a reform mayor on a businessman's platform, was able to reorganize the city finances as well as its police department and educational system. And in 1913, John Purroy Mitchel, as the mayoral candidate on a fusion ticket, defeated the Tammany Democrats' choice.

Outside of New York City, municipal reformers were also active. As early as 1889, Hazen S. Pingree, mayor of Detroit, campaigned against the substantial economic privileges enjoyed by the public utilities, especially the street railways. His most publicized venture, however, was his "potato-patch plan" to aid the poor by allowing them to cultivate vacant lots owned by the city. In Baltimore in the 1890's a reform uprising broke the power of the Gorman–Freeman ring. And in this same period Chicago, chastened by the actions of its city council in selling, for a fraction of their value, important traction rights to Charles T. Yerkes, a wealthy utilities magnate, turned to reform and organized the Municipal Voters' League. In 1897 the cause of clean government won over corruption, and Chicagoans elected Carter H. Harrison, Jr., who, although a regular party man, "was right on traction."

Two of the most forceful and dramatic municipal leaders in the United States at the turn of the century were from Ohio: Samuel M. Jones of Toledo and Thomas L. Johnson of Cleveland. Both men were unusual in that they were able to apply much of their idealistic personal philosophy to the practical cause of good government. Jones, who was first elected mayor of his city in 1897, had made a fortune as a pioneer manufacturer of machinery for the oil industry. An unconventional disciple of the Russian novelist Tolstoy's Christian anarchism, Jones attempted to conduct business and politics according to the biblical golden rule. As mayor he urged public ownership of municipal utilities, improved the city playgrounds, provided free concerts in the parks, added kindergartens to the school system, and substituted light canes for the policeman's traditional clubs. His efforts to apply Christian principles to municipal politics alienated all the conventionally respectable elements of Toledo, including the churches and two major parties. "Everyone was against him," Fred Howe noted, "except the workers and the underworld." Yet he was reelected three times on an independent ticket, and after he died in office in 1904 he was succeeded by his disciple and former secretary, Brand Whitlock. Whitlock, who shared Jones's general outlook, was able to secure a new city charter providing for the initiative, referendum, and recall as well as the direct popular nomination of candidates for city offices.

Like Jones, Tom Johnson made a fortune in private industry. Then, at the height of his career, the study of Henry George's economic philosophy persuaded him to forsake business for politics and reform. As congressman from 1891 to 1895 he could do little to further his ideas, but as mayor of Cleveland from 1901 to 1909, Johnson was able to bring the street railways under municipal control and reduce the fare to three cents. Other reforms included city planning and a reassessment of the real estate of the city. He was, said Lincoln Steffens, the "best mayor of the best governed city in the United States." Johnson was notable, too, for the devoted followers whom he inspired—men like Fred Howe and Newton D. Baker, who succeeded him as mayor of Cleveland and who later became Woodrow Wilson's Secretary of War.

Both Johnson and Jones were firm believers in the municipal ownership of public utilities—a policy widespread in European cities. The city's ownership of its public services, the Progressives hoped, would eliminate the graft and corruption that was the frequent companion of the sale of franchises and contracts to private interests. By the close of the Progressive Era most American cities, indeed, operated their waterworks and sewage systems. A much lesser number, however, experimented with municipal ownership of such utilities as gas, electricity, and public transportation. One circumstance, which lessened the value of the European example, was that certain of the state constitutions and city charters did not permit municipal ownership. Socialism, in any case, was not a complete answer to the city's problems.

For the more traditional liberals and good-government people, municipal reform remained a simple moral issue. It was sufficient merely to elect honest men and to prevent their corruption. In the smaller towns and cities, it was still no doubt true that the older liberal standards of American civic virtue and responsibility were strong enough to ensure decent government. But the modern twentieth-century metropolis, with its urgent social and economic problems and its mounting population, transcended the old morality. Both the gentleman–reformer engaged in politics as a leisure-time activity and the typical machine boss were being forced to step aside and yield at least a share of the stage to the professional student of public administration. The government of cities required specialized skills and a new ethic of social, rather than individual, morality. The individual, whether a feudal-type machine politician or a benevolent upper-class reformer, could not "do it alone." According to Fred Howe, surveying *The Modern City and Its Problems:*

> The city can only live by cooperation; by cooperation in a million unseen ways. Without cooperation for a single day a great city would stand still. Without cooperation for a week it would be brought to the verge of starvation and be decimated by disease.
>
> The city has destroyed individualism. It is constantly narrowing its field. And in all probability, cooperation, either voluntary or compulsory, will continue to appropriate an increasing share of the activities of society.

The revival of the old-fashioned sense of civic-mindedness, plus the need for social cooperation and professional skills in governing American cities, received dramatic illustration in 1900 when a giant tidal wave swept in from the Gulf of Mexico, drowning one-sixth of the population and destroying one-third of the property of Galveston, Texas, in a single night. To meet the emergency the citizens appealed to the state legislature and to the governor to allow them to replace their old and unwieldy council form of government with a special commission of five members. Given full control of the city, the commission enacted municipal ordinances, awarded contracts, and made appropriations and appointments. Each of four commissioners assumed responsibility for a major department, while the fifth acted as mayor and chairman of the commission. When the new system proved efficient, it was adopted in Houston and other Texas cities and spread in the early 1900's to a number of places in the South and Midwest. Meanwhile, George Kibbe Turner's article on "Galveston: A Business Corporation," published in *McClure's* in 1906, provoked wide discussion. And a year later Iowa authorized a more elaborate version of the Texas commission form of government for Des Moines and other cities in the state.

Further refinements of the commission plan to permit the addition of a professional city manager lessened certain weaknesses such as the lack of central responsibility in the Galveston-type government. Under this revised system, although all authority in respect to laws and policy remained in the hands of the commissioners, an appointed city manager administered the various municipal departments in their day-to-day operations. The city-manager plan was first tried by Staunton, Virginia, in 1908, and then, three years later, by Sumter, South Carolina. A home-rule amendment to the Ohio state constitution in 1912 permitted cities in that state to adopt the new version of municipal rule, which was first put into effect in complete form in Dayton in 1913. By that year the commission or city-manager types of municipal government, with certain modifications, were in force in over two hundred cities throughout the United States. Both systems proved popular in medium-sized cities in Texas, New England, and parts of the Middle and Far West. Each type of government reflected not only the Progressives' drive for municipal reform, but also the businessman's interest in efficient management. The prosperity of the modern city, measured in terms of its commerce, industry, and real estate, required new standards of professional government and public administration.

While the commission–manager form of city government was becoming a favorite of local businessmen, it was not without significant opposition. Critics attacked the whole concept of running the city as a business enterprise. Social concerns and public welfare, it was argued, even though they were expensive, were as vital to public needs as abstract standards of efficiency and economy. "Good health," one critic remarked, "is more important than a low tax rate." The old-line political machines in northern cities had obvious reasons for grievances against the commission–manager plan. But often the Socialist party, which in the decade after 1910 succeeded in electing municipal officers in over three hundred cities, led the opposition. Both the Socialists and the machine politicians understood that the citywide election of commissioners effectively eliminated the local ward representation on which the power of the machine and the hope of minority representation alike rested. Nonpartisan tickets also hurt the chances of Socialist or labor candidates. Finally city managers with professional standards of administration reduced the amount of the patronage on which the old political machines had thrived.

To put reform efforts on a more permanent and scientific basis, municipal research bureaus, reform leagues, citizens unions, and civic clubs were organized in some of the larger cities like New York and Chicago. The National Municipal League, established in 1894, developed a general educational program of information for cities, including advice on technical questions and blueprints of model charters, ordinances, and organizational plans. The New York Bureau of Municipal Research, formed in 1906, became the prototype for similar bureaus in other cities and states. It was also an example of the growing use of trained experts in public administration and of the application of the principles of political science to the needs of local government.

A matter on which there was near-unanimous agreement among the experts was the necessity for a larger measure of home rule for American cities. Under the federal system of checks and balances between the different levels of American government, local units often fared badly. They were dependent, in the first place, on charters or constitutions prescribed by the states. Legally, the city, as a municipal corporation, was the creature of the state legislature, exercising certain delegated functions, but absolutely under legislative control except as it might be protected by the restrictions of the state constitution. In conferring governmental powers on cities, legislatures were usually more parsimonious than generous. Thus cities were forced to seek authority, or even to beg funds, from state legislatures, and the latter, in turn, found themselves devoting time and energy to urban problems rather than to statewide concerns. In New York State between 1910 and 1915, out of a total of over four thousand bills passed by the legislature almost one thousand were special city measures.

Many state legislatures were guilty of unjustifiable acts of aggression upon the needful rights of city government. To curb the power of the city bosses, for example, state legislatures, dominated by rural interests and voters, and frequently no more honest than the urban political machines which they sought to displace, managed to deprive the cities of effective control over their own affairs. Thus few cities had the power to grant franchises for necessary public services in their own jurisdiction. It was true that home rule, simpler charters, and shorter ballots were not by themselves guarantees of good government, but they did offer cities an opportunity to become more efficient and to gain a measure of independence from unsympathetic state legislators. Home rule also promised city taxpayers control, not only over what they paid in the form of taxes, but also over what facilities or services they felt their municipality should provide. "With home rule secured," concluded Fred Howe, "with popular control attained, with the city free to determine what activities it will undertake, and what shall be its sources of revenue, then the city will be consciously allied to definite ideals, and the new civilization, which is the hope as well as the problem of democracy, will be open to realization."

The Progressive movement in the cities, building on the work of the earlier reformers of the 1890's, was able to achieve a systematic, concerted series of substantial improvements. City government was made more responsible and brought closer to the people via a more direct democracy. The urban reformers did not eliminate all evils or achieve utopia. But they were, for the most part, tough-minded, realistic reformers who shared a sincere concern for the social welfare of the teeming masses of workingmen and women who had become the American city's chief responsibility. By the close of the Progressive Era, it was a fact that American cities seemed better governed and that the flagrant corruption of which Bryce had complained was much less in evidence. More efficient administration and a renewed sense of civic responsibility thus strengthened democracy in the area of its greatest population growth and strongest challenge.

CHAPTER 7

The States as Laboratories of Reform

PROGRESSIVISM in the states was often an out-growth of reforms begun in the cities. Within the states, however, Progressivism was able to extend and broaden the movement for social and political changes and appeal to the middle classes as well as to the labor and ethnic groups concentrated in urban areas. In its efforts to reorganize American democracy, Progressivism, moreover, was able to utilize the states as laboratories of reform. Federalism, as James Bryce noted in his *American Commonwealth*, enabled the people "to try experiments in legislation and administration which could not be safely made in a large centralized country." In this way, each state served the nation as an experiment station, thereby fulfilling one of the important tenets of a federal system of government.

The states likewise provided a test for the novel theories of public administration being applied by the new regulatory commissions and planning bodies. Here a class of civil servants, dedicated to professional standards of governmental efficiency, and familiar with similar trends in Europe, was becoming a new elite. More significant accordingly than the tensions and status anxieties impelling the sons and daughters of the old gentry and professional classes to enter reform politics were the satisfactions now often engendered by holding public office. Moreover, the increasing emphasis on efficiency and the better training of governmental employees proved useful, as Samuel Haber points out, to many of the Progressives who were trying to create a reform program without stirring the social conscience or revolutionary feelings of the masses. Planning and social control via state regulation, in place of laissez faire, could be justified in terms of scientific principles and good public administration. "Efficiency," Haber adds in his book *Efficiency and Uplift*, "provided a standpoint from which those who declared allegiance to democracy could resist the levelling tendencies of the principle of equality."

Not all the states moved along with the Progressive tide; in the South black people, for example, failed to benefit from advances in democracy in their geographic area. Within the various states, Progressives themselves held conflicting views on such measures as prohibition and laws which restricted personal rights or privileges. Urban elements and Progressives with a libertarian point of view resented the kind of censorious restraints upon the individual exemplified in state morals legislation. Older liberals, moreover, discerned dangers to traditional freedoms in the growth of big government and in the way in which a mounting bureaucracy accompanied increases in social-welfare and regulatory legislation.

By the late nineteenth century, the corruption of America's state governments came close to equaling the shame of its cities. In reality the era of sordid materialism following the Civil War left no branch of American government untouched. Demands for special privileges characterized politics on all levels. In the states, as in the cities, corrupt political machines dominated by powerful bosses were the medium through which dishonest businessmen obtained franchises and contracts. Railroads, as the major economic interest in the country, received especially favorable consideration in the form of land grants and low taxes. In certain states—Missouri and New Jersey were unhappy examples—the railroad lobby controlled legislators and key officials who served its selfish demands rather than the public welfare. Western states, where the Granger movement had achieved some regulation of rates, were particularly dependent upon the railroads. In the Far West, the Southern Pacific Railroad—the *Octopus* of Frank Norris's novel—was popularly supposed to own the state of California. But almost everywhere there was the same unholy alliance of business and politics. A French map of the United States, published in the *Literary Digest* magazine in 1905, showed only six of the forty-five states as free from corruption. Twenty-five were depicted as wholly corrupt and thirteen as partially corrupt.

Like the good-government movement in the cities, the Progressive revolt against corruption in the states grew out of previous efforts at reform. Well before the turn of the century some of the states, particularly in the agrarian-dominated West, had approved laws regulating the railroads. In the industrial areas of the Northeast other states experimented with legislation affecting public health and sanitation or conditions of labor. In contrast to the general run of the city bosses who preferred to rule anonymously from behind the scenes, some of the state machine leaders occupied top political positions. Matthew Quay of Pennsylvania and Thomas C. Platt of New York were the dominant corporation voices in their states while they served in the United States Senate. It was Platt, nevertheless, who smoothed the way for

Theodore Roosevelt to run for governor of New York. Roosevelt, John P. Altgeld in Illinois, and Hazen S. Pingree in Michigan were noteworthy examples of nonmachine leaders who prepared the ground for the Progressive movement in their states. Pingree, who moved on to the governor's chair after serving as a reform mayor of Detroit, set a course followed by Joseph W. Folk of Missouri and Hiram W. Johnson of California, both of whom became state governors after first building reputations by exposing corruption on a local level.

Reform governors, like reform mayors, were usually confined to single terms while the machine regrouped and regained its power in the next election. In New York State, Roosevelt, after serving creditably as governor from 1899 to 1901, was chosen Vice President of the United States with most of his reform proposals still not approved. Conservative political opposition plus public apathy thwarted the early reformers, and it was not until Robert M. La Follette defeated the regular Wisconsin political machine in 1900 that Progressivism in the states really got started.

Forty-five years of age when he first became his state's chief executive, La Follette, with his tremendous energy and ambition, was able to build a powerful political following based on the small farmer in the interior and the workingman in the lakeshore cities. The regular wing of the Wisconsin Republican party opposed his initial proposals for reforms. But after he succeeded in gaining the election of a sympathetic legislature, La Follette inspired what George Mowry has termed "the most comprehensive reform program in the history of American state government down to 1933." A direct primary law, provision for a railroad rate commission, heavier railroad and corporation taxes, a civil service act, antilobbying law, conservation and waterpower act, and state banking measure were all passed at La Follette's urging. Later, after he had gone on to the United States Senate, the

Wisconsin legislature approved a state income tax, the first of its kind and a measure the passage of which was due almost entirely to his support. Originally within the Republican party, then later through their own Progressive party, La Follette and his political heirs, including his two sons, Robert, Jr., and Philip, established what was the most durable of any of the state reform administrations.

Wisconsin's Progressive reforms also owed much to the unique alliance between the state government and the state university. In Wisconsin the state and the university joined in advancing social democracy, and "The Wisconsin Idea" became a term used to describe the application of scholarship and theory to the needs of the people. In a real sense, the University of Wisconsin was a fourth department of the state government, cooperating with the legislative, executive, and judicial branches. Professors contributed their expert, specialized knowledge to the drafting and administration of state legislation, and much of what La Follette was able to accomplish depended upon the atmosphere of political freedom associated with the enthusiasm for learning and research fostered by the university.

Wisconsin was also an interesting Progressive state because, with its large immigrant population, it naturally looked to Germany for many of its ideas about reform. The high value placed on learning, the stress on civil-service reform and expert administration, plus such specific measures as a model workmen's compensation law, were important examples of Wisconsin's social democracy. La Follette, as the first Progressive governor, was aware of the new currents of reform in Europe, and contemporary writers described Wisconsin as fundamentally a German state. According to Fred Howe, it was "doing for America what Germany is doing for the world. It is an experiment station in politics, in social and industrial legislation, in the democratization of science and higher education."

Inspired, perhaps, by La Follette's success in capturing the Wisconsin governorship, Iowa, Minnesota, Missouri, and the adjacent states to the west, from North Dakota to Kansas, swept reform administrations into office. In Iowa in the fall of 1901, Albert Baird Cummins, a former railroad attorney who became dissatisfied with the treatment he had received from the state Republican machine, won his campaign for the governorship on an antimonopoly, antirailroad platform. In office he fought the conservative railroad interests in the state successfully, and then in 1908 he followed La Follette to the United States Senate. In 1904, Minnesota and Missouri elected reform Democrats, and in the latter state Joseph Folk, the new governor, continued to hold the liberal support that he had first gained in his struggle against the bosses in St. Louis.

Progressivism, although strongest in the Midwest, inspired similar, if not identical, political shifts in some of the states in the South. There a new generation of leaders took over much of the agrarian program and flamboyant political oratory of such Populists of the 1890's as Tom Watson of Georgia and Benjamin R. Tillman of South Carolina. Jeff Davis in Arkansas, James K. Vardaman in Mississippi, and Hoke Smith in Georgia—all southern rebels—gained the governorship in their states in the 1900's on reform platforms. Against the conservative, corporation-dominated Democratic machines, they appealed to the economic and racial prejudices of the southern poor whites. Thus, along with genuine reforms in the improvement of educational facilities and regulation of the railroads, the new southern leaders reinforced traditional patterns of racial discrimination and segregation in their states. By disfranchising the Negro through electoral

devices of dubious constitutionality, they were able to outvote
the old aristocratic classes who had controlled the blacks and
to bring about a revolution in southern life and politics.

Progressivism in the South, it should be noted, did not rest
entirely on demagogic appeals to class and race interests.
Governor Charles B. Aycock of North Carolina led a dig-
nified drive for better public schools and more effective
railroad regulation in his state. The South generally was in
the forefront in providing state railroad commissions. And it
also supported the commission form of government in the cities and a more direct popular democracy on the state level.
Although southern newspaper editors later provided important backing for Woodrow Wilson's New Freedom, the South
as a whole gave less support than other sections of the country
to the social-justice movement. And it was abundantly clear
that Progressivism below the Mason-Dixon line meant little
change in race relations; it remained a reform movement for
whites only.

In the more industrialized and urbanized states of the
Northeast, political Progressivism was less evident and less
spectacular than in the other sections. The reform movement
there rested to a greater extent on the crusade for social justice in the cities and on legislation in behalf of labor. Along
these lines much had already been accomplished in an older
state like Massachusetts well before the Progressive movement took hold in the West and South. Massachusetts set a
standard for other states by its legislation regulating public
utilities and railroad finances. It was, also, in 1888 the first
state to require the Australian, or secret, ballot. In New York,
Charles Evans Hughes achieved a national reputation for his
outstanding work as chief counsel to the legislative committee
investigating the mismanagement of the country's greatest
life insurance companies. As governor from 1907 to 1910, he
sponsored a direct primary law as well as public commissions

to regulate the utilities and railroads. Vermont and New Hampshire also chose reform governors from the insurgent wing of the Republican party. Most interesting of all the eastern states, however, was New Jersey, where first the Progressive Republicans, and then the Democrats under Woodrow Wilson in 1911, were able to push through a legislative program that helped to overcome the state's image as a haven of corporate power, boss rule, and corrupt politics.

A major characteristic of the Progressive movement was its faith in a direct appeal to the voice of the people. Even the most talented and conscientious leaders, like Senator La Follette, needed to build a loyal popular following similar to that of the political machines they sought to displace. Progressives had to keep their hold on the voters if they hoped to overthrow the established political and social order and push their reform ideas to completion. Confident that the people really wanted good government, the reformers proposed changes in the structure of the American political system designed to restore popular democratic rule.

In the early 1900's a number of state constitutions were amended to conform to Progressive conceptions of direct democracy. In general these changes gave added powers to the state governors, centralized administrative functions, and introduced the electoral reforms of a shorter ballot and secret voting. At the same time the functions of the legislatures, singled out by Progressives as the most corrupt branches of state government, were reduced in favor of special regulatory commissions. Thus representative government in the Progressive scheme of things seemed to be yielding to a combination of direct democracy and an administrative state.

Of all the democratic innovations in the Progressive Era, the initiative, referendum, and recall, the direct primary, woman suffrage, and the popular election of United States senators stand out as the most significant. "Give the government back to the people!" became a slogan of Progressivism in the states. A key figure, perhaps more responsible than any of his fellow Progressives in carrying forward the movement for popular democracy, was William S. U'Ren of Oregon, a disciple of Henry George. U'Ren never held a major political office, but during the 1890's he became interested in the system of direct government practiced in Switzerland. Utilizing his experience as a newspaper editor, lawyer, and Populist, U'Ren devoted his life to persuading Oregon and other states to adopt the direct primary, the referendum, the initiative, and the recall. Under the direct primary the voters rather than political meetings or conventions, often boss-ruled, nominated party candidates. The electorate was also empowered to initiate legislative action by petition, and to approve or reject legislation submitted to a popular referendum. The voters might also recall certain public officials before their terms of office expired. The recall as a device of direct government was, however, more popular in the cities than in the states. In the latter it was bitterly opposed by conservatives when it was extended to include the recall of judges as well as their particular decisions.

The degree of direct popular democracy put into practice by the states varied considerably. By the close of the Progressive Era, a majority permitted the people to call for a constitutional convention in addition to voting on proposals for constitutional amendments. South Dakota in 1898 was the first state to adopt the initiative and referendum for ordinary legislation, with nineteen other states following by 1928. The recall of elected officials was less widespread, but a number of states, beginning with Mississippi in 1902, adopted compulsory, statewide, direct primary laws. By 1916 only Rhode Island, Connecticut, and New Mexico lacked some form of a direct primary.

Also important in strengthening popular government

were the secret ballot and the shorter ballot. The latter permitted a more meaningful choice than when the voter was confronted by long lists of candidates for minor offices. The Australian, or secret, ballot was not a Progressive innovation, but its use grew in the 1900's so that by 1910 every state in the Union had adopted this device to protect the integrity of the vote. A number of states, beginning in 1905, also adopted some form of corrupt-practices legislation to limit the amount and kind of campaign contributions and expenses in elections.

Despite the high status historically accorded to women in the New World as distinct from the Old, the movement for woman suffrage in the United States developed slowly. It was also offset in large part by growing restrictions in the South on the Negro vote. By the turn of the century, four Rocky Mountain states permitted women to vote. Then before 1914 seven other states of the Middle and Far West followed their example. During the first world war the suffragist cause gained adherents and, with the adoption of the Nineteenth Amendment, achieved final success in time for the 1920 elections. Though regarded by many suffragists as a means to the end of further feminist triumphs, the attainment of the vote was also considered by some as the climax and culmination of their cause. In either case the Nineteenth Amendment proved disappointing to those who had predicted that its adoption would herald a thoroughgoing reformation of the American political scene.

As the states turned more and more to direct democracy, pressure mounted for the popular election of United States senators. By 1900 a number of state legislatures pledged themselves to select the popular senatorial candidate, but constitutionally the choice did not lie with the people. Finally, in 1913, popular election was accomplished by the Seventeenth Amendment. There is evidence that the Democratic city machines, usually regarded as opposed to Progressivism and reform, provided vital support to the cause of the direct popular choice of senators. Because the average urban dweller was underrepresented in the rural and Republican-controlled state legislatures, which had previously elected United States senators, a direct popular vote was more likely to give the Democrats a chance for victory. Thus partisan politics as much as Progressivism helped to strike this blow for democracy.

For Progressives, direct democracy provided a means of keeping government closer to the people and preserving popular control of public policy and administration. The initiative and referendum, for example, offered reformers an opportunity to arouse the minds of the public and educate the people on issues of exceptional interest and importance. "Nearly all the proposals designed to checkmate legislative abuses," Charles Beard pointed out, "have been based upon the assumption that the hope for better government lay in more democracy rather than less." Yet Beard wondered whether enlightened legislation could be secured if the majority of the voters, or their representatives, had to be polled on every issue. Students of government more conservative than Beard feared that direct democracy would lead to the tyranny of an ever-fluctuating majority of public opinion, and many decided that the courts offered the only sound bulwark against radical legislation.

While conservatives turned increasingly to the judiciary, and especially to the United States Supreme Court, to curb what, they felt, were the excesses of popular democracy in the states, Progressives urged instead the establishment of new governmental agencies and regulatory commissions. Through such administrative bodies they hoped to carry out their reform programs and answer the criticism that democracy was inefficient. If the state governments were to assume a broader range of regulatory functions in order to deal with the complex problems of an industrial civilization, their effectiveness might depend on the development of an impartial corps of public administrators—a bureaucracy of experts and intellectuals removed alike from the corrupting influences of business and politics. It was easier certainly, as many of the Progressives discovered, to create a bureau and shun responsibility than to devise a remedy and assume control. There was also an evident contradiction between the Progressives' confidence in extending direct democracy and their willingness to centralize political authority and interpose independent regulatory commissions between the people and their elected representatives.

In general, it seemed true that the Progressives had—as Marver H. Bernstein, a student of the commissions, wrote— "an abiding faith in regulation, expertness, and the capacity of the American government to make rational decisions provided experts in the administrative agencies could remain free from partisan political considerations. They consistently believed that regulation would overcome privilege, restore decency, and save industry from its own avarice and self-destruction." The difficulty, of course, was that the regulatory commissions and boards, which wielded great powers, often had no direct responsibility to the people. In the South, however, major commissions were usually elected rather than appointed. But in New York State, where there were nearly one hundred such boards, a contemporary critic observed: "The boards are practically irresponsible bodies. They are beyond the control of the people, or of anyone who is responsible to the people for their actions." According to Seth Low, the reform mayor of New York City, "state commissions for any other purpose than for inquiry are the most dangerous bodies, because they exercise authority without responsibility. Power without responsibility is always dangerous, but power with responsibility to a constituency, which can readily call it to account, is not dangerous." There was, moreover, the risk that a state public service commission might become, as the Citizens Union of New York reported in 1905, "merely political, and will *probably become a safeguard to the corporation rather than a protection to the public.*"

If governmental favors went to the largest investors, the administrative state promised, in fact, to become merely the tool of the special interests it was supposed to regulate. It would thereby impede, rather than advance, the cause of social and political justice.

For many of the states, especially in the industrial Northeast, one of the most striking achievements of the Progressive movement was the labor legislation passed in the decade before the first world war. In New York alone, Charles Evans Hughes, probably the outstanding Progressive-type governor in the East, signed over fifty model labor laws between 1907 and 1910. However, labor itself, and especially the American Federation of Labor in its formative years in the late nineteenth century, tended to be suspicious of governmental regulation and wary even of many social-reform measures. To labor, the power of the state in the post-Civil War decades was demonstrated in its intervention on the side of capital and in its use of federal and state troops as strikebreakers. Labor's main object accordingly was to organize its own trade unions and to elect state legislatures and governors that, if not favorably disposed toward labor, would at least be neutral. Trade unions, more than politics, offered the workingman the advantage of being a member of a social group having common interests. They also helped to overcome the loss of identity that resulted from working long hours at routine tasks as a mere cog on an assembly line.

Fear of the machine, or of what a later generation called technological unemployment, helped to arouse labor hostility to the scientific-management movement pioneered by Frederick W. Taylor, an industrial engineer and economic consultant whose ideas achieved importance and popularity in business and public-administration circles in the Progressive Era. Labor resented so-called Taylorism as still another attempt to dehumanize the worker through a system of speeded-up operations based on piece work and elaborate time-and-motion studies of individual tasks. As a device to increase efficiency and productivity by the better use of labor and machinery, Taylorism was likewise subject to the suspicion that it would decrease the need for labor and depress the average workingman's wages. Taylor's ideas seemed, in addition, to threaten the traditional wage and hour structure painstakingly achieved over the years by the trade-union movement. Although labor could not fight technological progress or avoid the overall impact of scientific management in industrial operations, it was able to get the federal government to refrain from using its methods in various Navy yards and arsenals scattered among the states.

The American Federation of Labor, from its founding in 1886, was designed as a parent body to provide state and national leadership for the skilled trade unions which made up its constituent membership. Its objects were businesslike rather than utopian, conservative rather than radical. During the nineties the Federation campaigned to limit the use of injunctions in labor disputes, and it also pioneered in the movement to abolish child labor. But it supported with less enthusiasm various measures for far-reaching social and economic reforms. Fearful of incurring public criticism as a radical movement, the Federation tended to limit its legislative demands to such essentially conservative issues as immigration restriction. Samuel Gompers, the president and driving force behind the A.F. of L. through its first thirty-odd years, adhered to the philosophy that he clearly stated in 1915: The labor movement, Gompers wrote, "undertakes to secure from government, both state and nation, the enactment of laws for the accomplishment of such things as working people cannot secure or enforce themselves."

Gompers's essentially conservative approach emphasized labor's own efforts through collective bargaining with employers. As a federation of skilled trade unions, the A.F. of L. stood in contrast to the radical Industrial Workers of the World with their syndicalist program of direct control by labor of the means of production. At the same time, Gompers kept the A.F. of L. apart from the socialist movement and political support of the Socialist party. Instead he cooperated with many of the intellectuals and social workers within the labor movement who encouraged better labor-capital relations, a modification of traditional business antagonism toward organized labor, and an end to employer paternalism. In keeping with his philosophy of cooperation in labor's relations with business, Gompers served as first vice president and labor's most important voice in the National Civic Federation. The federation, which was founded in 1900, was organized on the principle of a tripartite representation drawn from the ranks of business, labor, and the general public. It sought to establish reforms through cooperation and conciliation among these groups, as well as through the sponsorship of legislative and regulatory proposals designed to restore "that habitual normal sense of social solidarity which is the foundation stone of democracy."

National prosperity, organized labor's growing strength, and Theodore Roosevelt's Progressivism made the years of the early 1900's what one labor historian has called "a honeymoon period of capital and labor." Labor's own rise was reflected in the increase in the A.F. of L's membership from 278,000 in 1898 to 1,676,000 in 1905, when it leveled off before it soared again in the World War I years. By Roosevelt's second presidential administration, however, mounting labor dissatisfaction with the Republican party's national stand on labor matters modified the Federation's traditional nonpartisan political stance. Injunctions by state and federal courts prevented labor's use of the boycott against antiunion companies and hampered its right to strike. In 1906 the A.F. of L. accordingly took a more active role in trying to elect its friends to Congress. Then, two years later, after A.F. of L. delegates were rebuffed in their demands by the Republican national convention, Federation officials, including Gompers, campaigned openly for Bryan and the Democrats. In 1912 they again supported the Democrats, and in Woodrow Wilson's presidency labor seemed finally to achieve a number of its social and economic goals—especially the modification of the government's use of the injunction and antitrust laws as antiunion devices. By this time, too, the state federations had become more active in the movement for labor and social reforms. In New York, for example, organized labor took the lead in 1913 in securing an improved workmen's compensation law.

Instances of state action which divided reformers in the Progressive Era were the movements to arrest the spread of divorce and to bar the manufacture and sale of alcoholic beverages. Longstanding feminist efforts to liberalize state divorce laws were countered in the 1900's by other reformers' attempts to secure uniform marriage and divorce laws through a federal constitutional amendment or by uniform codes in the several states. Antidivorce sentiments remained especially strong in the Protestant churches, and few Progressive leaders were willing to challenge popular feeling on the issue. Theodore Roosevelt, while President, spoke out vigorously in defense of marriage and the family, and he also expressed concern over the declining American birthrate and the dangers of what he called "race suicide." Yet the divorce rate was growing, at the ratio of one divorce for every twenty-one marriages in 1850; one in twelve in 1900; one in ten in 1909; and one in nine in 1916 attested. Moreover, by the second decade of the 1900's, some of the traditional American reticence about sex began to break down. A symbolic and professionally significant event, foreshadowing the post-World War I popular interest in the subject, was the friendly American reception of Sigmund Freud's lectures on psychoanalysis during his first visit to the United States in 1909. Conservative as most Progressives seemingly were in the area of sex mores and customs, they proved unable to retard the growth of divorce by restrictive legislation or other political means.

Progressives generally were more successful as guardians of the nation's personal tastes and morals in the area of prohibition legislation. In the years preceding the first world war, a great wave of temperance sentiment swept across the nation, resulting in either local option or statewide prohibition laws. Because the saloon and liquor interests, licensed and taxed by the states and cities, were frequently involved in corrupt political practices, it was easy for the prohibitionists to justify governmental interference with what had traditionally been regarded as a matter of personal taste or private morality. The prohibition movement commanded its strongest support in those regions of the Middle West and South that were dominated by the old-stock, rural, Protestant middle class. Other Progressives, especially those identified with urban, labor, and immigrant elements in the large eastern cities, resisted the reform implications of the antiliquor crusade. The prohibition movement, which seemed an extreme instance of a misguided zeal to legislate private morality, was capable of provoking the Harvard historian Albert Bushnell Hart to declare in his book *National Ideals:* "No free people is more subject to the arbitrary will of the man in authority than the Americans."

To a sensitive liberal like Brand Whitlock, successor to "Golden Rule" Sam Jones as mayor of Toledo, the saloon was actually more an effect than a cause of social ills. He deplored therefore the inconsistency of those reformers who, though reluctant to disturb existing property rights, were agreeable to seeing the government interfere with every possible private and personal right in the field of moral conduct. In the opinion of the staunchly individualistic and libertarian Albert Jay Nock, the advocates of progressive democracy faced an insoluble dilemma. Recalling his own youthful doubts over Progressivism, Nock wrote: "The reformers themselves apparently did not see that the State, as an arbiter of economic advantage, must necessarily be a potential instrument of economic exploitation. . . . So I was sceptical about the reformers' projects, and the more they were trumpeted as 'democratic,' the less good to society I thought they boded."

In their complaint against overlegislation and censorious governmental regulation, old-fashioned liberals or conservatives like Nock defended a libertarian point of view for which there seemed to be increasingly less support in modern society. The ultimately successful opposition to prohibition, perhaps, represented an exception to this generalization. But, on the whole, it appeared that democratic America in the twentieth century was also becoming what a recent historian calls "the most highly organized nation in history."

*In Search
of a
National
Program*

CHAPTER 8

T.R.: The Leader of the Band

To the American people Theodore Roosevelt was the superman with the muckrake—the outstanding leader of Progressivism. From his accession to the presidency to his death in the first week of 1919, he was a controversial figure, always at or near center stage. "Pure act," Henry Adams complained in reflecting upon the abnormal drive for power and restless energy of his friend. Yet Adams felt even more depressed when, after seven years as President, Roosevelt took official leave of Washington. On March 2, 1909, the two men dined together for the last time in the White House. Later Adams also came across Lafayette Square from his own home for the final day. "I shall miss you very much," he said to T.R., no doubt voicing the feelings of much of the country.

Roosevelt, as Donald Richberg, a fellow Bull Moose Republican of 1912, wrote in retrospect, "expressed more accurately the mass sentiments of my generation" than Bryan,

La Follette, or Woodrow Wilson. He "spoke for this nation, as few presidents have spoken in our history," declared Walter Lippmann. According to his influential disciple, Herbert Croly, Roosevelt was even more of a nationalist than a reformer. And, like Croly, Frank Vrooman, the Kansas reformer, called him "the first man in a position of peculiar power or influence since Hamilton to see clearly and draw distinctly the natural line of cleavage between the democracy of individualism which threatened the very existence of democracy upon the earth, and the democracy of nationalism which offers the only rational and ethical alternative for socialism or individualism."

Like his distant relative a generation later, Theodore Roosevelt was a transitional figure. Both Theodore and Franklin D. Roosevelt served as presidents in eras when the American democratic tradition was undergoing great changes. Reformers, and even radicals, to many of their contemporaries, each was also, at least in part, a conservative less extreme in action than in rhetoric. Yet it was also true that both men played important roles in initiating what might be called a peaceful revolution in American life, and the vastly different condition of the country and the reaction that followed their respective deaths were measures of their enormous influence.

Theodore Roosevelt's early political career was significant mainly for the way that it kept open the path to the eventful last two decades of his life. Like a number of other young men of aristocratic family backgrounds, Roosevelt was distressed by the harsh, crude character of American business and politics in the post-Civil War generation. Yet, unlike Henry Adams, he did not remain aloof, disdaining any active participation in government. As a youthful state legislator, member of the National Civil Service Commission, police commissioner in New York City, and finally Assistant Secretary of the Navy under McKinley, Roosevelt gradually made a name for himself as a reformer without, however, alienating the ruling bosses in the Republican party. Still he could feel uncertain about his future. Aside from politics, his only professional interest and skill was in writing history. For business or the law, which attracted other able men of his class, he had little enthusiasm or aptitude. An aristocrat who scorned the plutocracy of new-rich money grubbers, T.R. was also a bureaucrat who valued government or military service as opposed to a career in industry or banking. Thus he criticized mere wealth-getting and the material comforts of the middle class, while he gloried in army life and upper-class culture. Later, when he traveled in Europe, it was this side of his nature that made him popular with the monarchs and nobility of the Old World.

In Washington, in the years before the Spanish–American War, Roosevelt was part of an intellectual circle of wealth and culture including such scholars in politics as John Hay, Thomas B. Reed, Henry Cabot Lodge, Elihu Root, and Albert J. Beveridge. Reed, Speaker of the House, and Hay, in his important diplomatic posts, were older men at the height of their careers, but the others were youthful and personally ambitious. Although ambivalent in their attitude toward liberal reform, the younger members of what Matthew Josephson has called "Roosevelt's salon" were united in their dissatisfaction with McKinley's conservative foreign policy. Their restlessness, manifested in an eagerness for imperialistic expansion, was finally resolved in the war with Spain.

To Roosevelt, with his adolescent fondness for violent adventure and his aristocratic admiration of the martial virtues, the war was especially welcome. Only forty years of age in 1898, Roosevelt might easily have been able to keep moving up the slippery ladder to greater political success, but the fact remains that it was the war with Spain that provided him with his prime opportunity. More correctly than his superior, Secretary of the Navy John D. Long, he discerned its significance. To Long's amazement, therefore, Roosevelt resigned as assistant secretary in order to take up active duty as Lieutenant Colonel of the First Volunteer Cavalry, popularly known as the "Rough Riders." Commenting in his diary on how absurd it might be if Roosevelt "should accomplish some great thing . . . ," Long later wrote over the original entry of April 25, 1898, "Roosevelt was right. . . . His going into the army led straight to the Presidency."

In the fall of 1898, the brief wartime heroics in Cuba won Roosevelt nomination and election as governor of New York. Two years later, when the Republican chieftains pressed the nomination for Vice President upon him, he accepted gracefully despite some personal misgivings, and then campaigned effectively against Bryan's so-called radicalism. President McKinley's death on September 14, 1901, a week after he was felled by an anarchistic assassin's bullet, completed the extraordinary cycle of events that had guided Roosevelt's road to the White House at the unprecedented early age of not quite forty-three years. Favored by a kind providence, T.R. had also made few mistakes. And more than almost any other President in American history he was thoroughly to enjoy the responsibility of the nation's highest office.

Despite the conventional polite assurances that he would continue his predecessor's policies, there was little doubt that Roosevelt wanted to be his own master. Although subject to many of the same anxieties and tensions that plagued most of his reform-minded friends who were in public life, Roosevelt, much more than the average mugwump type of liberal, had the capacity and desire for vigorous action. His previous experience had given him an appreciation of the importance of good administration. He liked hard work, was a good judge of people, and was willing to seek the counsel of experts and to delegate authority without abrogating his own ultimate responsibility. Blaming McKinley for his alleged complacency in the face of popular discontent at home and war abroad, the new President moved quickly to re-create a feeling of national unity.

Roosevelt's presidency benefited from the fact that the country needed a period of reassurance and security. The bitter class conflict of the nineties, followed by the war with Spain and McKinley's violent death, had given ample reason for alarm. In addition, the imperialism resulting from the war, and the rapidly mounting concentration and centralization of the national economy, brought to the surface problems that demanded positive action. At the same time, there was much popular hostility to the lingering radicalism of the Populists and socialists. Roosevelt himself, with his repeated denunciation of anarchists and socialists, admitted in 1901 that he had "an almost Greek horror of extremes." Responding to the uncertainty of the time, he was able to offer a combination of moderation and strong presidential leadership. In his search for a viable political program, he found that he could unite Americanism and Progressive reform. "It is an excellent thing to win a triumph for good government at a given election," Roosevelt had written while governor of New York, "but it is a far better thing gradually to build up that spirit of fellow-feeling among American citizens, which, in the long run, is absolutely necessary if we are to see the principles of virile honesty and robust common sense triumph in our civic life."

In his first annual message to Congress, Roosevelt combined the twin themes of patriotism and reform. His predecessor's assassination enabled him to denounce anarchistic speeches, writings, and meetings as "essentially seditious and treasonable. . . . Anarchy," he declared, "is a crime against the whole human race; and all mankind should band against the anarchist. His crime should be made an offense against the law of nations, like piracy and . . . the slave trade; for it is of far blacker infamy than either." Roosevelt denied that the anarchist was "the victim of social or political injustice," but the emphasis that he placed in his message upon the social problems resulting from the unprecedented urban–industrial growth of the country suggested the existence of a state of economic anarchy requiring both legislative and administrative action. "There is a widespread conviction in the minds of the American people that the great corporations known as trusts are in certain of their features and tendencies hurtful to the general welfare," he told the Congress.

As President, Roosevelt pursued what was essentially a compromise position in regard to the problem of monopoly and the trusts. He believed that only those combinations which engaged in unfair restraint of trade or competition should be subject to prosecution. Later he came to accept the point of view that favored governmental regulation and publicity rather than dissolution of the trusts. The Bureau of Corporations, established in 1903, helped Roosevelt to investigate corporate abuses and prosecute offenders. It put at his disposal a large measure of presidential discretion and power in the control of big business. Meanwhile several successful antitrust cases early in his Administration—notably the breaking up of the Northern Securities Company, a railroad combine put together by E. H. Harriman, James J. Hill, and J. P. Morgan—won Roosevelt a reputation as a trustbuster and staunch Progressive.

While the Northern Securities trial was being contested, Roosevelt had occasion to intervene dramatically in an important labor dispute. In contrast to some of his predecessors who had not hesitated to sanction the use of federal troops to quell strikes, Roosevelt proposed to make the government an impartial arbitrator. He was aware that the growth of big business heightened labor demands for the right to join trade unions and bargain collectively, but in 1900 only about 4 percent of the working force was so organized. Then in the summer of 1902, anthracite coal miners, under the leadership of John Mitchell, struck for an eight-hour day, wage increases, and union recognition. The owners of the mines aroused the ire of the public and the President by their refusal to accept arbitration, but Roosevelt was finally able to put enough pressure on the operators to secure a compromise settlement.

Though criticized by Senator Robert M. La Follette and some later historians for his willingness to yield basic Progressive reforms and settle too readily with conservatives in Congress for "half a loaf," Roosevelt's leadership contributed to such important legislation in his second term as the Hepburn railroad rate bill, the Meat Inspection Act, and the Pure Food and Drug Law. All three measures, with later amendments, remain on the statute books as laws of the United States. They served also to illustrate the Progressive tendency toward further centralization of power in the federal government at the expense of the individual and the states. Thus the legislation typified a conception of democracy that was nationalistic as well as reform-minded.

In his presidential policies Roosevelt, like other chief executives, was compelled on occasion to compromise or retreat from some of his more advanced ideas. Yet, in his years before the public, he was able to sustain the main outlines of his social philosophy. An offspring of the Darwinian generation, Roosevelt accepted both Social Darwinism's concept of competition and struggle and the Reform Darwinist's belief in man's ability to control his environment and effect beneficial changes. "The true function of the State as it interferes in social life," he declared, "should be to make the chances of competition more even, not to abolish them."

Hostile to the kind of radical reforms that, he believed,

expressed socialistic, anarchistic, or agrarian ideologies, Roosevelt, however, also deprecated conservative concerns over
the approach of any form of social democracy. "I have scant
sympathy," he wrote, "with the people who talk about the failure of the Democratic movement to justify the rosy hopes of
those who hailed its advent. In any movement of progress
and reform there are always a large number of well-meaning
enthusiasts who prophesy the impossible." A communistic
form of socialism spelled annihilation for the country, but
the doctrine of many "high-minded Socialists," T.R. agreed,
"is really only an advanced form of liberalism."

In deploring what he felt were selfish class interests,
whether radical or reactionary, Roosevelt set the stage for his
own conception of a strong national state acting as the arbiter
of the common interest and popular welfare. He adhered to
the position that the government had to provide a stable
social and economic order, efficiently administered, if there
was to be any hope of satisfactory social justice and reform.
Since there were obvious imbalances and inequities in the
modern industrial order, men turned to the state for solu-
tions. "Our steady aim," Roosevelt asserted in his 1905 annual
message, "should be legislation, cautiously and carefully undertaken, but resolutely persevered in, to assert the sovereignty of the National Government by affirmative action."

Increasingly in his second term, Roosevelt came to accept
the position that in a complex industrial society the private
combinations known as the trusts were inevitable. "The corporation has come to stay, just as the trade union has come
to stay." It was a misfortune therefore that the federal laws
on the subject had been "of a negative or prohibitive rather
than affirmative kind." Regulation of the great corporations
meant, of course, a certain increase in the powers of the federal government. "Let those who object to this increase in the
use of the only power available, the national power, be frank,

and admit openly that they propose to abandon any effort to control the great business corporations and to exercise supervision over the accumulation and distribution of wealth; for such supervision and control can only come through this particular kind of increase of power." Equally opposed to "unrestrained individualism" and "a deadening socialism," Roosevelt in his December 1908 message to the Congress concluded: "The danger to American democracy lies not in the least in the concentration of administrative power in responsible and accountable hands. It lies in having the power insufficiently concentrated, so that no one can be held responsible to the people for its use."

Roosevelt did not limit his belief in the need for more affirmative federal policies to the general question of regulating big business. His interest in conservation, for example, was evident in the ready support that he extended to Gifford Pinchot's efforts to preserve America's forests and other natural resources. Roosevelt and Pinchot were able to persuade Congress and the people that much of the land, water, mineral, and forest reserves within the public domain belonged to the nation as a whole rather than to the states or to individuals or corporations. Conservation, harmonizing with Roosevelt's own philosophy of government, provided perhaps the best example of Progressivism at work. But in other areas as well, the President called for positive governmental action. Although opposed to the principle of the closed shop for labor, he sought legislation to improve working conditions. To this end he urged the abolition of child labor, the extension of the eight-hour day to railroad employees, and an improved pension plan and accident compensation for all federal employees.

In the matter of race relations, Roosevelt moved no faster than most of the Progressives. At the outset of his Administration, he sought the advice of Booker T. Washington, president of Tuskegee Institute, in regard to federal appointments in the South. When T.R. also asked Washington to dine at the White House, he touched off a furor in the South. Outraged by the courteous presidential gesture to a prominent Negro leader, the southern press used the incident to express its racist sentiments and to embarrass Roosevelt politically. Although he angrily defended his action, Roosevelt did not repeat the invitation, and later he privately voiced regret over what he concluded had been a mistake. After 1903, Roosevelt also gave up his initial efforts to appoint Negroes to federal positions in the South, and thereby to reverse the Republican party policy of catering to the "lily-white" political machines in southern states.

Though he was willing to accept individual leaders like Washington, Roosevelt considered Negroes as a group an inferior race in contrast to the superior Anglo-Saxons. Moreover, he did not believe that the majority of black men was qualified to enjoy the vote. Thus he was annoyed at the pressure for equal rights maintained by liberals like Oswald Garrison Villard and the *Nation* magazine. If Roosevelt accordingly did little as President to help the black man, it was also, however, true that he was less outspoken in his criticism of the Negro as compared with certain other ethnic or minority groups that seemed to him to stand in the way of American nationality. In any event it was clear that Roosevelt, like most of the country, preferred to let the slow course of evolutionary change in the economic and social status of the black man work a gradual improvement.

William H. Harbaugh, his most thorough biographer, denies that Roosevelt was either a racist or a politician bent on achieving personal power. Despite the forced compromises of his last years as President, Roosevelt, Harbaugh contends, largely met the challenge of the times. As a Progressive-type reformer, he had little patience with the kind of liberal who offered merely negative criticisms without making some positive effort toward a practical solution. "The good citizen," Roosevelt wrote in 1910, "is not a good citizen unless he is an efficient citizen." This insistence on maximum efficiency from both government and individuals contributed to his low opinion of a President like Thomas Jefferson, whom he considered a poor administrator. On the other hand, he admired Abraham Lincoln as "an efficient leader of the forward movement," and said of Lincoln and Washington that "each was the efficient leader of the radicalism of the time."

The phrase the "Square Deal," which was affixed to Roosevelt's own Administration, expressed the theory of a strong government to administer a fair and impartial justice. In practice, however, the Square Deal, with its paternalistic overtones of centralized federal power and executive authority, led directly to the New Nationalism of the Progressive party. And Roosevelt as President, in anticipation of the program that he urged more extensively in 1912, took the first decisive steps toward the modern welfare state.

CHAPTER 9

The Uses of
Public Power:
Trustbusting and
Conservation

DESPITE the conventionally comfortable belief of
Republican party leaders in the McKinley era that
the United States had enjoyed ideal conditions
since the Civil War, it was evident that the tremendous industrial expansion of the country was creating new problems.
The federal government faced the increasingly difficult task
of trying to pass legislation to keep up with the growing needs
of an urban–industrial society. And Theodore Roosevelt, it
seemed, was the first President to confront frankly the less
happy implications of the country's vast economic growth. He
was also the first President to use the public power of the
United States for broad social and economic, rather than narrow fiscal or political, purposes.

By the year 1901, when Roosevelt was suddenly thrust
into the presidency, it was apparent that the national interest
demanded some clarification of public policy in regard to
social and economic issues. Despite the undoubted material

achievements of the past half-century, the growth of the trusts and big business was arousing increasing concern. In a number of key industries, intense competition was being followed by corporate mergers, with the consequent greater concentration of production and management. At the same time, popular resentment against big business, and especially the railroads, led to the demand for political action to meet the threat of still greater economic centralization. However, neither state laws prohibiting all combinations in restraint of trade nor efforts to invoke the old common-law doctrine of conspiracy against the community interest were able to gain general support. "To economists and sociologists, judicial attempts to force Benthamite conceptions of freedom of contract and common-law conceptions of individualism upon the public were," as Dean Roscoe Pound of the Harvard Law School stated, "no less amusing—or even irritating—than legislative attempts to do away with or get away from these conceptions are to bench and bar."

Although a number of judges were critical of monopoly and willing on occasion to affirm state and local regulation, on the whole the courts, as Dean Pound asserted, did not want to curb legitimate business enterprise or hamper the normal flow of commerce between the states. State laws against monopoly, if rigorously enforced, might cancel the possible economic benefits to be derived from large-scale enterprise. At the same time, federal court decisions made clear the probable unconstitutionality of most state attempts to regulate interstate commerce. Moreover, technological advances often encouraged larger manufacturing units, while federal patent laws and the operations of the protective tariff frequently served to foster monopoly and discourage new enterprises.

In the 1890's, hard times, plus the passage of the Sherman Antitrust Act, had slowed developments somewhat. The Sherman Act simply declared all combinations in restraint of trade or commerce among the several states illegal and authorized the government to take action to force their dissolution. However, the failure to define such terms as "trusts" and "combination," the lack of vigorous court prosecution, and the growing use of the holding company as a device to mask business mergers, plus the return of prosperity following the war with Spain, together encouraged the formation of a new group of even larger trusts. The 1900 census showed some 185 industrial combinations, 73 of them capitalized at $10 million or more and accounting for 14 percent of the nation's industrial production. In 1901 the United States Steel Corporation, representing a merger of the Carnegie steel companies and competing interests controlled by J. P. Morgan, became the first billion-dollar corporation in the United States. Three years later, in 1904, over three hundred trusts controlled two-fifths of the manufacturing capital of the country. Meanwhile continuing popular concern over the trusts was reflected in the publication in 1899 and 1900 of some two dozen books, more than 150 magazine articles, and the nineteen volumes of the official report of the United States Industrial Commission.

Among the wide range of suggestions for a public policy toward the trusts, the simplest and at first the most popular political solution was rigorous enforcement of the Sherman Act along the lines of President Roosevelt's own original plans for trustbusting. Although T.R. himself gradually lost interest in such a program, it appealed to many of his followers. Middle-class citizens, who felt hemmed in by the monopolistic corporations on one side and the rising labor and socialist movements on the other, wanted action against the trusts. Moreover, governmental regulation in the national interest promised a compromise between economic extremes and a check on the growing strength of both big business and organized labor.

Yet, despite its initial political popularity, trustbusting, as T.R. quickly recognized, was not an economic panacea. The trusts had developed, at least in part, as a natural result of the growing nationalization of the American economy. Paradoxically, trustbusting, too, reflected such a nationalizing influence, as when Roosevelt appealed for national support against "the malefactors of great wealth." But since business was increasingly national in scope, it seemed to follow that efforts at regulation or control should also be the responsibility of the federal government. Along with the pressure for reform coming from the country, business itself wanted government relief from economic instability and ruthless competition. Those very conditions had oftentimes led to the formation of industrial combinations in an effort to avoid economic chaos and achieve greater operational efficiency. Finally the Progressives had no desire to disrupt the national economy or hamper legitimate enterprise.

To Roosevelt and a number of his supporters, the use of public power to regulate, but not to destroy, the large private corporations was the most constructive alternative to laissez faire or socialism. John Bates Clark, an outstanding economist of the Progressive Era, took such a position, and in 1901 he published a collection of his more popular academic articles under the title *The Control of the Trusts*. A neoclassicist in economic theory, Clark believed in the workings of free competition and the laws of supply and demand. Monopoly, he feared, would destroy the dynamic forces of capitalism and the hope of progress in society. Yet, like Roosevelt, Clark did not want to curtail the productive powers of large-scale enterprise or surrender America's competitive position in world trade. "Success in the fierce rivalries into which nations are now entering," he predicted, "will come to those which utilize, for all that it is worth, the power that massed capital gives, without surrendering their economic freedom." Favoring

neither the "trust-smashing" of the laissez-faire school of indi-
vidualists, nor the government ownership advanced by socialism, Clark, during the 1904 presidential campaign, wrote that
the natural laws of economics dictated a system of "trust-
regulating."

As Clark noted, trustbusting could have an adverse effect
on America's comparative position in foreign trade. This
awareness of the advantage enjoyed by Europe's cartels in the
world market also led Roosevelt to advise caution in dealing
with the problem of the trusts in the United States. As early as
his first annual message, he pointed out to Congress that

> The same business conditions which have produced the great
> aggregations of corporate and individual wealth have made them
> very potent factors in international commercial competition. . . .
> America has only just begun to assume that commanding posi-
> tion in the international business world which we believe will
> more and more be hers. It is of the utmost importance that this
> position be not jeopardized, especially at a time when the over-
> flowing abundance of our own natural resources and the skill,
> business energy, and mechanical aptitude of our people make
> foreign markets essential. Under such conditions it would be
> most unwise to cramp or fetter the youthful strength of our Na-
> tion.

Although certain types of industrial combination were in-
valid in England, public policy in Germany was almost wholly
favorable to the economic cartels or trusts. Because big business could more easily absorb the higher costs and heavier
taxation entailed by rearmament and the welfare program of
the German social democracy, even labor was willing to accept
the growing concentration and centralization of industry. According to one observer, since Germany believed the cartels
both inevitable and desirable, it was "only a question of regulating the stream, not of damming it."

Under William Howard Taft, Roosevelt's chosen successor, the pace of trustbusting seemed to quicken. The prosecution of the American Tobacco Company and Standard Oil, initiated under Roosevelt, was continued along with action against the United States Steel Corporation and other large industrial combinations. But among Roosevelt Progressives trustbusting now yielded to the concept of a regulated monopoly. In this new form, the whole question of government–business relations became one of the major issues in the 1912 presidential campaign. Meanwhile Roosevelt's own position was best explained by George W. Perkins, his close friend and staunch political supporter. In an address at Columbia University in 1908, Perkins, a partner of J. P. Morgan, defended the corporation on the grounds of its efficiency and fitness. For example, it provided greater continuity than a hereditary family type of business, and by widespread stock sales it became a quasi-public interest. Such a preferred position warranted some government regulation of the corporation and this, indeed, according to Perkins, was not unwelcomed by the business community. At the same time, he explained that Roosevelt, in spite of widespread misunderstanding of his position, believed that "modern industrial conditions are such that combination is not only necessary but inevitable; that corporations have come to stay, and that, if properly managed, they are the source of good and not evil."

In recent years historians, in analyzing the Progressives' position in regard to the uses of public and private power, have suggested that much of the regulatory legislation of the early 1900's actually encouraged closer government–business relations. Thus Robert Wiebe has pointed out that the business interests of the country recognized by this time that

> Only the government could ensure the stability and continuity essential to their welfare. Its expert services, its legal author-

ity, and its scope had become indispensable components of any intelligent plan for order. And what they sought could no longer be accomplished by seizing and bribing. . . . They required long-range, predictable cooperation through administrative devices that would bend with a changing world. Nor were they thinking about a mere neutralization of the government, the automatic reaction many had given to the first flurries of reform. They wanted a powerful government, but one whose authority stood at their disposal; a strong, responsive government through which they could manage their own affairs in their own way.

Other historians, going further than Wiebe, have seen the cooperative relations of the businessmen and the Progressives as more than an effort to achieve superior organization and efficiency. Gabriel Kolko, for example, has argued in *The Triumph of Conservatism* that the departure from laissez faire indicated by governmental intervention in the economy can be interpreted as reform only if one assumes automatically that such action enhanced the general welfare. Business, he contends, continued to derive an attractive range of benefits and subsidies from the government. Even the reform proposals ascribed to Roosevelt's second term—railroad rate regulation, federal inspection of meat packing, the Pure Food and Drug Law, and conservation—were at best only halfway measures. "The dominant fact of American political life at the beginning of this century," Kolko asserts, "was that big business led the struggle for the federal regulation of the economy." According to such interpretations Progressivism was more than just a coincidence of similar needs and interests on the part of businessmen and reformers. It was rather business control over the economy in the form of helpful government regulation—private power in the guise of public power—and an important American step toward a European type of state socialism or state capitalism.

Historians who have interpreted Progressivism as an essentially middle-class, conservative movement dominated by a paternalistic philosophy of government have found those same qualities underlying much of the Progressives' enthusiasm for the conservation of natural resources. "The conservation movement," Samuel P. Hays, one of its recent historians, has written in *Conservation and the Gospel of Efficiency,* "did not involve a reaction against large-scale corporate business, but, in fact, shared its view in a mutual revulsion against unrestrained competition and undirected economic development. Both groups placed a premium on large-scale capital organization, technology, and industry-wide cooperation and planning to abolish the uncertainties and waste of competitive resource use." Other scholars, however, in their description of conservation as a conflict between public and private power, have contended that the "organized conservationists were concerned more with economic justice and democracy in the handling of resources than with mere prevention of waste."

Among the conservationists themselves at the turn of the century, there was also a diversity of opinion. For example, nature lovers and big-game hunters wanted the national forests kept inviolate as parks or game preserves, while stockmen and lumber companies favored the use of these lands for grazing and commercial timber. Both groups had already achieved some success in their attempts to influence government policy. Wildlife preserves and national parks helped keep nature in its pristine state. Yet, at the same time, conservation was also closely tied to the Progressives' urgings of an efficient use of natural resources under governmental controls.

Conservation, in this latter sense, did not become an important political and ideological question until the opening years of the twentieth century. As long as the United States possessed what appeared to be an inexhaustible reserve of lands and minerals in the West, the American people expressed little interest in either the preservation or conservation of the nation's natural heritage. During the nineteenth century there had been no lack of a romantic interest in nature, nor of enthusiastic exploration of the American landscape by writers, artists, and travelers. But America was too much a land of plenty to be worried over alleged or impending scarcities. Only the realization of the passing of the frontier—at least in the sense of the free and easy exploitation of the West—made conservation the serious concern of some Americans.

By the 1870's and 1880's, men like John Wesley Powell, the famed explorer of the Colorado River and director of the United States Geological Survey, were already reporting the need to preserve scarce resources and redeem desert areas by federal reclamation and irrigation projects. At the same time, American anxiety over dwindling forest lands resulted in the first federal action to investigate the state of the nation's timber resources. The knowledge of Europe's experience in first depleting and then attempting to restore its forests spurred Americans to organize a campaign for conservation. Carl Schurz, the most prominent of the German refugees who had come to the United States after the failure of the revolutions of 1848, was the first Secretary of the Interior to suggest stopping timber removal from the public domain. And Bernhard E. Fernow, the first professional forester employed by the federal government, was able to acquaint American conservationists with the longstanding German efforts at reforestation that he had observed at firsthand in his own training abroad. Under congressional authorization, presidents Harrison and Cleveland took action to create forest reserves on federal lands, but full presidential support for conservation was not achieved until Theodore Roosevelt entered the White House.

Always fond of camping and hunting, Roosevelt's first youthful contacts with nature and the wilderness were reinforced by his sojourn in the Dakotas in the 1880's after his first wife's death. Keenly interested in preserving the natural beauty as well as the rich resources of the country, he listened sympathetically to nature lovers like John Burroughs and John Muir, who accompanied him on presidential tours of the Yellowstone and Yosemite areas in the Far West. But Roosevelt's major contribution to the conservation movement was the practical political support that he gave in Washington to such already established conservationist leaders as Gifford Pinchot.

Pinchot, sometimes called America's first forester, had traveled in Europe observing and studying the latest scientific and practical methods in forest care. Success in his career as a forester for private interests led to his appointment in 1898 as head of the Forestry Division of the Department of Agriculture. Since forest reserves were still under the jurisdiction of the General Land Office of the Department of the Interior, Pinchot in the Agriculture Department was literally a forester without forests until 1905 when President Roosevelt was able to persuade Congress to place all federal timber resources under Pinchot's authority in the Bureau of Forests. Meanwhile, in behalf of his ideas of scientific timber cutting and reforestation practices, Pinchot lectured widely, wrote for several national magazines, and published *A Primer of Forestry,* of which eventually more than one million copies were distributed.

Pinchot, like Roosevelt, was a Progressive who recognized the need for publicity and political pressure in behalf of reform. To mobilize public opinion behind the cause of conservation, he made the Bureau of Forests the focus of an extensive information service, supplying literature, lantern slides, and various technical materials to speakers, schools, and nature groups. "Nothing permanent," he pointed out, "can be accomplished in this country unless it is backed by a sound public sentiment. The greater part of our work, therefore, has consisted in arousing a general interest in practical forestry throughout the country and in gradually changing public sentiment toward a more conservative treatment of forest lands."

Personally wealthy, Pinchot contributed some of his own funds to attract able men to government service and help make Forestry an extraordinary example of an efficient bureaucracy. Pinchot was accordingly a perfect example of the type of patrician reformer who cast his lot with the Progressives, not because of economic deprivation, but out of a desire for greater status, service, and power. A practicing member in what Richard Hofstadter has called a status revolution, Pinchot with his inherited wealth and sense of noblesse oblige was more inclined to accept Progressive reforms than the new rich class of businessmen and industrialists still intent on making their private fortunes. As the Progressive Walter Weyl observed in his contemporary book *The New Democracy,* "Once wealth is separated from its original accumulation, it slackens its advocacy of its method of accumulation."

Under the urgings of Pinchot and Roosevelt, federal appropriations for Forestry rose majestically: from $28,520 in 1899 to $3,572,922 in 1908. During this period the President, on Pinchot's recommendations, also drastically increased the number and acreage of forest reserves, approximately 46 million acres of forest lands in 41 reserves growing to 150 million acres in 159 national forests. Not surprisingly, Pinchot was sometimes accused by congressmen and newspaper critics of going too far in his enthusiasm for conservation. Yet, in most of its actions, the Forest Service was upheld in the courts, and Pinchot, who followed Roosevelt's belief in a broad and elastic interpretation of the Constitution and governmental powers, was most reluctant to yield his favorite ideas and projects. "It is the first duty of a public officer to obey the law," he declared. "But it is his second duty, and a close second, to do everything the law will let him do for the public good, and not merely what the law directs or compels him to do. Unless the public service is alive enough to serve the people with enthusiasm, there is very little to be said for it."

Conservation, of course, included more than Pinchot's crusade for scientific forestry. In 1902, Congress passed the Newlands Act, creating the Reclamation Service, and later Roosevelt appointed the Inland Waterways Commission to establish an overall plan for the water resources of the country. To further its work, and at the same time arouse greater public support for a broad conservation program, Roosevelt called together the famous Conference of Governors at the White House in May 1908. The two major themes at the conference were the impending depletion of natural resources and the necessity of their conservation as a matter of national patriotism. "I have asked you to come together now," the President told the governors, "because the enormous consumption of these resources, and the threat of imminent exhaustion of some of them, due to reckless and wasteful use, once more calls for common effort, common action." The American people, Roosevelt feared, did not understand that "conservation of our natural resources is only preliminary to the larger question of national efficiency, the patriotic duty of insuring the safety and continuance of the Nation." What neither Roosevelt nor the American people saw clearly in their concern with the national interest was the way the United States, under the policies of imperialism, was turning increasingly to the exploitation of the natural resources and native peoples of the hitherto less developed areas of the world.

By the close of Roosevelt's presidency, conservation, encouraged by patriotic pressures, was well on the way to becoming an organized national reform movement. The Conference of Governors led to the establishment of a National Conservation Commission as a coordinating and fact-finding body, and in December 1908 selected state and federal officials held a joint conservation conference. By now, the new practical conservationists led by Pinchot and fellow government officials overshadowed the older group of naturalists. Conservation involved important political and business interests which were no longer able to function on the historic assumption of an unlimited exploitation of the country's wealth. Conflicts such as the famous Ballinger–Pinchot dispute in the Taft Administration brought into the open the antagonism between differing conceptions of public and private power in the development of the nation's remaining resources. Pinchot, continued in office as head of the Forestry Bureau by President Taft, accused Secretary of the Interior Richard A. Ballinger of injuring the conservation program in order to aid corporation interests. Specifically at issue were the reopening of certain water-power sites in the West and the patenting of Alaskan coal lands to the Guggenheim mining interests.

Despite the public attention attracted to the Ballinger–Pinchot cause célèbre, what was really significant now was the way in which both government and business had come to accept conservation in terms of simple efficiency. Conservation to ensure profits and national security was the new Progressive goal. In the words of Pinchot's *Fight for Conservation:*

> The central thing for which Conservation stands is to make this country the best possible place to live in, both for us and our de-

scendants. It stands against the waste of the natural resources which cannot be renewed, such as coal and iron; it stands for the perpetuation of the resources which can be renewed, such as food-producing soils and the forests; and most of all it stands for an equal opportunity for every American citizen to get his fair share of benefit from these resources, both now and hereafter.

To this Pinchot added: "Conservation stands for the same kind of practical commonsense management of this country by the people that every business man stands for in handling of his own business."

The early conservation movement, which reached its climax with the end of the Roosevelt years, provided a good example of the use of public power. It was able to persuade the American people that the natural resources of the West, hitherto freely open to private exploitation, should belong to the nation and to the people as a whole rather than to individuals or corporations. In Pinchot's mind, conservation simply meant the more efficient, planned use of nature's resources. Interpreted in this way, it seemed to provide a popular scientific answer to the new national problems of the twentieth century. It appealed not only to the Progressive reformer's nationalism and patriotism, but also to his interest in social control and planning. It was democratic in a nationalistic rather than individualistic sense. In the opinion of Charles R. Van Hise, president of the University of Wisconsin, and author of the first history of conservation in the United States, "He who thinks not of himself primarily, but of his race, and of its future, is the new patriot."

In a certain sense, as one authority pointed out in commenting upon Theodore Roosevelt's Progressivism, "The trust-buster and conservationist are strange bedfellows." Monopolists, after all, were sometimes prosecuted for trying hard to limit production, a goal not inconsistent with the conservationists' own efforts. Yet, in broader perspective, it is clear that the Progressives, in their espousal of better government–business relations and the planned use of natural resources, were critical of the traditional American emphasis on competitive enterprise. Such an emphasis, they believed, led mainly to overproduction and extravagant consumption, with resultant waste and inefficiency. Wiser public policy, they concluded, demanded better organization as well as continued reforms. This whole problem of public power, including the trusts and conservation, became the major issue in the great popular referendum on Progressivism in the presidential campaign of 1912.

CHAPTER 10

The Solemn Referendum: 1912

THE election of 1912 was a solemn referendum mainly in an ironic sense. By near general agreement it is regarded as one of the more interesting and significant presidential campaigns in American history. Thus it joins that of Jefferson in 1800, Jackson in 1828, Lincoln in 1860, and the 1896 Bryan–McKinley battle of the standards. Yet, historians also concur in pointing out that all four principal candidates in 1912—Taft, Wilson, Roosevelt, and Debs—were in some degree Progressives. And, although Roosevelt was defeated, much of his program was subsequently enacted in the first Wilson Administration.

If there was a paradox accordingly in the ultimate triumph of Roosevelt's New Nationalism over Wilson's New Freedom, it is also nonetheless true that such post-election transfigurations have not been unusual in American politics. It is indeed partly for this reason that the presidential race of 1912 was so important. While the election of 1896 killed the

Populist movement, it was not clear at that time what might follow. Only belatedly is it possible to see that the Roosevelt–Taft years were largely a transitional period, the broader implications of which were not fully worked out until after 1912. In the confused rhetoric of the campaign, Wilson's New Freedom often seemed Jeffersonian; four years later it had become lost in the New Nationalism and the world war. Not the New Freedom then, but the reborn New Nationalism and the world war comprised the major heritage that Progressivism bestowed upon the twentieth century.

The solemn referendum on Progressivism in 1912 was in large part a contest centered on the personality and program of Theodore Roosevelt. The unusual nature of the campaign had its origins in a number of vital decisions that the ex-President made in the months before the election. While still in the White House puzzling over the choice of his successor, and particularly thinking about Charles Evans Hughes, the reform governor of New York, Roosevelt had written to Amos Pinchot, Gifford's younger and more radical brother: "If only I could be sure of the public sentiment I should feel easy as to what I should do." His own last year in office had not been a happy experience. Assailed by conservatives in Congress, where his domestic reform program ran into increasing opposition, Roosevelt was anxious to find a candidate who would unite the party and be a popular choice with the voters. By settling on William Howard Taft, the most available and politically plausible Republican, Roosevelt made what, in retrospect, was his first major pre-1912 error.

In light of the growing division between conservative and progressive Republicans, perhaps no one, not even Roosevelt himself, who had earlier toyed with the notion of a third term, could have enjoyed a successful presidency after 1908. But the fact remains that Taft, however great his promise and abilities, proved an inept administrator and politician. Somehow he managed, despite a good record in regard to the trusts, and even in the matter of conservation, to alienate completely the Progressives in the Republican party. Such key issues as the Payne–Aldrich tariff, the insurgents' fight against Speaker Joseph G. Cannon's control over the House of Representatives, and the Ballinger–Pinchot dispute in regard to leasing certain public lands, Taft bungled badly. In foreign relations his sincere concern with world peace was offset by his espousal of a dollar diplomacy by which he further antagonized those Progressives who were no longer beholden to the Rooseveltian nationalism and militarism.

To give Taft a clear track as President, Roosevelt did the sensible and courteous thing by departing on an African safari in the spring of 1909. Emerging a year later from the depths of the jungle, the former President inevitably captured the headlines on his leisurely trip home by way of a grand tour of Europe. There he immensely enjoyed the hospitality of the crowned heads of state. He reviewed troops with the kaiser in Germany, delivered several formal addresses, and talked seriously with the English liberals Herbert Asquith, Lloyd George, and Sir Edward Grey. Before embarking for Africa, Roosevelt had agreed to become a regular contributor to *Outlook* magazine, and now upon his return home these articles gradually became more political and controversial. Although Roosevelt's first wish was to restore Republican party unity, his campaign for some of the more progressive Republican candidates in the 1910 congressional elections forced him into a stance increasingly hostile to President Taft and conservatives in the party.

In the celebrated New Nationalism address on August 31, 1910, at Osawatomie, Kansas, Roosevelt developed further a number of the ideas of Progressivism which he had already begun to urge in his last year as President. "T.R. seems to have delivered the Osawatomie speech exactly as Gifford wrote it," Amos Pinchot observed the next day in a letter to their mother. And indeed, the address reflected the advanced Progressivism of both Roosevelt and Pinchot, now T.R.'s closest confidant among the political associates of the presidential years. Recalling for his Kansas listeners the images of John Brown and Abraham Lincoln, Roosevelt told the Grand Army of the Republic veterans in the audience that he wanted to revive the equality of opportunity and nationalistic faith exemplified by the Civil War. But giving every man a fair chance, he pointed out, "means that the commonwealth will get from every citizen the highest service of which he is capable. No man who carries the burden of the special privileges of another can give to the commonwealth that service to which it is fairly entitled." Roosevelt reiterated that his Square Deal, in its opposition to all special interests, favored effective control rather than prohibition of combinations in industry. More specifically, he advocated a tariff commission, graduated income and inheritance taxes, workmen's compensation acts, and other types of economic and social-reform legislation.

Roosevelt's phrase the "New Nationalism" typified the spirit of his address at Osawatomie. Conservation, for example, he saw as "a great moral issue" involving "the patriotic duty of insuring the safety and continuance of the nation." Though admitting that it was hardly necessary in his case, Roosevelt repeated his well-known belief in a strong army and navy, meanwhile warning all progressive-minded citizens "continually to remember Uncle Sam's interests abroad." The New Nationalism put the country's needs before personal or sectional advantage, but it was not synonymous with over-centralization. In broad terms it stressed national efficiency in government so that there would be no neutral ground for lawbreakers between the federal and state authority. Finally, invoking once more the memories of the Civil War, as well as the virtues of home and family, Roosevelt called for "a genuine and permanent moral awakening." In contrast to the older American liberal tradition of limited government, Roosevelt's New Nationalism was a manifesto of the modern, positive welfare state. Offering citizens a square deal, it expected in return their unswerving loyalty and obedience. Roosevelt's Progressivism embraced wholeheartedly the position, historically more identified with conservatism, that there were no individual rights without commensurate responsibilities and duties.

Well before his address at Osawatomie, Roosevelt's nationalistic Progressivism had already won important intellectual support in a book that was quickly recognized as the most systematic expression of the Rooseveltian philosophy. Herbert Croly's *The Promise of American Life,* published in 1909 while its hero was still in Africa, has been hailed as one of the few original works in American political theory. Roosevelt, who received a copy abroad, praised it enthusiastically and on his return home invited its author to lunch at Oyster Bay. Though the Croly–Roosevelt personal relationship waned, and though historians differ on the question of who influenced whom, there is little doubt that *The Promise of American Life* was a significant statement of the Progressive program and philosophy. In describing the book's major thesis, a contemporary reviewer wrote: "Nationality and democracy, now and forever, one and inseparable, is Mr. Croly's new battle-cry of enlightened patriotism."

Herbert Croly's father, David Croly, was a leading American disciple of Auguste Comte's positivist or scientific philosophy, and indeed both his parents provided their only son with an unusually cosmopolitan, European sort of intellectual background and education. At Harvard, where he took his degree in philosophy, Herbert Croly studied principally with Josiah Royce and George Santayana. But it was the pragma-

tist philosophy of James and Dewey, along with Royce's idealism, which seemed to influence his own thinking. A compe-
tent and cultured, though relatively obscure, man of letters
before the publication of *The Promise,* Croly in 1914 became
one of the founders and chief editor of *The New Republic* magazine. Together with his younger co-editors like Walter Lippmann, Croly, therefore, remained a significant intellectual
force in American reform journalism.

Ten years in preparation, *The Promise of American Life*
added to the familiar Progressive attack on laissez faire the
frank plea that traditional Jeffersonian individualism be replaced by a more realistic political philosophy. Much like
Roosevelt in his preference for the Hamiltonian over the Jeffersonian position in history, Croly contended that American
nationalism and American democracy were not incompatible
or contradictory values. But the traditional philosophy of
equal rights and of no governmental interference in private
enterprise lead inevitably to the conquest of the weak by the
strong. The opportunities of a frontier society no longer existed in the United States, and government therefore must
become a partner of the American people, while liberal followers of Jefferson would have to take over Hamilton's nationalistic methods. What was necessary, accordingly, was
open governmental intervention in the economy and a redis-
tribution of wealth.

> The Promise of American Life is to be fulfilled—not merely
> by a maximum amount of economic freedom, but by a certain
> measure of discipline; not merely by the abundant satisfaction of
> individual desires, but by a large measure of individual subordi-
> nation and self-denial. . . .
> Whatever the national interest may be, it is not to be asserted
> by the political practice of non-interference. The hope of auto-

matic democratic fulfillment must be abandoned. The national government must step in and discriminate; but it must discriminate, not on behalf of liberty and the special individual, but on behalf of equality and the average man.

Roosevelt won Croly's praise as a reformer who was in the tradition of Hamilton's strong nationalism. In contrast to a figure like Bryan, Roosevelt realized that reform could not be separated from nationalism. "He has, indeed," wrote Croly, "been even more of a nationalist than he has a reformer." T.R., to Croly, was a Hamiltonian with the difference that he accepted democracy and then emancipated it from its Jeffersonian heritage of anti-statism.

In his discussion of specific reforms, Croly took issue with some of the shibboleths of the average Progressive. Majority rule, he felt, should not always be morally or nationally binding, while the secret ballot, direct government by the people, and more frequent elections might only damage democracy by making it less workable. In the same way, civil-service reform hurt efficiency by enabling employees to become independent of their superiors. The political boss he condoned as necessary in an age of increasing specialization in order to overcome "a separation of actual political power from official political responsibility."

In the matter of government relations with business and labor, Croly was essentially Rooseveltian. He wanted the federal government to cease its war on the large corporations, substituting a national incorporation law for the Sherman Antitrust Act. At the same time, he recognized that government had a responsibility for dealing with the problem of monopoly. This might be exercised, he believed, through a system of regulation and inspection, by higher graduated corporate income taxes, and finally through the offsetting power of stronger labor unions to which the government would extend "legal recognition" as well as a measure of federal control.

Not unexpectedly, Croly was criticized by contemporaries for advocating socialism, and by some later historians for anticipating fascism's corporate society. Most Americans, he readily admitted in *The Promise,* would no doubt consider his program "flagrantly socialistic both in its methods and its object." Unconcerned, however, "with dodging the odium of the word," Croly stated that his definition of democracy was socialistic only "if it is socialistic to consider democracy inseparable from a candid, patient, and courageous attempt to advance the social problem towards a satisfactory solution." On the other hand, he pointed out that there were some doctrines, frequently associated with socialism, which were inimical to his own conception of democracy and some which should more properly be characterized not so much as socialistic, but "as unscrupulously and loyally nationalistic."

In all phases of his program, Croly distinguished between his conception of nationalism and a European type of centralization. But he also felt that the United States, coming more and more to resemble the society and government of Europe, must copy European ways. In the realm of foreign affairs, he accepted the need of a larger army and navy to go along with American interests abroad, and he defended war as a sometimes useful agent of civilization. Croly, however, was less bellicose than such Progressives and imperialists as Roosevelt or Senator Beveridge, or figures like Admiral Mahan and Senator Lodge. Toward the American imperialism that followed the Spanish–American War he took a somewhat equivocal attitude. Foreign domination of primitive peoples might be justified in terms of the progress of civilization, but Croly nevertheless disliked United States policy in the Philippines. Acquisition of the islands, he suggested, might be valuable chiefly in advancing America's long-range interests in the Far East.

Together, Croly's *Promise of American Life* and Roosevelt's New Nationalism offered Progressives a program and helped define the issues confronting the American people in 1912. Much less clear was the means of maneuvering T.R.'s own return to political leadership and the presidency. The congressional and state elections in 1910 were almost a complete disaster for the Republican party. At the same time, the results offered no conclusive mandate for Roosevelt's own political future. Although Progressive Republicans triumphed in the West, the two candidates closest to Roosevelt—Senator Beveridge in Indiana and Henry L. Stimson, Republican nominee for governor of New York—met defeat. Most significant of all was the Democratic party's resurgence and the election of Woodrow Wilson as a reform governor in New Jersey and potential national leader for 1912.

For Roosevelt personally the signs were indeed mixed. Although at this stage, in 1910, he believed that Taft could be renominated, he also felt that the Republicans were doomed to defeat and that he should neither be a candidate in 1912 nor give his endorsement to any individual. Radicals like the Pinchots were disappointed, in turn, by Roosevelt's continued straddling and efforts still to support both conservative and progressive Republicans. At a meeting in January 1911 the Republican insurgents, despairing for the present of Roosevelt as a possible leader, organized the National Progressive Republican League for the purpose of defeating Taft and nominating Senator La Follette for President. La Follette, whose main political strength was among farmers and small businessmen in the West, reflected the old Populist element in the Progressive movement. He was, therefore, hardly the kind of candidate to appeal to the more nationalistic Progressives like Roosevelt or Croly.

Roosevelt and La Follette's relations, although cordial at first, deteriorated steadily under the pressure of their respective political ambitions. La Follette, led to believe that he had the Colonel's unofficial blessing and could thus win the nomination, was forever embittered as his own supporters continued to look hopefully to the former President. Although convinced, like those who backed him, that the Republicans could not win in 1912 with either Taft or La Follette as their nominee, Roosevelt waited until the fall of 1911 before giving direct encouragement to the behind-the-scenes efforts to put across his own nomination. A key factor then in T.R.'s decision was President Taft's initiation of antitrust proceedings against the United States Steel Corporation. Since Roosevelt as President had approved, tacitly if not actually, the steel corporation's acquisition of the Tennessee Coal and Iron Company during the Panic of 1907—the basis of the government's suit—the whole matter reflected unfavorably on his integrity.

Privately Roosevelt denounced what he felt was Taft's bad faith. And publicly, in *Outlook* for November, he attacked the steel case as an unfortunate attempt to force an archaic system of competition upon American industry. The article, which enabled T.R. to regain some of the confidence in business circles that he had forfeited with his radical Osawatomie speech, also helped renew the possibility of his candidacy. A number of business leaders now felt that Roosevelt was the safest of the so-called Progressives. Frank A. Munsey, the newspaper and magazine publisher, and George W. Perkins, a Morgan partner and old Roosevelt friend, became open supporters; even more importantly they promised to back Roosevelt's campaign with their checkbooks.

By February 1912, La Follette's chance for the nomination dissolved tragically. A poor speech in Philadelphia, haranguing the country's publishers at their own meeting, provided an excuse for his followers, including the Pinchots and a number of Progressive politicians, to turn to the Roosevelt bandwagon. That same month Roosevelt threw his cowboy hat in the political ring. At Columbus, Ohio, in a major address, he appealed to the mixed and varied groups whose support was vital to his cause. Advised by Frank Munsey to stress a frank statism, Roosevelt offered businessmen his conception of a paternalistic type of government regulation as a contrast to Taft's trustbusting. At the same time, however, Roosevelt also encouraged the more radical Progressives by announcing a controversial plan for the recall of state judicial decisions. Although essentially conservative in its message, the Ohio speech seemed to indicate that there were two Roosevelts: the moderate-type Progressive acceptable to business interests and the radical Progressive who symbolized the social and economic reforms of the New Nationalism.

Unfortunately for T.R., his opponents seized upon the issue of the judiciary, exaggerating his views to imply that he favored the recall of all judges as well as specific court decisions. Already a subject of much scholarly controversy among political scientists, the debate over an independent judiciary continued throughout the 1912 campaign. The recall of judges, Elihu Root, United States senator from New York, declared, "sets at naught the great principle that justice is above majorities." As defined by Root, judicial independence ran counter to the whole Progressive theory of direct popular rule. It contradicted the force of public opinion in a democracy. An indirect result of the heated political battle was the later publication, in 1913, of such pertinent works as A. Lawrence Lowell's *Public Opinion and Popular Government,* Charles Beard's *An Economic Interpretation of the Constitution,* and ex-President Taft's *Popular Government.* With their nostalgia for an older America, it appeared to conservatives like Root and Taft that Roosevelt's challenge to the judicial status quo threatened all remaining traditional values. Roosevelt, in turn, denied that his proposal "for the exercise of the referendum by the people themselves in a certain class of decisions of constitutional questions" was "putting the axe to the tree of well ordered freedom." In France and the British Commonwealth of Nations, all governed by parliaments akin to the American Congress, he pointed out, it was the legislative body which made the final decision on constitutional questions.

The vigorous, uncompromising nature of his speeches in the spring of 1912 indicated that Roosevelt was in the presidential race to stay. In the face of Taft's ability to force his own renomination via control of the Republican party machinery, Roosevelt's continued candidacy meant that he would probably have to create a third party and run as an independent. Even if the Republicans were by some chance to choose Roosevelt, he could hardly campaign on the radical platform he had set forth at Osawatomie. Yet as a third-party candidate he realized, of course, that he could not hope for the backing of any but a small proportion of the staunch Republican regulars. Hitherto always careful to stay with his party, and unfailingly critical of the mugwump type of independent reformer, Roosevelt now, however, rejected the advice to wait until 1916. Buoyed by his victories in the states holding presidential primaries, and convinced that the Taft forces had cheated him out of the nomination by refusing to recognize the credentials of many of the Progressive delegates at the Republican convention, T.R. stood by the decision to form a new party.

Politics makes strange bedfellows, but it was still an amazingly diverse band of loyal disciples who gathered at Chicago in August to nominate Roosevelt for President on the Progressive party ticket. Missing, however, were most of the liberal Republican governors and senators who had originally coaxed Roosevelt to run. At the point of no political return, they dared not jeopardize their futures by splitting the Republican party on the state and local level. Historian John Blum writes correctly that "the Progressive party—Roosevelt's creature—was a politician's Gothic horror. . . . It was a party with only three assets, all transitory: enthusiasm, money, and a Presidential candidate."

The trouble, of course, was that too many of the faithful, like Jane Addams and her fellow social workers, were not politicians at all. While the pacifist reformers cheered their militant hero to the strains of the "Battle Hymn of the Republic" and "Onward Christian Soldiers," the scattering of professional politicians and business leaders tried to take charge. Thus George W. Perkins, for example, was able to delete an antitrust plank from the party platform, and Roosevelt's own essentially nationalistic spirit gained predominance over the radical, socialistic planks in the Progressive program. Nevertheless it was still the most advanced platform that any major American party had yet presented to the electorate. It embodied a broad program of social-welfare legislation, including a minimum wage for women, the prohibition of child labor, workmen's compensation, and social-insurance legislation. To secure a more direct democracy, the Progressives called for the adoption of the initiative, referendum, and recall, the recall of judicial decisions, a nationwide presidential primary, and publicity for all campaign contributions and expenditures. To meet the economic challenge of the trusts, the Progressives advocated their version of national regulation—rather than destruction—through a strong federal administrative commission. In this regard, the party platform noted that "Germany's policy of co-operation between government and business has, in comparatively few years, made that nation a leading competitor for the commerce of the world." It was imperative therefore to the welfare of the American people, the Progressives believed, that their government by a similar encouragement of business "enlarge and extend our foreign commerce."

Both George W. Perkins and Frank Munsey, it is well to note, were admirers of a strong administrative state and of German nationalism. Together they contributed almost half a million dollars to the organization of T.R.'s campaign, and Munsey also helped with his newspapers and magazines, even at the cost of circulation and profits. As early as March 1912, *Munsey's Magazine* confidently declared: "The radicalism of Roosevelt . . . has already mellowed into conservatism. . . . Of all the progressives, Roosevelt is today preeminently the biggest and sanest conservative—a progressive conservative." And in August it observed that the Progressive party "does not believe in the destruction of big corporations, but it believes in controlling them and making sure they do not destroy the competition of the small man or smaller concerns."

It was not surprising that Donald Richberg, one of the dedicated youthful workers in the Bull Moose campaign, in looking back upon the relations of T.R. and his business supporters, commented that "the party did not come from the grass roots." Except perhaps in the Midwest, Richberg's comment was correct. Although Roosevelt ran better in the cities than in rural areas, the Progressives generally could not organize enough mass support to add to the votes that Roosevelt was able to attract through his own personality. Norman Hapgood, the muckraking editor of *Collier's Weekly*, who supported Wilson instead of T.R., believed the intellectual foundations of Roosevelt's campaign were too weak to sustain his reform followers' enthusiasm. The conservatives took the party away from the Progressives, and Wilson was able to force Roosevelt on the defensive in regard to such issues as the tariff and the trusts.

Between the Republican and the Progressive conventions

in Chicago, the Democratic party, meeting in Baltimore, nominated Woodrow Wilson on the forty-sixth ballot in what Arthur Link calls "one of the miracles of modern American politics." Wilson's switch only two years earlier from the presidency of Princeton University to the New Jersey governorship was now climaxed by his successful uphill fight for the nomination against the popular Speaker of the House of Representatives, Champ Clark. Despite the Democrats' drawnout struggle, the choice of Wilson as the nominee was admirably suited to bring harmony to the party. Better than any of the other possible candidates, Wilson appealed to all sections of the country. Moreover, he was progressive enough to win Bryan's support without alienating the reactionary state and city bosses. Finally, the split between Taft and Roosevelt gave the Democrats good reason to believe that with Wilson at the head of a united party they would elect the next President of the United States.

As the fourth-ranking candidate in a crowded field, the Socialists—returning to Indianapolis, where the party had been born in 1901—again nominated Eugene V. Debs, party standard-bearer in 1904 and 1908. Although prosperous, with over one hundred thousand paid-up members and delegates from every state except South Carolina, the Socialists faced a struggle between the left and right wings of the party that only Debs's personal popularity was able to surmount. Thus the convention, in amending the party constitution to rule out violence and sabotage in industrial disputes, set the stage for a split among the more radical Socialists and the expulsion a year later of William Haywood and his followers in the I.W.W. Throughout the campaign, however, Debs managed to present an advanced socialist program in American dress. Like Roosevelt, a politician with immense voter appeal, Debs succeeded in making his radical position acceptable to many non-Socialists.

Although Taft, the Republican choice, was by no means the servile creature of big business depicted by his Progressive opponents, he and Debs were soon relegated to the extreme right and left of the political spectrum, while Roosevelt and Wilson competed for the mass support of the broader middle range of American voters. Taft's fears of all-powerful government and his dislike of the Progressive version of direct democracy stated positions which Wilson was also able to use effectively against Roosevelt. Yet the election of 1912 was more complex than a simple referendum between the New Freedom and the New Nationalism.

An old-fashioned, Jeffersonian liberal before he became a progressive Democrat and reformer, Wilson was also a strict Calvinist and Puritan. Reared in the South as the son of a much-respected Presbyterian minister, Wilson's liberal inclinations were reinforced by his admiration of the nineteenth-century English Whigs or Liberals. His academic training in history and political science broadened his intellectual horizons, but his general philosophy remained centered in an Anglo-American, Presbyterian tradition. Until he became President, Wilson took little interest in political developments abroad. He was, however, a keen student of domestic politics in an academic sort of way. Thus he looked to the leadership of a well-educated elite trained for government service and public administration. Civil-service reform and a sound system of taxation, as opposed to patronage and subsidies, would help keep the government innocent of the corrupting influence of special interest groups. This rather limited view of the function of modern government was modified in Wilson's case by his growing belief in the importance of the office of the President, especially in the conduct of foreign relations. While Wilson's talk of the need of individual goodness and morality in public affairs undoubtedly made him attractive to some conservative Democrats, looking for an alternative to Bryan's Populism, it also enhanced his popular appeal as a reformer and spokesman for the New Freedom.

Although Wilson, like Roosevelt, moved from an essentially conservative position to a more advanced type of Progressivism, he was reluctant to accept the idea of positive government. The regulation of business, he pointed out in 1907 and 1908 while president of Princeton, was really socialistic. The comprehensive, expert knowledge needed to regulate business would lead the government "actually to order and conduct what it began by regulating." Arguing in good Whig fashion for the "reign of law rather than the reign of government officials," Wilson stated: "I can see no radical difference in principle between governmental ownership and governmental regulation of this discretionary kind. Advocates of governmental regulation talk of it as a necessary safeguard against socialistic programmes of reform, but it seems to me to be itself socialistic in principle."

In his 1912 campaign speeches, Wilson maintained that freedom and competition in American life were being endangered by the growth of special privilege and monopoly. Often, where competition continued to exist, it was more like a warfare between pygmies and giants rather than a true competition between nonmonopolistic forms of economic enterprise. Dissenting from the whole idea of an alliance between government and business, Wilson contended that the federal government had to remain more powerful than business. Yet he believed that social betterment arose historically from a sense of social justice on the part of the people themselves. "Liberty," he declared in a passage that Roosevelt took up and quoted largely out of context, "has never come from the government. Liberty has always come from the subjects of the government. The history of liberty is a history of resistance. The history of liberty is a history of the limitation of governmental power, not the increase of it."

From Louis D. Brandeis, the liberal attorney and foe of monopoly who offered his advice and support, Wilson developed the concept of a regulated competition as an offset to Roosevelt's regulated monopoly. Regulated competition, Wilson was careful to point out, differed from the old-fashioned competition that had built up the mammoth corporate combinations and monopolies. Wilson adopted, too, Brandeis's notion of "the curse of bigness." "There is no point of bigness," he said, "where you pass the point of efficiency and get to the point of clumsiness and unwieldiness." Without espousing the specific proposals for social and economic justice in Roosevelt's New Nationalism, Wilson, however, agreed during the course of the campaign that "if Jefferson were living in our day he would see what we see: that the individual is caught in a great confused nexus of all sorts of complicated circumstances, and that to let him alone is to leave him helpless as against the obstacles with which he has to contend; and that, therefore, law in our day must come to the assistance of the individual." Although opposed to paternalism, Wilson conceded that government was needed to ensure fair play for the individual. "Freedom to-day," he concluded, "is something more than being let alone. The program of a government of freedom must in these days be positive, not negative merely."

Over much of the debate between New Freedom and New Nationalism, or regulated competition versus regulated monopoly, there was a kind of semantic confusion and lack of reality which gave point to the economist Richard T. Ely's complaint, after listening to him on an earlier occasion, that Wilson "could speak beautifully and say nothing, if he wished." Though deeply moved by the future President, Ely was annoyed that he could recall nothing of the substance of what he said.

Still, as Roosevelt asserted, Wilson's program was unlike his own. Wilson was a good man who would probably make a better President than Taft, Roosevelt complained, but he was "not a Nationalist" and had no convictions on issues that T.R. deemed vital. For example, Wilson's belief in the limitation of government, though correct historically, no longer applied to the day when "governmental power rests in the people . . . and what people sorely need is the extension of governmental power." The two men differed, as John Blum has written, "about the nature and obligation of government, the concentration and use of power. Merging Brandeis's political economy with the political theory of his youth, Wilson made the New Freedom, as he put it himself, 'only the old revived and clothed in the unconquerable strength of modern America.' "

"Rural Toryism," Roosevelt called Wilson's position, but to the more sympathetic *Nation*, Roosevelt was an uncritical proponent of centralization and monopoly. "This issue of centralized power and regulated monopoly is not only the one great and explicit feature of the Roosevelt platform as formulated at Chicago; but it is also the one issue with which his personality and record are profoundly and unmistakably identified."

It was a stirring campaign, and Roosevelt especially waged a magnificent personal battle. By the middle of October, however, it was evident that Wilson would easily win the uneven contest. As Arthur Link points out, "The significant development of the campaign was Roosevelt's failure to unite progressive Republicans and progressive Democrats." Like Brandeis, too many Progressives believed that the new party was primarily Roosevelt's personal vehicle and only afterward a true Progressive party. Wilson also received the support of numbers of reformers and liberals who could not trust T.R. and who particularly feared his militarism and imperialism. Even in the Midwest and West, where Progressivism was strongest, there were many old Populists and La Follette supporters who could not accept Roosevelt's views on the tariff and trusts, nor approve the sophisticated Croly–T.R. version of the New Nationalism. Much of Roosevelt's backing in the western states, George Mowry suggests, came in spite of his program, not because of it.

Although the electoral vote was a Wilson landslide, his popular margin was less impressive. Debs's large vote, the highest percent of the total ever received by the Socialist party, presumably drew in part from large groups of disaffected Progressives who might have cast their ballots for Wilson or Roosevelt. In any case, the Debs total of 901,873 made the others' combined votes less than the major-party share of the ballots in 1908. Wilson polled 6,293,019, 42 percent of the total. Roosevelt's 4,119,507 put him ahead of Taft, who received only 3,484,956. Since even Taft denied that he was a conservative, the results could be regarded as a Progressive victory. Only Woodrow Wilson, however, had to confront the task of translating the contradictions of the solemn referendum of 1912 into a meaningful reform program.

PART

FIVE

*Imperial
Democracy*

CHAPTER 11

Hands Across the Seas

 IMPERIAL democracy—the notion that the American republic was destined to become a great world empire—assumed new reality after the Spanish–American War. In 1898 the United States exchanged its place as a republic equal in all its parts for an empire of noncontiguous areas which were relegated to an inferior political status. Already an important national state by the mid-nineteenth century, and indeed a strong new nation almost from birth, the United States now also became in the twentieth century an imperial world power. In an era of change and ferment, the novel, imperial and worldwide interests of the United States developed swiftly. Between the war with Spain and the first world war, a radical transformation took place in both American foreign and domestic policy. Expansion abroad, like reform at home, became a means of rationalizing the economy. As William Leuchtenburg has pointed out, Progressivism and imperialism flourished together, not as opposites, but as "expressions of the same philosophy of government, a tendency to judge any action not by the means employed but by the results achieved, a worship of definitive action for action's sake. . . ."

To enthusiastic proponents of American expansion abroad, particularly Theodore Roosevelt and political friends like Henry Cabot Lodge and Albert J. Beveridge, the new worldwide interests of the United States were as inevitable as they were deemed to be desirable. On the other hand, to many of those whose beliefs about foreign policy were rooted in the older liberal tradition of American democracy, imperialism represented an unfortunate departure from the ideals of the early republic as well as a monstrous interference with alien peoples living in distant lands. In the words of the popular humorist Finley Peter Dunne—Mr. Dooley—paraphrasing Senator Lodge, it was a policy of "hands acrost th' sea an' into somewan's pocket."

By the latter decades of the nineteenth century, imperialism was an integral and accepted feature of world politics. As the industrial revolution reached maturity in the major countries of Western Europe, there was a scramble for markets overseas. The old colonial empires, founded in the original expansion of Europe in the sixteenth and seventeenth centuries, took on added importance as sources of raw materials and as consumers of manufactured goods. On the continents of Asia and Africa, England, France, and later Germany, sought new colonial possessions or spheres of influence. Economic progress based on industrial expansion encouraged a materialistic philosophy and a diplomacy of *realpolitik,* while economic nationalism at home led in turn to national imperialism and capital investments abroad.

The United States, preoccupied after the Civil War with the economic development of its last frontier in the trans-Mississippi West, deferred until the close of the century its own imperial ambitions. But except in the direct sense of the acquisition of overseas possessions, American expansion was, of course, neither a new policy nor a sudden interest. Isolationism in the nineteenth century had not precluded the quest for foreign trade and markets. At the same time, the idea of an American mission to encourage the peaceful spread of democracy focused national attention upon revolutionary movements and political changes abroad. Although the earlier American territorial expansion of the nineteenth century had been a continental thrust into sparsely settled wilderness areas, there had been an element of imperialism in United States relations with the Indians and Mexicans. The phrase "American Empire" had been used by some of the Founding Fathers to describe a growing American dominion over a larger area and population. But what Jefferson called "an empire for liberty," and what later historians termed agricultural imperialism, was generally peaceful in intent.

Despite the Mexican War and the aggressive American efforts to gain Cuba in the early 1850's, continental expansion and manifest destiny created a nation–state, not an imperialistic empire. Even the purchase of Alaska hardly signified a departure from the pattern of acquiring contiguous territory on the North American Continent that could someday be added to the Union as a state. Thus expansionistic tendencies toward an imperialist empire were not fully realized until the war with Spain and the acquisition first of the Hawaiian Islands and then the Philippines, Guam, and Puerto Rico.

By the 1890's economic penetration into the less developed, outlying areas of the world became a more attractive possibility for the United States. As the balance of foreign trade shifted in America's favor, the percentage of manufactured goods in its exports rose steadily. In 1897 the value of manufactured articles exported exceeded that of those imported for the first time. That same year the margin by which the value of exports exceeded imports was the greatest in history, and a year later, in 1898, the margin had doubled. The ever-increasing American population, which rose more than 100 percent in the generation between the Civil War and the war with Spain, was able to consume nine-tenths of American products, but the other tenth was far from unimportant and amounted to perhaps a billion dollars by 1897. Together these statistics gave point to Albert J. Beveridge's famous exhortation before a group of Boston businessmen in 1898. "American factories," the future Progressive Republican senator declared, "are making more than the American people can use; American soil is producing more than they can consume. Fate has written our policy for us; the trade of the world must and shall be ours."

For probably the larger share of the American public who supported McKinley and voted Republican in 1900, expansion abroad, if it was necessary to preserve private enterprise and free competition at home, was preferable to European concepts of socialism and drastic government regulation. The economic stewardship implied in the business philosophy of Andrew Carnegie's Gospel of Wealth, when carried overseas, became a part of the white man's burden. In the same way, political philosophies of benevolent aid or paternalistic regulation of business were easily projected to cover an official expansionist policy of securing new outlets and markets for American domestic surpluses. Tariff reciprocity to widen markets for American exports was as logical a policy as high duties to protect infant American industries.

Though an expansionistic program seemed to offer a plausible solution to some of the economic ills of the 1880's and 1890's, the business and producing classes were not the most ardent spokesmen for American imperialism. Instead, its first and most articulate support was found among an interesting elite of publicists and politicians, missionaries and navalists, professors and moral philosophers. The expansionistic ideology that met with the favor of these influential individuals was a mixture of the philosophies of manifest destiny, Darwinian evolution, Anglo-Saxon racism, economic determinism, militarism and navalism, nationalism and patriotism. Already in the 1880's, John Fiske, the popular historian and Darwinist, and the Reverend Josiah Strong propounded the thesis that world leadership henceforth was to be exercised by the Anglo-Saxon race of nations. In Fiske's eyes, the coming imperialism was to be peaceful and benevolent, a result of American industrial power and Anglo-Saxon political ideals rather than war. Strong, whose book *Our Country* reached a wide audience, believed that the Anglo-Saxon race, the divine depository of the eternal principles of Christianity and civil liberty, was destined to spread over the earth. As the principal home of this race, the seat of its coming power and influence, it was the duty of the United States to assume the leadership and responsibility for the future progress of the world.

Well before the turn of the century, as Ernest R. May has shown in his book *American Imperialism*, the leading figures in the American business and political establishment were familiar with European imperialism and were often close associates on friendly terms with their counterparts in Europe, where they were also frequent visitors. Although anticolonialism remained dominant among these American leaders until 1898, it was fast weakening, and the mass of the American people were being persuaded to change their views. The easy victory over Spain, McKinley's arguments of duty and destiny, and the patriotic appeal of men like Roosevelt, fresh from his exciting experience in Cuba, were all potent psychological portents. A vigorous foreign policy accompanied by the return of prosperity also offered a hopeful contrast to the bitter class conflict and hard times of the nineties. Signs were not

wanting, therefore, that the United States was ready to follow
Europe and adopt an imperialistic policy. Foreign trade, colonies, navalism, and even war, were all now suddenly more attractive and important in American life.

"At no time have the Old World and the New had so much
in common," wrote Leo S. Rowe in describing the influence of
the war with Spain upon American public life. According to
Professor Rowe, writing in *Forum* magazine in 1899, the new
position of the United States carried with it

> obligations from which we cannot escape. Closer contact with the
> Far East will make clear where the great commercial opportu-
> nities lie. The peculiar conditions of trade in that portion of the
> globe demand that our Government pave the way for commer-
> cial supremacy. Our merchants and manufacturers will no longer
> remain indifferent to the scramble of the European Powers for
> special trade privileges. Thus, little by little, the negative attitude
> of the American people toward Government will give way to a
> more positive interpretation of its *role*. Non interference with Eu-
> ropean affairs will no longer be interpreted as isolation from Eu-
> ropean contact. In short, the doctrine of political isolation, based
> on the Monroe Doctrine, is likely to be set at rest by the force of
> recent events.

On both sides of the Atlantic by the turn of the century, a
growing number of influential scholars, journalists, and politicians repeated the arguments for imperialism, linking together the interests of the United States and Great Britain
and suggesting an ideology of American foreign policy that
was to prove congenial to most American Progressives. On
the whole, British opinion interpreted the Spanish–American
War and ensuing imperialism as evidence that the United
States had emerged from its relative isolation in the nineteenth century. For example, Edward Dicey, a prominent and
scholarly English publicist, stated that "the instinct of the

ruling race," though always present in the United States, had been subordinated previously to domestic concerns. Now, however, an American democracy without foreign markets could no longer, according to Dicey, resolve such growing social evils as poverty and urban slums. The United States Constitution would have to be amended or ignored in order to make possible the acquisition of colonies. A number of English liberals, including James Bryce, frankly regretted the changing course of American foreign policy; they warned the United States therefore against the dangers of imperialism. But Dicey, reflecting what seemed to be the more popular British view, congratulated the United States for having "preserved the ideal of an Imperial mission"; and for preparing "to carry out that manifold destiny which is the birthright of the Anglo-Saxon race."

In British imperialist circles, McKinley's re-election in 1900, hailed as a "victory of imperialism," implied support for England's own policies. During the presidential campaign it was true that Bryan had expressed sympathy with the Boers in their war with the British in South Africa, and the Democratic party platform denounced the "ill-concealed Republican alliance with England." But the British government understood that the United States officially took no such pro-Boer stand. Moreover the American people, immersed in their own imperialistic struggle with the Filipinos, took little interest in the Boer cause and were not overly critical of Britain's repressive policy.

Most interesting was the attitude toward imperialism of the British Socialists, including the Fabians, for whom the Boer War created formidable problems. Against general socialist demands for denunciation of the government's Boer policy, a majority of the Fabians deserted the Socialist ranks and stood with the Liberal imperialists. George Bernard Shaw, supported by Sidney and Beatrice Webb, drafted his

manifesto *Fabianism and the Empire,* providing a socialist rationale for the union of national reform and imperialism.
Until the socialist federation of the world became a fact, Shaw
contended that imperial federations like the British Empire
must prevail. He wrote:

> The problem before us, is how the world can be ordered by Great
> Powers of practically international extent. . . . The notion that a
> nation has the right to do what it pleases with its own territory,
> without reference to the interests of the rest of the world, is no
> more tenable from the International Socialist point of view—that
> is, from the point of view of the twentieth century—than the no-
> tion that the landlord has a right to do what he likes with his own
> estate without reference to the interests of his neighbours. . . .
> The State which obstructs international civilization, will have to
> go, be it big or little.

Shaw's argument, rejecting the old liberal pacifism that
was still strong in British socialism, undoubtedly shocked
many of his friends. Most of those in the Liberal and Socialist
parties were probably still anti-imperialist in their sympathies
after 1900, but British popular sentiment was now increasingly both jingoistic and reform-minded.

Fabian Socialist support of the Boer War had a parallel in
the stand of certain American radicals, Populists as well as Socialists, regarding the war with Spain. American Socialists
vacillated between the orthodox Marxist groups opposed to
the war and the American Fabians and Bellamy Nationalists
who were prowar. W. J. Ghent, an independent socialist,
maintained that English Liberals and later-day American Jef-
fersonians like William Jennings Bryan were unrealistic and
reactionary sentimentalists in their nostalgic longing for individual liberty and hostility to imperialism. Invoking Ben-
tham's dictum of "the greatest good for the greatest number," Ghent, like George Bernard Shaw, contended "there is

every justification for the use of force in establishing orderly and decent government in the Transvaal and the Philippines. The question comes home: Will the authority of America in the one and of England in the other make for order, for democracy, for civilization, for justice, for the 'individuation' of the downmost man?" In justification of American policy in 1900, William A. Peffer, the former Populist senator from Kansas, went so far as to assert:

> The trouble in the Philippines has been occasioned by Aguinaldo and his associates. Americans are there of right, and they ask nothing of the natives but to be peaceable, to obey the laws and to go ahead with their business; they will not only be protected in every right, but will be aided by all the powerful influences of an advanced and aggressive civilization.

William Jennings Bryan, who stood before the voters on the question of imperialism in the 1900 presidential campaign, was typical of these Democrats and Populists who had used the Cuban issue to embarrass the McKinley Administration. Enthusiastic over the war with Spain as long as it was a humanitarian crusade to free Cuba, Bryan and many of his followers, however, opposed it when it became an imperialistic adventure. The more formidable and costly struggle against the Filipino insurrectionists they condemned as unnecessary and unjust. And the Democratic platform censured President McKinley's policies for placing the United States, "previously known and applauded throughout the world as the champion of freedom, in the false and un-American position of crushing with military force the efforts of our former allies to achieve liberty and self-government."

The anti-imperialist movement, though never well-organized outside Boston and a few other large cities, included some of the most distinguished statesmen and men of letters in America. William Dean Howells, Mark Twain, William Vaughn Moody, and Thomas Bailey Aldrich all opposed colonial expansion, while Samuel Bowles, Edwin L. Godkin, and Finley Peter Dunne were important journalistic critics. In the Democratic party eight members of Cleveland's Cabinet, including the former President and his Secretary of State Richard Olney, were ranged against imperialism. Among Republicans it was mostly the liberal reform element of elder statesmen carrying on the old antislavery traditions who protested against McKinley's annexationist policies. Typical of this group was Carl Schurz, one of the German forty-eighters, who denied the imperialist argument that the United States had a mission to serve those outside its own boundaries. He recognized that America naturally desired to advance its own principles of government, but he believed that if his adopted country assumed a universal responsibility for the progress of civilization, American democracy itself would break down.

On the whole the anti-imperialist movement was based more on abstract political and ideological principles than on economic, religious, constitutional, or humanitarian considerations. Imperialism was opposed as contrary to the traditions of American democratic government as stated in the Declaration of Independence, Washington's Farewell Address, and Lincoln's Gettysburg oration. The abandonment of these principles in favor of imitating the ways of the Old World, the anti-imperialists believed, would destroy the republic.

The anti-imperialists, frequently dismissed as unrealistic idealists, out of step with direction of world politics in the twentieth century, were actually often quite discerning in their awareness of the affinity between Progressivist and imperialist ideologies. Particularly attentive to this phenomenon were a number of academic figures, old-fashioned liberals or conservatives, who were suspicious of the recent and growing tendencies toward more governmental power.

Paul S. Reinsch, professor of political science at the University of Wisconsin, and later United States minister to China and legal adviser to the Chinese government, was one of those who saw the significance at home of the new international currents abroad. In his book *World Politics,* a volume in the Macmillan Citizen's Library published in 1900, Reinsch stated that the exaggerated nationalism of the nineteenth century was now being transformed into "the age of national imperialism." Everywhere the spirit of individualism and the old cosmopolitan sense of European unity were being sacrificed to a Machiavellian and Hegelian philosophy of nationalism and statism. In England the liberalism of a Gladstone, with its checks on the power of government, was nearly dead. "The simple questions of national greatness and glory, and of such social legislation as that of old-age pensions, are of greater interest to the new democracy—and of these two, the former, with its constant appeals to patriotic feeling, has the stronger hold on the masses." Despite the popularity of social reform, Reinsch feared that the governing classes in both Europe and America would ultimately subordinate home affairs to imperial interests. "A nation that is rapidly expanding is quite likely to suffer in its social and political well-being at home." Mindful of the needs of the average American citizen, Reinsch warned that "the central government should not be turned into an instrumentality for advancing powerful centralized interests."

While Reinsch tended still in 1900 to think of imperialism as a possible threat to social reform, others perceived that Progressivism might instead try to unite all interests through the instrumentality of a strong, centralized national state. "The socialist development of Liberalism paved the way for Imperialism," Leonard T. Hobhouse, the English philosopher and journalist and the first professor of sociology at the University of London, wrote in his book *Democracy and Reac-*

tion. "So non-intervention abroad went by the board along with laissez faire at home; national liberty was ranked with competitive industrialism as an exploded superstition; a positive theory of the State in domestic affairs was matched by a positive theory of Empire, and the way was made straight for Imperialism. . . ." William Graham Sumner, author of the anti-imperialist essay *The Conquest of the United States by Spain,* was an American counterpart of Hobhouse in much of his thinking. In his famous anthropological study *Folkways,* Sumner noted that, under the modern optimistic philosophy of progress of which he was dubious, "the philosophical drift in the mores of our time is towards state regulation, militarism, imperialism, towards petting and flattering the poor and laboring classes, and in favor of whatever is altruistic and humanitarian." According to the economist Franklin Pierce, Sumner's New Haven neighbor, and like him a conservative in his social views, governmental paternalism and imperialism were intimately associated. "Everywhere in every direction," he observed, "we are putting on the airs and adopting the customs of a monarchical form of government, and we are doing this because we have become an empire and because our people are given over to the spirit of materialism."

In his *Reminiscences of an American Scholar,* the political scientist John W. Burgess deplored the evil effect of the Spanish–American War on the national character. "We started then on the road of imperialism and we have not turned back. The exaggeration of government at the expense of liberty made a mightier spring forward than at any preceding period in our history. . . ." Burgess, one of Theodore Roosevelt's professors at the Columbia University School of Law, and himself a firm admirer of German scholarship, believed that the United States, in its adoption of imperialism, an income tax, and direct democracy, was aping Europe. America, he feared, was moving steadily away from liberty of the individual toward despotic government at home as well as abroad.

The contemporary American rationale for imperialism, as professors like Sumner and Burgess complained, seemed to anticipate and parallel Progressivist ideology. Thus the democratic government sought by Progressives, it was believed, could also prove beneficial abroad. Exhortations of reform and self-sacrifice at home as the means of simple justice for the less fortunate classes of society were readily translatable into demands that the American people should shoulder the white man's burden and embark on missionary crusades overseas. The popular magazines of the early 1900's—*The Independent, Outlook, Century, Harper's,* and *North American Review,* for example—were all filled with articles in support of imperialism, not only in terms of American economic interests, but as the democratic duty and world responsibility of the United States. Down in the heart of all Americans, the editor of *Century* magazine wrote in April 1903, was "a sense of national superiority, as to our governmental system and our actual condition, that needs only slight excitation to make it vocal."

As early as 1900, Franklin H. Giddings, professor of sociology at Columbia University, in a book called *Democracy and Empire,* maintained that the two forms of government were not incompatible. Via imperialism the United States would spread its ideals of liberty and equality to the rest of the world. In an address before the annual meeting of the National Education Association in 1899 titled "An Educational Policy for Our New Possessions," William T. Harris, like Giddings, urged the benefits of imperialism. To Harris, the United States Commissioner of Education, it seemed obvious that "if we cannot come into contact with lower civilizations without bringing extermination to their people, we are still far from the goal. It must be our great object to improve our institutions until we can bring blessings to lower peoples and set them on the road to rapid progress. . . . Such a civilization," Harris stated, "we have a right to enforce on this earth. We have a right to work for the enlightenment of all peoples and to give our aid to lift them into local self-government."

Imperialism was frequently justified in terms of Anglo-Saxon racist arguments. These arguments were well suited to both the Progressives' paternalistic conception of social reform and the growing rapprochement in American and British foreign policy. Josiah Strong, clergyman and social reformer, whose book *Our Country* had predicted the Europeanization of America and then the Anglo-Saxon conquest of the world, in his later work *Expansion,* published in 1900, rejoiced that his predictions were coming true. Strong illustrated the bellicoseness of American Protestant churches—what Julius Pratt has called "the imperialism of Righteousness."

Even so fair-minded and tolerant a Progressive as William Allen White, in editorials (partly satirical) in 1899, also stressed the white man's burden of the Anglo-Saxon race. White, in an interesting example of youthful exuberance, wrote in his *Emporia Gazette* on the first anniversary of the sinking of the battleship *Maine:*

> It was probably intended in the beginning that the Anglo-Saxon should conquer the Latin. . . . And yet, thousands of people cannot help longing for the old order. They cannot but feel that something good is gone and that this deepening of responsibilities brings a hardship with it and a loss of the old-time individual freedom. For every American is not only his own master now—as he was a year ago—but he is master, so much as a man can ever be another's master, of twenty million people of lower races and inferior intelligence. And the master has lost the freedom the slave has found.

A month later, commenting on the news of riots in Havana, White expressed the opinion that the United States would have to keep policing the island. The Cubans were not, and could not be, really free. Only Anglo-Saxon nations could really govern themselves. In an editorial that, some twenty-five years later, he remarked, sounded like "the squawk of the hardboiled chicken that has not pipped the shell," White stated:

> It is the Anglo-Saxon's destiny to go forth as a world conqueror. He will take possession of all the islands of the sea. He will exterminate the peoples he cannot subjugate. This is what fate holds for the chosen people. It is so written. Those who would protest will find their objections overruled. It is to be.

Against a narrow Anglo-Saxon interpretation of imperialism, Booker T. Washington, the conservative Negro educator, offered a view more in harmony with his own philosophy for an accommodation between the races in the United States. Under the heading "Signs of Progress Among the Negroes," Washington suggested optimistically that the experience of the South "will prove most valuable in elevating the blacks of the West Indian Islands. To tell what has already been accomplished in the South under most difficult circumstances is to tell what may be done in Cuba and Porto Rico." Washington, however, also warned that how the United States might treat the native peoples in its new possessions would prove an interesting question. "Certainly," he wrote in the January 1900 issue of *Century,* "it will place this country in an awkward position to have gone to war to free a people from Spanish cruelty, and then as soon as it gets them within its power to treat a large proportion of the population worse than did even Spain herself, simply on account of color."

Within the influential circle of expansionist politicians and intellectuals, Theodore Roosevelt and Brooks Adams, whom Daniel Aaron in his study of American reformers calls Pseudo-Progressives, were outstanding. Brooks, like his brother Henry, was concerned with the issues that he propounded in his book *The Law of Civilization and Decay* (1895). In tracing the progress of civilization along the great strategic trade routes in history, Brooks had reached the conclusion that the ever-accelerating pace of economic concentration was such that, he feared, "the elasticity of the age of expansion is gone." Imperialistic expansion, however, offered the United States the means of forestalling the kind of capitalistic concentration and centralization that was already affecting adversely the prospects of Europe.

In *America's Economic Supremacy*, published in 1900, Adams depicted the British scepter passing to the United States. Even though he was confident that the United States could gain a temporary haven for its economic institutions via imperialism, he feared that the eventual thrust of the dominant economic forces would be a competition of the Eastern and Western continents "for the most perfect system of state socialism." The Anglo-Saxon had been the most individual of races, but as expansion ceased and competition quickened, men consolidated into denser masses and individualism declined. American prosperity had been due to "the liberal margin of profit" resulting from frontier expansion. Now, however, the time had come when the domestic surplus had to be sold abroad. "To-day the nation has to elect whether to continue to expand, cost what it may, or to resign itself to the approach of a relatively stationary period, when competition will force it to abandon the individual for the collective mode of life."

Theodore Roosevelt refused to accept Brooks Adams's pessimistic notion that capitalism could not escape his law of civilization and decay, but in other respects he shared Adams's view of world history and politics—particularly in regard to China's economic potential and the menace of Russian expansion in the Far East. In contrast to such conservative Republican party leaders as Mark Hanna and McKinley, Roosevelt was an early advocate of what his friend John Hay termed the "splendid little war" with Spain. To a correspondent early in 1898, T.R. confided: "I have been hoping and working ardently to bring about our interference in Cuba." More important, Roosevelt's own temperament and energy made him a leading proponent of the so-called large policy of 1898 by which the United States carried the war over Cuba to the Philippines and the Far East. The United States, he wrote in *The Strenuous Life*, could not afford to adopt a passive, isolationist Chinese role.

> If we are to be a really great people, we must strive in good faith to play a great part in the world. We cannot avoid meeting great issues. All that we can determine for ourselves is whether we shall meet them well or ill. In 1898 we could not help being brought face to face with the problem of war with Spain. All we could decide was whether we should shrink like cowards from the contest. . . .

As President, Roosevelt, whom Henry Demarest Lloyd called an admirable instrument for the Americanization of the world, pursued in foreign policy the same aggressive course that he displayed in domestic affairs. Though his remark "I took Panama" was an exaggeration, Roosevelt did live up to his slogan "Speak softly and carry a big stick" in United States relations with the governments of Europe and Latin America. To protect American interest in the Caribbean area, he added his so-called corollary to the Monroe Doctrine to the list of classic presidential pronouncements on American foreign policy. By Roosevelt's injunction, the

United States asserted the right to interfere in the internal affairs of the Latin American republics if this became necessary to prevent outside intervention by a European power. In practice the United States proposed to act as a collector when financial or political disorders in Latin America endangered its debts to European creditor nations. In the Western Hemisphere, Roosevelt declared, "the adherence of the United States to the Monroe Doctrine may force the United States, however reluctantly, in flagrant cases of such wrongdoing or impotence to the exercise of an international police power."

Although generally a confident imperialist, Roosevelt in his later years seemed to have some doubts. Like a growing number of American business and political leaders, Roosevelt came to consider American expansion more in terms of trade and markets than in colonies or further territorial acquisitions. Thus he worried over the relations of democracy to empire and the general problem of ruling colonial peoples. He wondered whether an imperial power could extend the machinery of democratic government abroad and still maintain democratic ideals at home. Colonies might even in time become burdens, offering no substantial material rewards. And from a military standpoint, Roosevelt suspected that the Philippines might "form our heel of Achilles." Earlier than Roosevelt, Henry Adams, never as enthusiastic an imperialist as his brother Brooks, despaired of the possibility that America could run the world. "I incline now," he wrote to Brooks in 1901, "to anti-imperialism, and very strongly to anti-militarism. I incline to let the machine smash, and see what pieces are worth saving afterwards. I incline to abandon China, Philippines, and everything else. I incline to let England sink; to let Germany and Russia try to run the machine, and to stand on our own internal resources alone."

In contrast to the Adams family's faculty for the bleakest

sort of intellectual pessimism, Roosevelt was, of course, primarily a man of action and hope. In this light, his most striking departures from past isolationist traditions were his personal efforts at global peacemaking, both in regard to the Russo–Japanese War and in the dispute between France and Germany over Morocco. For his success in bringing the Russians and the Japanese to the peace table at Portsmouth, New Hampshire, he was awarded the Nobel Prize in 1906. Roosevelt was sure that America must exercise a new and increasingly important role in international politics. "In foreign affairs, we must make up our minds that, whether we wish it or not, we are a great people and must play a great part in the world. It is not open to us to choose whether we will play that great part or not. We have to play it. All we can decide is whether we shall play it well or ill." At the Algeciras Conference, where the United States cooperated to help avert the partition of Morocco, German prestige suffered when the United States continued its policy of moving toward closer relations with England and France. The net effect unfortunately was to strengthen the European rivalries leading away from peace and toward the first world war. Thus the outbreak of the war, though delayed perhaps by Roosevelt's informal intervention at Algeciras, was not halted.

The Rooseveltian practice of power politics reflected his imperialistic outlook. He had a keen sense of the importance in diplomacy of cooperation among the strong powers, with which, he believed, "there is but little danger of our getting into war." Resentful accordingly of anti-imperialist pressures in favor of smaller nations, he wrote in 1905 that the United States "is too apt to indulge in representations on behalf of weak peoples which do them no good and irritate the strong and tyrannical peoples to whom the protest is made." Rooseveltian imperialism was more opportunistic than economic in base, motivated by his stress on political and military security, but security along nationalist and imperialist lines through an extension of American power abroad.

Howard K. Beale, the most thorough student of Roosevelt's foreign policy, concludes that he was generally astute and realistic in international affairs. Despite his fondness for military and naval display and his belief in power politics, he opposed resort to a policy of bluff in pushing American interests abroad. More rational than romantic, despite his occasional play-acting and love of war, Roosevelt was also more successful than Taft or Wilson in gaining the support of American Progressives for the policies of imperialism and dollar diplomacy. Senators like Robert M. La Follette, who remained apathetic or who managed to go along with T.R. on foreign policy, later broke with Taft and refused to follow Wilson. Finally, the close association of social-reform politics and an aggressive foreign policy, so evident on both sides of the Atlantic in the 1900's, underscored the nationalistic elements in American Progressivism and European social democracy. Thus American Progressives were able, on the whole, to accept Roosevelt's strong leadership in foreign as well as in domestic affairs.

CHAPTER 12

The New Navalism and Incipient Militarism

AMERICA'S imperial democracy, though undoubtedly a source of pride for many citizens, was also a heavy national responsibility. Colonial possessions and growing commitments overseas entailed burdens as well as benefits. Imperialism, however much its apparent popular appeal, was not to be achieved without cost. As the anti-imperialists had argued, it carried a high price in terms of traditional American values and institutions. This was especially the case with regard to questions of national defense. The United States now faced demands for a larger navy and more sizable standing army. Although the war with Spain had hardly lasted through the summer of 1898, the signing of the peace treaty did not enable the country to return to its old, prewar isolationism. Revolt in the Philippines, new naval bases in the Pacific, the occupation of Cuba, plus intervention elsewhere in the Caribbean, all required units of the United States military or naval forces. In a word, Americans were confronted by the unpleasant fact that imperialism meant a new navalism and incipient militarism for the United States.

The United States Navy, historically the country's first line of defense, had gradually come to assume an expanded role in the last decades of the nineteenth century. The American republic, it was true, had not reached the stage in history that had already impelled the European powers to stay armed against each other, but its own changing economic interests and modern technology suggested the need for revising traditional naval policy. "Without foreign commerce," the Secretary of the Navy reported already in 1877, "we must sink into inferiority; and without a Navy amply sufficient for this purpose, all the profits of our surplus productions will be transferred from the coffers of our own to those of foreign capitalists." In the 1880's, Congress accordingly authorized the construction of ironclad vessels capable of protecting American maritime commerce in offensive action on the high seas. The shift to the new-type vessels was inevitable, but certain segments of the American economy, notably the iron and steel industry, now gained a vested interest in naval expansion.

In the opinion of contemporaries as well as of later scholars, Alfred Thayer Mahan became at this juncture the most effective exponent of the new navalism in the United States. Although his father, Denis Hart Mahan, taught military science at West Point, the younger Mahan preferred to become a naval officer. At first opposed to an aggressive program of American expansion abroad, Mahan, however, turned by the late 1880's to his lifelong advocacy of seapower as the mainspring of a realistic foreign policy for the United States. He accordingly championed the view, increasingly popular in naval circles, that a powerful American battle fleet should be built to protect American exports and foreign markets. His first major book, *The Influence of Sea Power upon History,* published in 1890, launched him upon a unique career as a distinguished scholar, publicist, and propagandist as well as high-ranking naval officer.

A popularizer as much as an engineer of the new navalism, Mahan was able to win added support for his ideas through key friendships with such rising politicians as Henry Cabot Lodge and Theodore Roosevelt. Roosevelt, while lecturing at the new Naval War College in 1887, had met Mahan, stationed there as an instructor; and Roosevelt, Mahan, and Lodge soon began to exchange views on their common concern in building a stronger American Navy. Under Benjamin Harrison, the first outspoken presidential advocate of a "big-navy" policy, the Secretary of the Navy, Benjamin F. Tracy, expressing ideas attributed to Mahan, called in his first annual report in 1889 for a building program that included twenty battleships and sixty fast cruisers. More revolutionary, however, than Tracy's vast building program was the recommendation of his newly appointed Naval Policy Board that special attention be given to the creation of a fleet of long-range battleships. The policy board thus urged abandonment of the tradition under which the Navy had been confined largely to American waters.

Defense of the American coasts, though naturally the chief justification for the Navy in the popular mind, was a thin reed for securing public approval of a naval preparedness program of the dimensions envisaged by staunch imperialists like Mahan. The continental United States actually enjoyed an enviable defensive position, enhanced even more by America's growing diplomatic rapprochement with Great Britain. Since the United States was secure against any likely coalition of enemy powers, the advocates of naval expansion emphasized such emotionally charged goals as American interests and ideals abroad, the preservation of Anglo-Saxon civilization, and the fulfillment of America's manifest destiny. Mahan's contention that the protection of the American merchant marine and foreign trade required naval control of the high seas seemed to strain the meaning of the word "defense," stretching it almost to its bursting point—at least until the war with Spain provided a new rationale for both navalism and imperialism.

In the 1900's, in the postwar vision of American naval strategy, a canal across the Isthmus of Panama was deemed necessary for quick access to the outlying American possessions in the Pacific. Bases in the Caribbean and on the Hawaiian Islands were needed at the same time to protect American approaches to the canal. And finally, of course, a larger navy was considered vital to the maintenance of its own lengthened line of communications. Mahan and his disciples thus neatly linked together navalism and imperialism, each serving as cause and effect. As Robert Osgood points out in *Ideals and Self-Interest in America's Foreign Relations,* Mahan and the imperialists' "pleas of self-defense were sustained by motives more akin to ambition, pride, or covetousness than to fear or apprehension. Mahan's own writings clearly demonstrate that this observation applies to him."

The somewhat contradictory nature of Mahan's views was lessened in part by his outspoken contention that imperialism and navalism were both justified by America's rapid industrial development and overseas interests. Aware that expansionism was frequently criticized for not being in the true national interest, he frankly faced the dilemma. "Let us not shrink," he wrote, "from pitting a broad self-interest against the narrow self-interest to which some would restrict us." In a constant stream of articles in leading magazines, Mahan urged America to venture beyond the confines of its own protected, but limited, home market.

Whether they will or not, Americans must now begin to look outward. The growing production of the country demands it. An increasing volume of public sentiment demands it. The position of the United States, between the two Old Worlds and the two great oceans, makes the same claim. . . . The tendency will be maintained and increased by the growth of the European colonies in the Pacific, by the advancing civilization of Japan, and by the rapid peopling of our Pacific States. . . .

In the years around the turn of the century, Mahan's justification of navalism and imperialism gained widespread attention. The able exponent of trends already in being, he equaled Theodore Roosevelt as a leading spokesman for expansionism and preparedness. Members of Congress who supported a big navy plagiarized his statements on seapower, while merchants, shipbuilders, big-navy men, armaments manufacturers, naval personnel, expansionist statesmen, and publicists all used the Mahan theories for their own ends. Mahan himself was primarily interested in indoctrinating his own countrymen, but his influence extended abroad and served as an ideological stimulus for naval building in Great Britain, France, Germany, and Japan. Especially acclaimed in England as a great naval authority, Mahan in an 1894 visit to the center of world seapower was asked to dine by Queen Victoria, the Prime Minister, and the First Lord of the Admiralty. During the same visit the universities at Oxford and Cambridge conferred honorary degrees upon him. And five years later, President McKinley appointed Mahan as one of the American delegates to the First Hague Conference.

At the conference Mahan, a staunch believer in the philosophy that vital national interests should never be compromised or arbitrated, stated that the United States was not prepared to discuss the question of any limitation of armaments. Since his own writings had played no small part in encouraging naval rearmament in Germany and Britain, Mahan could be credited with a certain personal responsibility for the failure of the great powers to prevent the navalism and militarism which proved so characteristic of the 1900's. The naval preparedness which Mahan's writings encouraged and which he associated with the highest national patriotism also bore an obviously close relationship with the national rivalries that led the world to war in 1914. From almost any point of view, therefore, his ideas offered little incentive to American hopes of world peace.

Mahan's philosophy of seapower and foreign policy, apparently vindicated and carried to victory during the war with Spain, achieved its greatest practical triumph and widest popular influence during the presidential years of his friend Theodore Roosevelt. Roosevelt's own strong belief in preparedness and his admiration for the martial virtues that he had demonstrated with the Rough Riders in Cuba were of course well known. Disturbed by the number of men in the United States who, he felt, were lacking in a sufficiently robust patriotism, Roosevelt warned that there was no place in the world "for nations who have become enervated by soft and easy life, or who have lost their fibre of vigorous hardiness and manliness." "All the great masterful races have been fighting races," he told the Naval War College in 1897, "and the minute that a race loses the hard fighting virtues, then . . . no matter how skilled in commerce and finance, in science or art, it has lost its proud right to stand as the equal of the best." "No triumph of peace," he proclaimed, "is quite so great as the supreme triumphs of war."

Beginning with his annual message to Congress in December 1901, Roosevelt repeatedly urged a broad program of naval rearmament upon the country. Backed in the Senate by such longstanding enthusiasts for a big navy as his friend Henry Cabot Lodge, Roosevelt also gained important outside support from the new public interest in naval affairs. Helpful in arousing popular concern was the Navy League of the United States founded in 1903. The American Navy League was modeled after similar societies in Europe which had been established already in the 1890's in England, France, and Germany. In the latter country, the German Navy League enjoyed a membership of some half-million persons, but in the United States the league functioned through an elite of statesmen, businessmen, and naval officers. Thus it was able to exercise an influence upon Congress and the country out of proportion to its own relatively slender financial resources and limited membership.

Meanwhile, the country's rising martial spirit, whetted by hostilities with Spain, was enhanced by the prolonged Filipino insurrection and the growing involvement of the United States in world affairs. Aided in this way by the course of events, and spurred on by his own intense desire for a big navy, Roosevelt was able to overcome the still strong anti-imperialist, isolationist, and pacifist forces in Congress. From 1901 to 1905, Congress authorized ten battleships as well as numerous smaller vessels, while naval appropriations soared from $85 to $118 million per year, an increase without peacetime precedent.

The naval appropriation bill for 1905 marked the completion of the first Roosevelt building program. It also placed the United States in the first rank of naval powers, second only to Great Britain and, perhaps, France or later Germany. Meanwhile rising anti-Japanese agitation in California, plus British development of the all-big-gun battleships of the *Dreadnought* type, led to demands for adding similar ships to the American Navy. President Roosevelt gave his enthusiastic backing to the new-type vessel and in December 1907 astonished the country with a message calling upon Congress to appropriate additional funds for four battleships, all of the big-gun class.

The latest Roosevelt request for the Navy precipitated a bitter debate in Congress and the country. A reaction against the Roosevelt–Mahan views had already occurred. Peace leaders now were reinforced in their opposition by conservative business groups alarmed at the high costs of modern navalism. The National Association of Manufacturers, for example, pointed out that Roosevelt's conservation program would become impossible "if our money is to be squandered in so lavish measure upon battleships and militarism." In the Senate, while younger Progressives led by Albert J. Beveridge supported the T.R. four-battleship proposal, the Republican "Old Guard" took its revenge and joined with the Democrats to vote down the naval bill. Roosevelt, however, had carried through his plan to send sixteen battleships of the American fleet in an around-the-world cruise by way of Japan. Congress also relented sufficiently in its opposition to vote approval for two instead of four battleships. Since this exceeded the normal replacement policy of building one new battleship each year, Roosevelt could claim at least a partial victory in his determination to build a more powerful American Navy.

In the period of William Howard Taft's four years as Roosevelt's successor, opposition to the Republicans' naval program was intertwined with criticism of America's so-called dollar diplomacy of promoting business interests overseas. Although Taft was much less martial a President than Roosevelt, he likewise felt that the United States had to keep pace with contemporary European rearmament and he, too, was anxious to use foreign policy to further American economic interests abroad. While the Roosevelt–Taft navalism conflicted with the American tradition of the Navy as a primarily defensive force, the American people remained unwilling to accept wholeheartedly a military and naval policy based on the premise that another war was inevitable. Despite the discouragement engendered by the failure of the Second Hague

Conference on disarmament, and by the unsuccessful attempt by Taft to secure Senate approval of a series of bilateral
arbitration treaties, there was still a strong peace sentiment in
the country.

Even more than in the case of the Navy, the Progressive
Era saw revolutionary changes in the development of the
American Army. In the nineteenth century the American
people, enjoying what C. Vann Woodward has called an era
of free, or at least near-free, security, had associated a large
army—especially a large standing army—with European militarism, Caesarism, and despotism. Separated by the oceans
from both Europe and Asia, the United States had no need
for more than a minimal military establishment. Only rarely,
Woodward points out, were as many as 1 percent of American males between the ages of twenty-one and thirty-nine in
the armed forces, and in the last third of the nineteenth century, between Reconstruction and the Spanish–American
War, there was no year in which the figure was as much as one
half of 1 percent. With good reason, therefore, the American
Republic was celebrated as a haven of refuge for the young
men fleeing the wars and military conscriptions of the Old
World.

"The freedom of American youth from the long period of
training in military discipline that left its mark upon the
youth of nations where it was a routine requirement could
hardly have failed," Woodward writes, "to make some contribution to the distinctiveness of national character." Many
of the traits customarily attributed to the influence of the
frontier or of free political and economic institutions may
perhaps, therefore, be just as well ascribed to the kind of national security that enabled the United States to do without a
strong military establishment for the greater part of its history. Liberal values of individual freedom and initiative, of
democracy in political life, of free enterprise in business, and

of optimism in personal and social relations all owed much to the fact that America never needed to become a garrison state.

The American antimilitarist tradition inclined even so martial a President as Theodore Roosevelt to recommend reductions in Army appropriations at the same time that he called for increases in naval expenditures. Yet it was clear after the war with Spain that an emerging militarism, as well as navalism and imperialism, threatened historic American conceptions of peace and security. The generally anti-imperialist and pacifist *Nation* magazine, for example, asserted that Americans who had formerly criticized Europe for strapping soldiers on the backs of the people were now inflicting upon themselves the same burden. Under Roosevelt, it claimed, the country was merely "strapping on a sailor instead."

The outstanding political figure in the reorganization of the American Army in the early 1900's was Secretary of War Elihu Root, whom Walter Millis has described as responsible for bringing a "managerial revolution" to United States military policy. Root, a highly successful New York corporation lawyer, had been appointed by President McKinley in 1899 with an injunction to straighten out the departmental confusion and lack of preparedness revealed by the war. The difficulty in getting the American Army and supplies from Florida to Cuba, much publicized by T.R. and the Rough Riders, had led to the resignation of Russell Alger, Root's predecessor. Although not a professional soldier or close student of war, Root nevertheless was by inclination and philosophy a military-minded civilian. He sympathized with many of the so-called martial virtues and admired the soldier's discipline. He also believed in the Progressives' urging that public-spirited citizens assume more responsibility for efficient governmental administration. Continued as Secretary of War by President Roosevelt after McKinley's assassination, Root quickly became the chief architect in working out the details, not only of Army reorganization, but also of America's colonial policies in conjunction with the occupation of Cuba and suppression of the Filipino revolt.

In 1905, after a brief return to the private practice of law, Root went back to Washington to become Secretary of State. By this almost unprecedented combination of successive cabinet posts in war and state, Root illustrated the new articulation of American military and foreign policies. Thus it was Root who drafted the clauses in the Platt Amendment, affixed to the Army Appropriation Act of March 2, 1901, which assured the United States a preferred position in its relations with the Cuban Republic. Although never rivaling Admiral Mahan's literary charisma or international reputation, Root contributed as effectively to the progress of the American Army as Mahan did to the Navy.

Following the war with Spain, American soldiers—volunteers as well as regulars—were compelled to fight a bitter colonial war against the Filipino insurrectionists. The Army, like the Navy, was engaged in the defense of the United States in the new imperialist sense of overseas operations far from American shores. By 1902, however, the withdrawal of American troops from Cuba and the gradual abatement of fighting in the Philippines enabled Root to give his full attention to long-range military reforms. As Secretary of War he played a master role in securing legislation which provided for an increase in the size of the regular Army, the creation of a general staff and Army War College, and the federalization of the state militia. Although Congress authorized a standing Army of 65,000 men in contrast to the pre-1898 force of about 25,000, Root accepted it as axiomatic that the regular Army would never be sufficient by itself in wartime. Moreover it was war overseas, rather than Indian fighting or police duties, that henceforth would be the likely major responsibility of the United States Army. Efficient planning, training, and organization as well as additional manpower were accordingly destined to be the accouterments of modern military policy.

European experience dictated the value of a general-staff type of organization for the Army. The prescribed list of duties for the American General Staff in 1903 was taken directly from a German treatise on the subject, while French and English concepts also found their way into the American military command. The General Staff, with the Chief of Staff the Commanding General of the Army, was to provide both future war plans and continuity in the overall day-to-day direction of Army operations. Although Root envisaged the General Staff as means of civilian control of the military, in practice war was becoming too technical to be understood by nonprofessionals. Moreover, under an aggressive Chief of Staff like General Leonard A. Wood, Roosevelt's old colonel in the Rough Riders, the General Staff was able to impose its military point of view upon both Congress and the civilian Secretary of War. The General Staff could even usurp some of the historic responsibilities of the President. United States experience therefore seemed to duplicate that of Europe where the general staff organization for military planning furnished a ready means of militarist intervention within the government.

Almost as revolutionary as the law setting up the General Staff was the Root militia bill, or Dick Act of 1903, which provided for calling up a portion of the state militia to serve as a National Guard under federal authority and pay. Later, in 1908, the Dick Act was amended to enable the guard to serve "either within or without the territory of the United States." Although similar attempts to provide greater federal control over the state militia had been defeated in the past, the Dick Act, like the general staff legislation, was passed by an almost unanimous Congress. Some of the popular missionary implications of the militia reorganization measure were indicated by Root himself in an address on May 4, 1903, before the National Guard Association. Looking into the future, Root told his listeners that the regular Army would continue to perform the work of a central organization, embracing quartermaster duties and similar functions. But, he added, "when you come to the creation of the military spirit among the youth of the country, to the education and training of that military spirit, there you step in; that is your function of preparation, for that cannot be done at the center—that must be done all over this country."

Root's federalized militia or National Guard was a move toward a new type of American Army. The Militia Act of 1903, as Root recognized, was a valuable instrument for influencing public opinion on military matters. As a means of preparedness, it came as close as possible to providing a standing army without incurring the public resentment traditionally directed against that body. And, because it utilized the old state militia, it conformed with the popular idea of a citizen army, even though most military men understood that Root's federalized National Guard was not a citizen army in the nineteenth-century sense of that term.

Root himself believed that United States military policy should be based on a regular Army, expanded or reinforced in wartime by units of the National Guard and a system of conscription. In support of his position, he caused to be published as a government document Emory Upton's *Military Policy of the United States,* the classic argument for a standing army of regulars. With the addition in the first world war of the principle of selective training and service, the American tradition of the military amateur and volunteer was supplanted almost completely by professionalization and conscription. But it was Root's so-called reforms that paved the way. And without that contribution, it was possible that United States participation in the war, as Walter Millis wrote, "might never have taken place at all."

Elihu Root, no less than Theodore Roosevelt and Admiral Mahan, deserves to stand as a herald of modern American militarism and imperialism. Although conservative on most domestic issues, Root and Mahan were able to win support among Progressives for their essentially innovative ideas on military and foreign policy. Much of their philosophy, more European than American in its conception of enhanced state responsibility and power, was in almost perfect accord with the strong nationalism of the Progressive movement. The chief objection to their views came, therefore, from the more traditional liberal and pacifist segments of American thought.

CHAPTER 13

The Paradox
of Peace

The nineteenth century, often called the Century of Peace and Progress, was marred on a number of occasions by the outbreak of war. Yet, in the long span of the one hundred years between Napoleon's defeat at Waterloo and the coming of the first world war, there was no major conflict that engaged more than two or three of the most powerful nation–states. At mid-century the Crimean War, American Civil War, and Franco-Prussian War were all confined to the countries originally and immediately involved. And even European imperialism in the last third of the century, though constantly threatening to plunge the world into a general war, resulted in no such widespread struggle. The feeling grew—encouraged by the popular faith in the concept of progress—that the world was too civilized to engage in a general war. Many now believed, with Herbert Spencer, the English Social Darwinist, that war was an anachronism, incompatible with the forces of modern technological and industrial progress. The advances of science also seemed to bring the nations of the world closer together—at least in terms of speedier communication and diminishing travel time.

Despite these hopeful portents, the Sino-Japanese, Spanish-American, Boer, and Russo-Japanese wars around the turn of the century successively underscored the fragile nature of the world's peace. Great Britain and the United States, the two nations most admired for their advanced progress and established peace movements, were involved in colonial wars against weaker powers. Elsewhere around the globe—in Europe, Asia, and Africa—opposition to war conflicted with the desire of many peoples for national self-determination—to be free and united. Thus there was the continuing paradox of an uncertain peace, rendered even more precarious by mounting armaments and renewed threats of war.

In the United States, the Civil War had dealt the heaviest blow to the peace cause. Though the strict pacifist condemned all wars, most Americans, including many peace leaders, found it relatively easy to justify a conflict that involved no foreign nation and that could also become the means of ending the hated slave power in the United States. After Appomattox, the weakened peace movement faced an uphill struggle against the postwar forces of violence and militarism that lingered on, especially in the South. Gradually, however, new organizations and new issues won a measure of popular support. The Universal Peace Union, created in 1866, stressed American cooperation with the peace movement in Europe, and in 1882 the National Arbitration League was founded in Washington. In Europe, in 1889, two major organizations, both stressing the propagation of internationalist ideals, were formally established on the centennial of the French Revolution: the Interparliamentary Union, composed of members of national legislative bodies, and the Universal Peace Congress. The participation of American delegates at the meetings of both groups reflected the growing national interest in world affairs and in the peaceful adjudication of international disputes. One such dispute flared up in 1895 and 1896 over the boundary line between Venezuela and British Guiana. This gave the peace forces in the United States and England the opportunity to help restrain the bellicose public sentiment aroused by President Cleveland's aggressive assertion of American concern in the affair. But two years later the peace movement proved unable to ward off the war with Spain and the ensuing imperialistic conflict in the Philippines.

On the whole, the advent of the twentieth century offered what seemed an uncertain prospect for the advocates of peace. Fighting in the Philippines, American occupation troops in Cuba and the Caribbean, a President more militant and bellicose than any of his predecessors, and a growing spirit of imperialism, navalism, and militarism all provided ample grounds for discouragement. Nevertheless, the Progressive years from 1900 to 1914 also comprised the period that Merle Curti, in his history of the peace movement, characterizes as "Toward Victory." Despite its failure to prevent the annexation of overseas colonies, the anti-imperialist movement brought new allies into the struggle for peace. Gradually, too, the enthusiastic champions of a bigger and better Navy, in the face of an adverse public reaction, were forced into partial retreat.

Most significant was the rising popular support for a number of new peace societies, and the American government's participation in the international movement for arbitration, mediation, and disarmament. Despite the clearly paradoxical nature of their coexistence, it seemed true, as the pacifists themselves believed, that the juxtaposition of peace and war afforded grounds for hope as well as despair. It was the menace of war, after all, that provided the chief incentive for a strong peace movement. In fact, anti-imperialism and pacifism both became respectable again in the 1900's. Opposition to militarism and navalism took on something of the same evangelistic, missionary spirit that already characterized the advocacy of imperialism and the white man's burden. Peace-minded internationalists as well as aggressive militarists could agree on the concept of an American world mission. For, as Robert Osgood pointed out, "both combined the appeal of universal values with the lure of national destiny." And finally, in the arbitration movement, peace suddenly seemed to become a practical political and international possibility.

Each summer, beginning in 1895, a select group of prominent scholars, international lawyers, businessmen, and publicists interested in peace and arbitration met together at Lake Mohonk, New York. There in the serene Catskill Mountain resort hotel of Quaker Albert K. Smiley, educators and diplomats discussed the implications of America's new internationalism and the prospects of gaining greater organized popular backing for world peace plans. The Mohonk Conferences symbolized anew the traditional role of the United States as an example of the ideal, if not always the practice, of world peace.

For example, the American federal system of government suggested a means of adjusting conflicts of interest among separate political entities. Peace leaders also pointed to the United States Supreme Court as a model for some sort of world court to arbitrate international disputes. Scholarly and legal support for the cause of world peace was also evidenced in the founding in 1905 of the American Society for International Law, with Secretary of State Elihu Root as its first president, and in the formation, five years later, of the American

Society for the Judicial Settlement of International Disputes. Probably the leading American expert in the field was John Bassett Moore, professor of international law, counselor of the State Department, and later a member of the Hague Tribunal and a judge of the World Court. Moore was also editor of the impressive multivolume publications based largely on American examples: *History and Digest of the International Arbitrations to Which the United States Has Been a Party* (1898) and *Digest of International Law* (1906).

In the Progressive Era the American peace movement had come to embrace a wide variety of positions. Religious, nonresistant followers of Tolstoy's Christian pacifism and radical socialist opponents of capitalistic wars competed for public attention with the new businesslike, politically oriented peace organizations. Some of the latter, endowed by wealthy philanthropists, and enjoying the security of large memberships, demonstrated in large part the triumph of efficient management over sincerity. Thus the New York Peace Society, founded in 1906, drew many of its members from the social elite of the city, with Wall Street bankers as well as clergymen enrolled. Andrew Carnegie, the retired steel-master, contributed generously and also served as president. The American Society for the Judicial Settlement of International Disputes was similarly an upper-class organization in which Elihu Root, among other political leaders including President Taft, was a prominent participant.

Conflicting interests and emotions in the peace movement were illustrated in the tendency for certain well-known political and intellectual figures to accept membership in both the conservative peace societies and organizations like the Navy League. Perhaps the most striking instance of such a paradox was the case of Lyman Abbott, an eminent clergyman and editor of *Outlook*. Abbott, despite his belief in peace as an ideal, had, like his friend Theodore Roosevelt, long been an advocate of stronger armaments to avert national weakness. His Christian rationale of war and imperialism before popular audiences made Abbott a pariah among his more pacifistic associates, but it was not until 1913 when he signed a Navy League appeal for more battleships that the American Peace Society removed his name from its list of honorary vice presidents. Inconsistency, though seldom as blatant as in Abbott's case, nevertheless remained a characteristic of the membership of the major peace societies. Radical pacifists as a result were suspicious of the quasi-official peace groups. But they seldom were able to communicate their inner doubts to the larger public, which accepted uncritically almost all the peace societies as worthy contributors to their cause.

Particularly impressive to the American people was the new-found philanthropic support for peace in the Progressive Era. In 1910, Edward Ginn, the textbook publisher, established the World Peace Foundation with his gift of a million dollars. The foundation accordingly was able to finance an effective program of educational work, distributing its literature among youth, women's, and labor organizations. Also in 1910, Carnegie took the lead in creating the Carnegie Endowment for International Peace, of which Elihu Root was named first president. Carnegie and such co-founders of the endowment as Nicholas Murray Butler, president of Columbia University, were fearful of being classed as extremists. But the endowment, by placing its primary emphasis on scholarly study and publication, easily avoided all suspicion of radicalism.

Oldest of the pacifist groups in the United States was the American Peace Society, which, however, had consistently refused to take an absolutist or radical position. During the 1900's the society was able to expand its general influence and support. Woodrow Wilson was one of those who joined, retaining his membership until it seemed inappropriate after he became President. In 1912, while still governor of New Jersey, at a banquet given in his honor by the Universal Peace Union in Philadelphia, Wilson stressed the connection between domestic and foreign policy. Peace in the sense of justice and freedom, he pointed out, was as necessary at home as abroad if it was to be a useful guide to a country's foreign policy. Aggressive, autocratic governments could not be trusted to cooperate in a true concert of nations. Thus internal peace was a prerequisite for international peace.

Wilson's biographers have shown that there was much in his background and training that inclined him to accept leadership in a crusade to carry American ideals abroad. A dedicated Christian, fond of emphasizing the duty of the scholar, he was able to become both an advocate of peace and an apologist for the white man's burden and imperialism. Wilson's views which, of course, became all-important after his elevation to the presidency also served to illustrate some of the contradictions growing within the peace movement. These became more apparent as the United States moved away from its historic nineteenth-century isolationism.

Despite the succession of imperialistic wars which marked the passing of the Century of Peace, Americans were able to take hope from the developing worldwide interest in new forms of international conciliation. Diplomatic relations, traditionally regarded as a medium for negotiating vital national interests in the struggle for power, might also offer, it now seemed, a means of greater mutual cooperation among nations. International conferences and treaties to prevent, rather than merely conclude, wars suggested alternatives to each country's preoccupation with its own selfish national interests. In 1899 the First Hague Conference, called at the invitation of Czar Nicholas II of Russia, failed to achieve its ostensible objective of reducing world armaments. The United States, imbued with Admiral Mahan's navalist philosophy, was no more ready than the other great powers to cut back its military and naval strength. Although later the Second Hague Conference in 1907 also proved unable to surmount national suspicions and rivalries in regard to armaments, the assembled signatory nations had already managed to establish the Permanent Court of International Arbitration. The United States cooperated with other powers to support the court, and Americans also took satisfaction in its arbitration of a number of disputes, including the financial claims which Germany and Great Britain had pressed upon Venezuela in 1902.

Under presidents Roosevelt, Taft, and Wilson, the United States negotiated a series of treaties looking toward the peaceful arbitration or mediation of certain types of conflicts with other nations. Although objections by the United States Senate forced drastic limitations in the kind of disputes that could be considered for arbitration, over twenty such restricted agreements were signed by the close of Roosevelt's second Administration. Despite strong public support, President Taft was unable to persuade the Senate to go further and approve what he regarded as model pacts with England and France. These pacts provided for the arbitration of all "justiciable" questions, including ones in which American "vital interests" and "national honor" were involved. Privately, Taft blamed Roosevelt for the Senate's intransigent attitude. T.R., Taft wrote to Secretary of State Knox, "is obsessed with his love of war and the glory of it. That is the secret of his present attitude. . . . He would think it a real injury to mankind if we would not have war. . . ."

In the succeeding Wilson Administration, Secretary of State Bryan was more successful in negotiating thirty of his so-called "cooling-off" treaties. Technically conciliation rather than arbitration agreements, Bryan's pacts provided that otherwise insoluble disputes be referred to special international commissions for factual investigation. The signatory nations were then to refrain from all hostilities pending the receipt of a recommendation, usually within one year, from the agreed-upon mediation body.

Although siding with Henry Cabot Lodge and the Senate in their nationalistic opposition to the Taft treaties, former President Roosevelt had earlier helped to publicize international cooperation when he was awarded the Nobel Peace Prize. In his deferred acceptance speech at Christiania, Norway, in May 1910, Roosevelt urged the adoption of some of the concepts long espoused by the American peace movement. Thus he advocated a league to enforce peace, extension of the Hague Tribunal, arbitration treaties, and international agreements to check the world arms race. Roosevelt at the same time, however, also defended American foreign policy against charges of imperialism, and he was careful as well to exclude from his recommendations for international jurisdiction any points deemed vital to American national interests and sovereignty. For these reasons also, he later opposed Bryan and Wilson's "cooling-off" treaties.

Roosevelt, along with many of the more internationally minded peace leaders, welcomed American participation in world affairs. Though not for peace at any price, they recognized that a major war would threaten the existing social order and disrupt the international business community, with socialism and revolution the chief beneficiaries. Peace, on the other hand, would ensure the preponderance of the United States. With its ever-mounting economic strength, the country could look forward to becoming, not only the world's greatest power, but also its leader in the cause of international peace.

Encouraged by the evidence, however tenuous and slight, of increasing international cooperation, the peace forces in the United States attempted to lessen support for the war system at home. The continuing American political concern over the problem of preserving national interests and honor demonstrated the importance of Woodrow Wilson's contention that a climate of peace and justice at home must precede the spread of such ideals abroad. To counter the War Department's efforts to spread military training and preparedness in the nation's schools and colleges, the peace organizations extended their own work. Most educators resisted the trend toward militarism, believing it an inappropriate interference with educational ideals. The Intercollegiate Peace Association, founded in 1904, soon was able to claim over one hundred chapters on college campuses. The American School Peace League, established three years later, was successful by 1912 in securing the cooperation of the United States Commissioner of Education in distributing its literature. Important peace books, notably Norman Angell's *The Great Illusion* (1910), an indictment of the idea that wars were profitable, also helped to refute the militarist point of view of writers like Admiral Mahan.

Though not a book with the sensational popular appeal of *The Great Illusion,* which was translated into twenty languages, Jane Addams's *Newer Ideals of Peace* (1907) was an important expression of the more idealistic side of the Progressive movement. Famous for her efforts to alleviate human misery and poverty through the organization of the neighborhood settlement house in urban slum areas, Miss Addams was also alive to the broad nature of the causes of social injustice. Thus she stressed the dynamic aspects of peace as a factor in social change, in contrast to the way militarism supported the status quo. Government, she suggested, confined itself traditionally to the purely negative function of law enforcement. Instead of developing the citizens' interest in a genuinely peaceful society, the state was concerned merely with their fitness for military service and war.

The ties between militarism or the war system and the existing economic arrangements of society, deplored by the more pacifist-minded Progressives like Jane Addams, were also a significant part of the socialist case against capitalism. In contrast to Herbert Spencer and the nineteenth-century laissez-faire liberals who believed that war and militarism were incompatible with modern industrial progress, the socialists fixed the blame for war upon capitalism and imperialism. Radical socialists, moreover, were sometimes critical of pacifism as a bourgeois liberal movement, and they accepted, too, the Marxist doctrine of class war, while linking national wars to capitalism. Although opposed to the Root legislation revamping the American militia system and creating a general staff organization for the Army, some socialists favored the idea of a citizen army to keep weapons in the hands of the people. For example, Morris Hillquit, the Socialist party leader in New York City, in his book *Socialism in Theory and Practice* (1909), called for a genuine democratic militia as a substitute for a regular army. To this end he cited and explained the Swiss militia system, although he also admitted that any army service was apt to demoralize the individual soldier and deprive him of his civil rights.

Other socialists and radicals were more critical of both the militia and a traditional regular army. John Macy's *Socialism in America* (1916) questioned the democracy of the Swiss militia system and noted that the Swiss Socialists themselves opposed it. Labor spokesmen pointed out that the militia as well as the regular army was used against the worker in strikes. The Industrial Workers of the World, the IWW, denied its membership to anyone who joined the militia and at its first convention in 1905 passed a resolution condemning "militarism in all its forms and functions" and blaming it for "jeopardizing our constitutional rights and privileges in the struggle be-

tween capital and labor." Emma Goldman's anarchist magazine, *Mother Earth,* in a 1911 article entitled "Young Man,
Beware!" stated:

> The mission of the soldier is no different from that of the
> professional cutthroat who kills a man to order, except that the
> soldier receives less pay for his service, though he must be pre-
> pared not only for one murder but for wholesale killing. . . .
> The military uniform that seems so gay hides nothing but subjec-
> tion and humiliation for the common soldier, and provides only a
> very meagre existence.

In contrast to the hopeful view of state action shared by
most American Progressives, a number of socialists and anarchists brought to the United States radical and Marxian assumptions as to the nature of the capitalist state and its coer-
cive force upon the working class. They also added new
arguments to the peace cause by their contention that capitalism leads inevitably to militarism and war. In general, however, the peace movement, despite its internal confusion, continued to work for its goals within the framework of the
American political system. Liberal pacifists, indeed, felt justified in looking ahead with real enthusiasm to the inauguration of Woodrow Wilson and the New Freedom.

*New
Nationalism
or Lost
Freedoms*

CHAPTER 14

Woodrow Wilson: The Promised Land

For many liberal and progressive-minded Americans, the incoming Wilson Administration offered what seemed a promised land. Failing with the Populists and Bryan Democrats, disappointed by Roosevelt, and frustrated by Taft, they turned to the New Freedom as the last alternative to some Old World version of socialism or state capitalism. The promise of the New Freedom, however, was hardly fulfilled, and with the first world war disillusionment again crept over the land. Even in 1970, a modern young playwright–historian, Roland Van Zandt, condemning what he believes to be the late President's shortcomings and duplicity, has entitled his tendentious, satirical drama "Wilson in the Promise Land."

Historically we know that the turn from the philosophy of the New Freedom to that of the New Nationalism or the New Competition, plus the repression and hysteria following America's entrance into the first world war, conveyed equally to many of Wilson's own contemporaries this same sense of broken promises and lost freedoms. The indictments, both past and present, though harsh, have been justified in considerable measure by events. Yet Wilson's so-called failures need to be understood and explained as well as criticized. For example, the New Freedom, however noble an ideal, appears retrospectively to have been an unrealistic goal in twentieth-century America. And, in the same way, it is doubtful whether the world war could possibly have realized the high expectations entertained at its inception. Tragic for Wilson, the reality of unfulfilled promises and impossible ideals was a tragedy also for the American people.

The New Freedom, as it was spelled out by Wilson and his advisers in the 1912 campaign, did not preclude strong presidential leadership, with the government playing its part in the crusade for social justice and reform. Wilson early in his own career had urged the better training of civil servants through special schooling in public administration. He denied that such education would create a bureaucratic elite because, in a democracy like the United States, government officials had to be sensitive to public opinion. At the same time, the continuing evidence of inefficiency in popular government was raising serious questions over both the desirability and continued practicability of democracy. While education and better communication were stimulating the natural organic growth of democracy, it was also true, Wilson stated, that "democratic institutions are never done; they are like living tissue, always a-making. It is a strenuous thing, this of living the life of a free people; and our success in it depends upon training, not upon clever invention." Moreover, the mass of the people could not possibly govern themselves efficiently. Thus Wilson concluded: "This vast and miscellaneous democracy of ours must be led; its giant faculties must be schooled and directed. Leadership cannot belong to the multitude; masses of men

cannot be self-directed, neither can groups of communities."
Central to the Wilsonian political philosophy was the conviction that the first reform must be the elimination of privilege and monopoly from the national economy. Frederic C.
Howe, the Ohio municipal reformer and Wilson supporter,
summed up much of this thinking in his 1912 book *Privilege
and Democracy in America*. Monopolization of the land, Howe
argued, had been followed by other forms of economic privilege and self-aggrandizement. Necessary now, however, was
not more paternalistic governmental regulation, but industrial and economic freedom for the mass of the people. "Liberty," he wrote, "involves no complicated organization of society, no bureaucracy, no increase in the functions of the state.
Liberty involves rather repeal; it involves the abolition of the
privileges which have been created by Congress, the state
legislatures, and city councils."

Traditionally the mother of special privilege and monopoly in America was the protective tariff, pushed higher in
each succeeding bill passed by the Republicans since the Civil
War. As a southern Democrat imbued with his party's historic
low-tariff position, Wilson's first pledge was his promise to
call upon Congress to enact lower duties. To dramatize the
issue, the new President summoned the House and Senate,
each now controlled by the Democrats, into special session
and appeared in person to deliver his message. Recalling for
his listeners the responsibility laid upon the party by the principles of the New Freedom, Wilson declared:

> We must abolish everything that bears even the semblance of
> privilege or of any kind of artificial advantage, and put our
> businessmen and producers under the stimulation of a constant
> necessity to be efficient, economical, and enterprising, masters of
> competitive supremacy, better workers and merchants than any
> in the world. Aside from the duties laid upon articles which we

do not, and probably can not, produce, therefore, and the duties laid upon luxuries and merely for the sake of the revenues they yield, the object of the tariff duties henceforth laid must be effective competition, the whetting of American wits by contest with the wits of the rest of the world.

Wilson was unsparing in his denunciation of the tariff lobby that had killed previous Democratic efforts at reform. He also persuaded western Democratic senators, concerned over the protection of their section's sheep farming and beet sugar interests, that American agriculture could compete successfully with foreign imports of wool and sugar admitted duty free. Going beyond the mild bill already approved in the House, the Senate, traditionally the graveyard of lower tariff measures, effected further reductions to an overall general level of rates down some 25 percent. At the same time, Congress, with the authority granted by the recently adopted Sixteenth Amendment, enacted a federal income tax to make up the expected revenue losses from the reduced tariff schedules.

In the middle of its work on the tariff, Congress also began the even more complex task of overhauling the country's monetary system, which dated back to the Civil War National Bank Act of 1863. The so-called bankers' Panic of 1907 and the congressional report in 1913 of the Pujo investigation of the alleged money trust in the United States, widely portrayed as a spider web of interlocking Wall Street directorates, called public attention to the pressing need for banking and currency reform. Leading bankers and a number of financial experts favored a highly centralized system directed by private interests with a minimum of governmental regulation. Progressives led by Bryan and Brandeis insisted, on the other hand, that the government alone must control the banking structure of the country. In agreement with their position, Wilson told Congress: "The control of the system of banking and of issue which our new laws are to set up must be public, not private, must be vested in the Government itself, so that the banks may be the instruments, not the masters, of business and of individual enterprise and initiative."

As finally passed in December 1913, the Federal Reserve Act, though a composite of many divergent views, enacted most of the Progressives' demands short of outright government ownership and management of the nation's banking system. Rather than a central bank there were twelve regional Federal Reserve Districts. All national banks were required to join the system, and Federal Reserve notes issued on gold and bank holdings became legal tender with the backing of the United States Government. Since overall policy was determined by the Federal Reserve Board in Washington, on which the government rather than the bankers had the entire voice, the amount of the currency in national circulation could now be expanded or contracted in response to the board's decision.

The Federal Reserve Act, characterized by Arthur Link as "the greatest single piece of constructive legislation of the Wilson era," and the Underwood Tariff were the two major achievements of Wilson's first year. At the same time, the Administration had to deal with other pressing issues which put to the test the New Freedom's dictum of "special privileges to none." It was inevitable, too, that the varied Progressive interests and organizations, multiplying steadily since the turn of the century, should make an effort to realize their particular plans and panaceas. Such notable works—all published during the intense political excitement of 1912—as Walter Weyl's *The New Democracy,* Arthur Eddy's *The New Competition,* and Charles R. Van Hise's *Concentration and Control* outlined the demands of the Progressives in both parties for positive, and even radical, social reforms.

Advanced Progressives of the Croly–New Nationalism variety complained that Wilson was still wedded to a rationale of old-fashioned liberalism or laissez faire. In his new book *Progressive Democracy,* published in 1914, Croly asserted that "The 'New Freedom' looks in general like a revival of Jeffersonian individualism." In contrast, he suggested that plans of social legislation that would formerly have been dismissed as culpably "paternal" should now be considered as a normal and necessary exercise of the police powers of the new Progressivism. To hold its own against the complex, modern, centralized economic system, a revised Jeffersonian localism of a states-rights sort would have to "strip the agencies of big business of every shred of governmental favor." It would be more economical and efficient instead, Croly believed, to adopt Progressivism's example and revise the old Republican rule of special privileges for all by weighting it in favor of such previously disadvantaged groups as the workingmen and small wage earners.

Croly, out of his radical conviction that government must discriminate by granting special favors to previously underprivileged groups, was unimpressed with his friend Roosevelt's emphasis on equal rights. On the other hand, neither Roosevelt nor Croly could go along with Brooks Adams's apocalyptic visions of a coming social revolution and collapse of capitalistic government. Although T.R. had really done little to disturb the capitalists ranged against him at the Republican 1912 convention, so Brooks believed, they nevertheless resented his platform of equality by law and suggestions for limiting the practice of judical review. Roosevelt, in his discussion of the Progressive party's future in *Century* magazine for October 1913, expressed doubt that Wilson's New Freedom had any meaning at all. He agreed with Adams and Croly that the old doctrines of "extreme individualism" and of "a purely competitive industrial system" had broken down.

In setting forth his own program for "Social and Industrial Justice" via such economic reforms as wage-and-hours legislation, Roosevelt declared: "The growth in the complexity of community life means the partial substitution of collectivism for individualism, not to destroy, but to save individualism."

Striving to preserve the liberal tenets of the New Freedom against the pressure of its Progressive critics, Wilson resisted what he felt was class legislation dictated by special interest groups. A measure to exempt labor and farm organizations from prosecution under the antitrust laws and a long-term rural credits bill met with Wilson's disapproval in 1913. The President also withheld support from a model bill for a federal child-labor law and from the agitation to enact woman suffrage. In line with his philosophy of liberalism, he vetoed repeated congressional attempts to restrict immigration to the United States by imposing a literacy test upon new arrivals. One Progressive measure of social justice to which he gave his consent, however, was the La Follette Seaman's Act to enforce safety restrictions and fair labor standards in the American Merchant Marine. Wilson was apparently persuaded to sign the bill as a result of the convincing pleas of Senator La Follette and Andrew Furuseth, president of the Seaman's Union, to Secretary of State Bryan and other administration officials.

In contrast to his approval of the Seaman's bill, Wilson remained largely deaf to Negro pleas for a sympathetic review by the Administration of the whole problem of race relations. A number of important Negro leaders were by this time much disillusioned over the progress of their race. In 1905 a group called together by W. E. B. Du Bois, to form what became known as the Niagara Movement, had protested the growing curtailment of Negro political and civil rights. Du Bois himself appealed especially to that educated minority, which he considered the Negroes' "talented tenth," to oppose

Booker T. Washington's gradualistic philosophy of an accommodation between the races. In the early 1900's, Washington's own hopes seemed controverted more than ever by the spread of violence and lynchings, in the North as well as in the South. Then in August 1908 the entire country was shocked when at Springfield, Illinois, the home of Abraham Lincoln, a white mob, incited by a false accusation of rape against a black man, ran amuck. Negro homes and places of business were destroyed, and in the final count two black men were lynched, four white men were killed, and more than seventy persons were injured. Their sensibilities aroused by the affair at Springfield, certain liberal friends of the Negro cause began a series of exploratory meetings which resulted in 1909 in the organization of the National Association for the Advancement of Colored People, dedicated to the goal of equal rights and opportunities for all.

To Du Bois and his liberal colleagues in the NAACP it was apparent that the Republican party, historically their benefactor, could no longer be trusted to back the black man's political aspirations. For example, Theodore Roosevelt, despite his initial friendly attitude toward the Negro—in accord with traditional Republican practices—changed under the pressures of his own drive for re-election in 1904. In enormously popular political tours across the South and in personal contacts with the section's leaders, T.R. went out of his way to accept the southern point of view on the race question. In 1906 there was an especially ugly racial incident as a result of which his friend Booker T. Washington criticized him when Roosevelt, without considering their disclaimers of responsibility, ordered three companies of black troops dishonorably discharged in the aftermath of a riot in Brownsville, Texas.

Rooseveltian attempts at sectional conciliation, coupled

with frank Republican overtures to the white South, were continued after 1909 in the Taft Administration. It was a "lily-white" policy made demonstrably easier by the fact that the Negro was by this time effectively disfranchised in the southern states. As an aftermath of the Populist revolt of the 1890's, the section had united to preserve white supremacy and concert the means to prevent Negroes from voting. No longer was it worthwhile accordingly for Republicans to base their political hopes in the South on the black man's suffrage. But, at the same time, there was now also little reason for northern friends of the Negro to remain wedded to the Republican party. The possibility that Negroes in the North would move away from their customary blind fealty to the Republicans seemed more realistic, therefore, in 1912 than at any time since the Civil War.

In the 1912 presidential campaign, Roosevelt's Bull Moose party, though refusing to seat southern Negro delegates at its convention, had appealed for the votes of the black man in the North. Wilson, too, sought Negro support, and his frank appeals helped to win the largest number of black votes given to a Democratic presidential candidate up to that time. Such important spokesmen of racial democracy as Oswald Garrison Villard and Du Bois had been persuaded by Wilson's liberal views and vague promises to work for his election. At the same time, however, it was not lost upon Wilson or the Democratic party that 1912 offered the South its first opportunity in half a century to play a conspicuous and perhaps decisive role in American political life. And certainly Wilson's southern supporters, though progressive on many issues, were not disposed to question their section's traditional arrangements on the race question. In the new Administration it was hardly cause for surprise, therefore, that the city of Washington after 1912 appeared to be more than ever a southern town, and that a southern accent was evident in both Wilson's Cabinet and in the Democratic leadership in Congress.

For liberals, impressed by Wilson's New Freedom and hopeful of renewed steps toward racial justice, the first shock of disappointment was the President's refusal to act on Villard's ambitious plan for the appointment of a national race commission. Much worse, however, was the news that certain cabinet members had instituted racial segregation in federal offices, toilets, lunchrooms, and government services. Barely a month after inauguration day, Postmaster General Albert S. Burleson, a native Texan, suggested such a segregationist policy without arousing any protest from his fellow cabinet members. Soon thereafter a number of government bureaus followed Burleson's lead, while Post Office and Treasury officials in the South began to dismiss or downgrade Negro employees.

Segregation had previously existed in federal agencies, but it had been informal and unofficial. Now the official approval extended by the Administration aroused consternation among Negro leaders and their friends. Booker T. Washington observed that he had "never seen the colored people so discouraged and bitter as they are at the present time." Oswald Garrison Villard, the influential publisher of *The Nation* and New York *Evening Post,* taking advantage of his friendship with Wilson, protested bitterly against the segregation policy in his personal letters to the President. As a result of such pressures and continuing adverse publicity, the Treasury Department removed its offensive segregationist signs from the rest rooms, but Negro employees who returned to using the regular toilets were reprimanded. The President appealed to Villard to understand the delicate political problems he faced over the race question, not only in the South, but also in respect to anti-Japanese feeling on the

West Coast. Although concerned over justice for the Negro, Wilson reiterated to Villard that he would "never appoint any colored man in the South because that would be a social blunder of the worst kind." With regard to segregation in governmental offices, Wilson noted that "there was a social line of cleavage which unfortunately corresponded with a racial line."

Whatever the President's explanation, Villard in reply stressed the danger of the precedents that Wilson and Secretary of the Treasury William Gibbs McAdoo, like his chief a native Southerner, were permitting to become established by their race policy. "Because you are a Southerner, and your Administration is largely Southern," he told Wilson, "your subordinates are going about it in a high-handed way."

Villard and Negro leaders were relieved that the Sixty-third Congress, responsible for the passage of the key legislation of Wilson's New Freedom, adjourned on March 4, 1915, without approving a single one of the anti-Negro bills presented. The Administration also made some effort to halt the spread of discrimination and segregation within governmental departments, but Jim Crow had now become a settled policy in most federal bureaus in Washington. Even staunch Wilsonians felt that they had cause to doubt the President's commitment to liberalism, while Negro leaders concluded that their race had no party to turn to. Not only did the loss of federal jobs, anti-Negro bills in Congress, antimarriage bills in northern state legislatures, increases in lynchings, and segregation in governmental departments all indicate a decrease in Negro status, but such steps also marched backward from the progressivism and idealism of both the New Nationalism and the New Freedom. Moreover, racist precedents were now more than ever firmly established, ones that the country would find it difficult later to overcome.

Of the legislation in the Wilson era which seemed to move

in the direction of Roosevelt's New Nationalism the most significant was that pertaining to business and the trusts. By December 1913, following the passage of both the Underwood Tariff and Federal Reserve acts, Wilson was ready to proceed on the third major commitment of the 1912 campaign. Although convinced that his Administration could not rest content with a simple clarification of the Sherman Antitrust Act, Wilson was also determined to resist the New Nationalist and business pressures for the kind of paternalistic regulation demanded in both the Republican and Progressive party platforms in 1912. At the same time, Wilson did not want to undermine business confidence in his Administration or add to the economic recession already becoming evident in the country. Conciliatory and moderate accordingly in his January 1914 message to Congress, Wilson suggested that "the antagonism between business and government is over." In detail, he urged legislation prohibiting interlocking corporate directorships, the stiffening of the Sherman Act's criminal provisions against officials and companies deemed guilty of malpractices, and the establishment of a federal commission, replacing the Bureau of Corporations, to give advice but not to "make terms with monopoly or . . . assume control of business."

Wilson's general program for the trusts was embodied in a series of bills that emerged finally as the Clayton Antitrust and Federal Trade Commission acts. However, instead of the rigorous antimonopoly measure desired by a large minority of Democrats loyal to Bryan's agrarian views, the Clayton Act merely made more specific the original Sherman Antitrust Act's stipulations against unfair business practices in restraint of trade. A compromise provision in the Clayton Act refused a blanket exemption from the antitrust laws for labor and farm organizations, but did provide for restraints on the issuance of injunctions in labor disputes. Though organized labor, which in the case of the A.F. of L. had supported Wilson in 1912, protested vehemently that the Democrats had reneged on their campaign promise to exempt labor organizations from the Sherman law, Samuel Gompers optimistically called the modified anti-injunction clause in the Clayton Act "labor's Magna Charta."

The serious modifications of the New Freedom signaled by the weaknesses of the Clayton bill in its progress through Congress were made still more plain in the Wilson Administration's stand regarding the Federal Trade Commission measure. Wilson himself seemed confused by the political and economic arguments marshaled by proponents of the New Nationalism or the New Competition in favor of government regulation, rather than prosecution, of monopolies. Even Louis D. Brandeis, engaged in advising the government on antitrust matters, had moved by 1914 to support the idea of a strong federal trade commission to regulate business as the most practical solution regarding monopoly. With the help of his close friend and associate George L. Rublee, who had backed Roosevelt's New Nationalism in 1912 and who served on the United States Chamber of Commerce's trust committee, Brandeis drafted a bill reflecting these ideas and won Wilson's acceptance. Approved in Congress with the aid of pressure from the White House, the Federal Trade Commission measure became law on September 26, 1914. Three weeks later, Wilson completed the Administration's antitrust program by also signing the Clayton Act.

The Federal Trade Commission, a bipartisan body of five members, replaced the old Bureau of Corporations of the Roosevelt and Taft administrations. By investigation, publicity, and direct orders—subject to broad court review—the new commission was expected to curb unfair business practices which suppressed competition. Theory, however, was not always practice. And historians of the Progressive move-

ment as divided in their general interpretation of its significance as Arthur Link and Gabriel Kolko nevertheless agree
that the Federal Trade Commission Act indicated the surrender of the New Freedom to the ideology of Roosevelt's New
Nationalism. Brandeis, "the people's attorney," who like Wilson had originally opposed the strong trade commission idea,
believed now that it would be impossible to define by statute,
and thus prosecute successfully, corporate violations of the
antitrust laws. A discretionary regulatory agency, governed
by congressional guidelines and empowered after hearings to
issue "cease and desist" orders to business, seemed a more viable, realistic approach. To Brandeis's dismay, however, Wilson's pro-business appointees to the Federal Trade Commission thwarted its regulatory function. As Robert Wiebe
demonstrates in his book *Businessmen and Reform,* corporate
spokesmen quickly were able to gain the confidence and
cooperation of the FTC. Wilson himself, of course, had
warned earlier that governmental agencies required to work
closely with business would invariably end up by becoming
identified with the interests supposedly being regulated. Melvin Urofsky, the most recent historian of the Wilson Administration's economic policies, concludes that the adoption of the
Federal Trade Commission bill

> marked the end of the New Freedom. It displayed, as did no
> other measure of the Wilson Administration, how disjointed the
> Wilsonian dream was from the realities of the American econ-
> omy. The President and his advisors came to adopt, in form if
> not always in principle, the main tenets of the New Competition.
> The practical details of his major legislative accomplishments
> before 1915 all bore the imprint of business thought as embodied
> in the New Competition.

To the consternation, therefore, of many of his most loyal
supporters, Wilson turned away from the kind of liberalism

and progressivism he had espoused in the first months of his Administration. His appointment of conservatives friendly to banking and business interests on the Federal Reserve Board and the Federal Trade Commission meant that neither agency could fulfill the expectations of the New Freedom. Worried over the downturn in business in 1914, and upset still more by the outbreak of the war in Europe and the death of his wife, Wilson yielded the promise of the New Freedom for the reality of the New Nationalism. This compromise with liberal principles, moreover, had the advantage of entailing no embarrassing conflict of interests when later America decided to enter the war in Europe.

CHAPTER 15

Troubled
Neutrality

THE outbreak of the war in Europe came as a profound shock to the American people. "A general war is unthinkable," an editorial writer for *The New York Times* of July 28, 1914, noted on the day that the Austrian troops invaded Serbia. "Europe can't afford such a war, and the world can't afford it, and happily the conviction is growing that such an appalling conflict is altogether beyond the realm of possibility." Four days later Germany declared war against Russia, and within a week the major European powers were at each other's throats. Although the American people were astonished by the sudden onsurge of a conflict so terrible, the United States in less than three years found itself drawn into the holocaust of the first general war in the world in a century.

The initial effect of the European war was to strengthen isolationist and peace sentiment in the United States. Writers in the popular American magazines saw the war as an inevita-

ble result of the militarism and navalism that had been growing steadily in the Old World. This was the view of the historian Albert Bushnell Hart, whose hastily written book *The
War in Europe: Its Causes and Results* was published late in the
fall of 1914. Hart's Harvard colleague President Charles W.
Eliot, in a series of letters to *The New York Times,* later published as *The Road Toward Peace* (1915), also blamed large armaments and conscript armies as the twin evils that had made
the European war possible.

There was little question in 1914 that America wished to
remain neutral and keep out of the European power struggle.
Despite the nineteenth-century expansionist course of what
most Americans had conceived as their manifest destiny, and
the new worldwide imperial interests of the United States in
the early 1900's, the weight of the overall national experience
was still heavily on the side of peace. Isolationist feelings
remained strong, especially among Progressives in the West
and South. Almost everywhere in the nation liberal sentiments, in spite of the paradox of talking peace in the midst
of mounting navalism and incipient militarism, continued to
hold fast to pacifism and to stand against all war. Many Progressives, even those with a predilection for an aggressive-
type diplomacy, feared that war would weaken the reform
impulse at home and do irreparable damage to the crusade
for social and economic justice. More pacific-minded Progressives, those who, like Jane Addams and Oswald Garrison
Villard, later took the lead in 1917 in opposing American entrance into the war, believed that such a step would encourage reaction at home and destroy individual freedom.

Woodrow Wilson himself, in large part, shared the liberal
case against war even though his Administration continued
the Republicans' interventionist diplomacy in Latin America.
Certainly the President had no desire to see the country
embroiled in European politics or involved in what was, at

least initially in 1914, a purely European war. "It would be the irony of fate if my administration had to deal chiefly with foreign affairs," he had remarked to a Princeton friend before he went to Washington. In his new duties in the White House, he conceived of his responsibilities primarily in terms of the domestic reforms spelled out in the New Freedom. Thus it was clear that the European imbroglio posed an unwanted problem and an unhappy dilemma for both Wilson and the American people.

Even before the outbreak of the great war in Europe, the Wilson Administration had been confronted with difficult diplomatic problems related to American interests in the Far East and Latin America. Though motivated seemingly by the best intentions, illustrated in Secretary of State Bryan's desire to negotiate conciliation treaties with the other major powers, the Wilson Administration nevertheless became entangled in a complex maze of military intervention in Latin America, dollar diplomacy in China, and race feeling toward Japan. In practice, therefore, what Arthur Link calls the Wilson Administration's missionary diplomacy and desire to help other nations differed little from the alleged imperialism of its Republican predecessors.

The conflict of high ideals and unfortunate realities was perhaps most evident in the case of Wilson's ambiguous policy toward Mexico. When the 1911 revolution there eventuated in a military coup, two years later, against the new constitutional government, Wilson refused to recognize the insurgent Huerta regime, although it was in fact the only government in Mexico. Eventually Wilson was forced to compromise and accept outside mediation to resolve the explosive Mexican situation in which the United States had bombarded and occupied the city of Vera Cruz. President Victoriano Huerta, it was true, abdicated in favor of a new government acceptable to Washington, but the United States, by virtue of its full-scale punitive expedition against the forces of Pancho Villa in northern Mexico, again came close to war with its southern neighbor in the spring and summer of 1916. Wilson's policies had meanwhile aroused the suspicions of the Latin American states and provoked bewilderment at home. The American people, impressed by the idealism of the President's repeated avowals of faith in peace and justice, were at a loss to understand his bellicose attitude toward a sister American republic. United States intervention was all the more tragic because Wilson, though interfering in Mexico's domestic affairs, had little sympathy with the American commercial interests there which sought to undo the Mexican revolutionary movement. Nor did Wilson try to profit politically and ensure his own re-election by going the whole way to war, as he might have in the military campaign against Villa in 1916.

President Wilson's strong sense of an American mission to bring peace as well as law and order to Mexico underscored the dilemma that he faced vis-à-vis the much greater conflict in Europe. America, he knew, could hardly remain indifferent to the struggle taking place on the Continent, and, indeed, there was little doubt that the country, despite the prevailing sentiment for neutrality, was more generally sympathetic to the Allies than to Germany and the Central Powers. After the invasion of Belgium and the quick successes of the German armies, Americans came to consider European militarism and war guilt an exclusive German responsibility. As the weight of material and sentimental factors in behalf of England and France gradually gained ascendancy in their thinking about the war, they found it harder to adhere to the President's original injunction to "be impartial in thought as well as action."

The war in Europe and the fighting in Mexico led inevitably to calls in Congress and the press for American preparedness. For Wilson, beset by the delicate problem of preserving

American neutral rights in the face of the German submarine and the British blockade, the demand at home for greater military and naval preparedness appeared as a challenge to his own careful presidential leadership. In his annual message to Congress in December 1914, the President accordingly made a strong answer to those of his critics like Theodore Roosevelt who were demanding more vigorous military and naval preparations. Preparedness, the President pointed out, was a relative term, and he reminded his listeners that the traditional American policy was one of peace and hostility to standing armies. Under his Administration, he declared, the United States would prepare "to the utmost; and yet we shall not turn America into a military camp. We will not ask our young men to spend the best years of their lives making soldiers of themselves."

To the President and his friends it seemed illogical to suppose that the European nations, tied down by their own fighting, could threaten the security of the United States. The cry for preparedness was at odds, not only with the antimilitarist traditions of the Republic, but it was also open to question as a selfish movement governed by the hope of economic or political rewards on the part of its sponsors. It was this aspect of the preparedness cause that was censured by Nicholas Murray Butler of Columbia University, who, together with Eliot of Harvard and David Starr Jordan of Stanford, was one of the prominent university presidents defending Wilson's peace policy.

In December 1914, President Butler created a stir by giving a press interview in which he criticized the preparedness organizations in Washington as insincere and not really concerned with so-called national defense. He declared his belief that Europe's large-scale armaments had led directly to war, and he rejoiced that the country had in the White House a

President able to withstand the preparedness pressure. "In modern democracies the functions of the army and navy are police, philanthropic, and sanitary," Butler asserted, and he urged the American people to "put behind us forever the notion that we must arm in peace as a preventive of war, and that we must be perpetually defending ourselves or getting ready to defend ourselves against new enemies. No people will be hostile to us unless we, by our conduct, make them so." Reaffirming his opposition to preparedness in a letter to *The New York Times,* Butler wrote: "It must not be forgotten that militarism has its origin in a state of mind and that in reality it is a state of mind."

The pacific admonitions of President Wilson and his university supporters, backed though they were by the initial common sense of the country, proved unavailing in the face of the demands by the advocates of a stronger military preparedness. On May 7, 1915, a German submarine sank the *Lusitania* off the coast of England. The fact that the great British passenger liner carried munitions and other contraband as a part of its cargo did not condone the loss of 1,200 lives, including 128 Americans. But the attack on the *Lusitania,* in the eyes of those Americans who were determined to hold fast to neutrality, hardly justified the strong notes of protest which President Wilson addressed to the German government. They feared that by holding Germany to strict accountability for its submarine warfare Wilson implied a threat of war. With Secretary of State Bryan, who resigned after Wilson's second *Lusitania* note, they accepted, even if the President later regretted, the noble idealism of his message to some four thousand recently naturalized citizens at Philadelphia on May 10. There, in the short interval between the sinking of the *Lusitania* and his first note of protest, the President exclaimed:

The example of America must be a special example. The example of America must be the example not merely of peace because it will not fight, but of peace because peace is the healing and elevating influence of the world and strife is not. There is such a thing as a man being too proud to fight. There is such a thing as a nation being so right that it does not need to convince others by force that it is right.

For Bryan the contradiction in American foreign policy, holding Germany to strict accountability, while ignoring the substance of the British blockade, was unacceptable. His resignation, as Ernest R. May points out in *The World War and American Isolation,*

> was one symbol, indeed, of the administration's gradual shift from indrawn pacifist reformism to Progressive nationalism. Bryan had been a spokesman not only for appeasement but for isolationism. He had contended that the United States should not defend any interest at the risk of war, and he had argued for policies that would leave the power of decision in Washington—that would, in other words, permit the United States to make concessions without complete humiliation. It was these policies, as well as his specific recommendations, that the President had rejected, and Bryan resigned because Wilson had chosen to close the avenues of retreat, to threaten war, and to stake America's prestige on the success of his diplomacy.

In the midst of the *Lusitania* crisis and Bryan's leave-taking, a veritable stream of books, articles, speeches, and moving pictures depicted America as defenseless against a naval attack or an invasion from Europe. The National Security League, founded the previous December with a membership drawn largely from New York attorneys and businessmen, cooperated with the Navy League and other superpatriotic organizations in a far-flung and intensive propaganda drive.

Strong support for preparedness came from Army and Navy officers who saw an opportunity to gain an expanded military and naval establishment, as well as from industrialists who envisaged governmental defense contracts.

More persuasive than the propaganda of persons with an economic stake in preparedness was the work in its behalf by men like Theodore Roosevelt, General Leonard Wood, and Henry L. Stimson, who had been Secretary of War in the Taft Administration. Part of a New York or northeastern group of Progressives and Republicans who were now concerned mainly with foreign affairs, these critics of the President's neutralist policy considered preparedness a necessary preliminary step toward a desired American intervention in the war on the side of the Allies. Otherwise, if America was as weak as the preparedness advocates said again and again, simple logic dictated a Bryanesque conciliatory policy with a minimal risk of hostile incidents likely to lead to war—even if this meant yielding American neutral rights and foreign trade. Thus the American people might have been warned to stay off belligerent ships, especially those carrying contraband.

Whether the American people would have accepted the sacrifices that were likely to be needed if their farms and factories could no longer supply the Allied war machine is more doubtful. Organized labor, for example, though its leaders continued to decry war and militarism almost to the eleventh hour of America's final decision, was just as reluctant as the business and financial community to yield the benefits derived from the country's inflated foreign trade. Thus in November 1915 the Executive Committee of the A.F. of L. reported that American neutrality, carried to the point of an embargo on arms and munitions, would be disastrous to the average workingman, then just recovering from the effects of the country's economic setback in 1914. The committee asserted that war, despite its horrors, was no worse than the type of despotism that sought to prevent a people from realizing their own destiny. Samuel Gompers, the Federation president, although he had considered himself a doctrinaire pacifist, was the first prominent labor leader to espouse preparedness. Fearful of the economic hardships that a rigorous neutrality might entail, he helped to wean labor away from its traditional hostility to a large army and navy.

Theodore Roosevelt was, of course, the biggest gun in the arsenal of the preparedness advocates. The former President exemplified, better than any of his political contemporaries, certain militaristic and nationalistic values that a good many Progressives were now happy to accept. Like the less radical among American Socialists who welcomed the "startling progress in collectivism" in wartime England and Germany, Roosevelt and his Progressive friend ex-Senator Beveridge also admired Germany's military efficiency. Necessary to that achievement in England as well as in Germany, Roosevelt pointed out, was the merging of social and industrial justice with military preparedness—"two sides of a common program."

Roosevelt, together with a number of university presidents, extended enthusiastic backing to General Leonard Wood's program of voluntary summer military training camps for college students and businessmen. Regularly scheduled military training in the nation's schools and colleges also gained new support from the preparedness movement and the Progressive-type arguments linking it with American democracy. Denying the validity of the traditional liberal attack on universal service as a Prussian concept, Brooks Adams praised the French and German masses going off to war as an example of the democratic ideal in practice. Harvard philosopher Ralph Barton Perry, a disciple of William James, also defended conscription in his essay "The Free Man and the

Soldier," published in *The New Republic*. Roosevelt, too, contended that universal service represented "the true democratic ideal."

As Walter Millis subsequently was to point out in his book *Arms and Men*, "Preparedness was an inspired idea. There was something in it for everyone. It provided all the excitement and glamour of war, while promising to keep the country out of combat." Yet, though Roosevelt's "progressivism could hardly be discerned through the clouds of his perfervid patriotism, it was there nonetheless, insistent and real," historian Charles Hirschfeld writes. "In his preparedness philippics, he always demanded, within the context of his 'large Americanism,' social justice for all as well as adequate military defense. We could not, he argued, have a sound foreign policy 'unless there is also a sound relationship among our own citizens within our own ranks.' Reform and strength," Hirschfeld continues, "thus went together in the context of international crisis and war—an equation also accepted by Roosevelt's admirers among the leaders of the foundering Progressive Party in 1916."

Before it expired within the fold of the Republican party in 1916, the Progressive party adopted a platform calling for universal military training—a plank which incidentally Senator Lodge could not get his fellow Republicans to approve. Also the National Committee of the Progressives, after listing recent gains in Progressive legislation, observed that the war had brought

> an issue deeper than national advance, the issue of national unity and the nation's existence, of Americanism and of Preparedness. The Progressive Platform of 1916, therefore, placed foremost as our immediate need preparedness in arms, industry and spirit. . . . The Progressive National Committee recognized that such are now the issues that immediately confront the country and *looks only to the duty that arises* therefrom.

To Woodrow Wilson, agonizing in the White House over
the problems of American neutrality and the struggle to stay
out of war, the Progressive demands for preparedness and
reform posed a threat to his own prospects for re-election in
1916. To prevent as many of the Progressives as possible
from returning to the Republican party, the Democrats' obvious strategy was to move still further in the direction of the
New Nationalism via advanced measures of social justice.
Anxious to convince the Progressives that the Democratic
party was an acceptable vehicle of reform, Wilson defied conservatives early in 1916 with his nomination of Louis D. Brandeis to the Supreme Court. Moreover, under presidential
prodding, Congress now agreed to pass measures that Wilson
himself had previously opposed. Thus it approved the rural
credits bill, a workmen's compensation law for federal employees, the Adamson Eight-Hour Act for all interstate
railroad workers, and the Keating–Owen child-labor act.
Completing the metamorphosis in Democratic policies inaugurated with the passage of the Federal Trade Commission
Act of 1914, the Wilson Administration by the fall of 1916
had enacted, as Arthur Link points out, "almost every important plank in the Progressive platform of 1912." The new legislation, going beyond the political necessities of securing Wilson's re-election, brought the national movement for social
justice to its peacetime peak and also helped to unite the
country in the face of possible war.

Just as Wilson in his domestic policy forsook the ideals of
the New Freedom for the program of the New Nationalism,
so he moved from his essentially pacifist stand of 1914 to
espouse the preparedness position advocated most promi-
nently by his political enemies. The sudden reversal, confusing
to friends as well as to political foes, occurred sometime in
May 1915, although it was not revealed publicly until that
summer. Then in November, the President, at a dinner of the

Manhattan Club in New York City, explained the Administration's plans for an expanded Army of a half-million trained troops and a Navy second only to that of the British Empire. "We have it in mind," Wilson declared, "to be prepared, not for war, but only for defense."

Wilson's speech was immediately attacked by Bryan and others who questioned the likelihood of a threat to the security of the United States. Across the Atlantic, Lord Rosebery, the former Liberal Prime Minister, lamented that the President's defense plans would add to the world's armaments burdens and heighten the tragedy of the war. "I know of nothing more disheartening," he said, "than the announcement recently made, that the United States—the one country left in the world free from the hideous, bloody burden of war—is about to embark upon the building of a huge armada destined to be equal or second to our own." At home, William Lyon Phelps, the famous Yale professor of literature, in a letter to *The New York Times* interpreted Wilson's speech as evidence that the United States was ready to embark on "the dance of death." A similar view was expressed by Emma Goldman, the celebrated anarchist, who saw preparedness as "the road to universal slaughter." Voicing her disappointment that Wilson had succumbed to the same methods and techniques used forty years ago in Germany by Bismarck, she concluded sadly that there was little essential difference between Theodore Roosevelt, "the born bully who uses a club," and Wilson, "the history professor who wears the smooth polished university mask."

In the President's own party there was strong opposition to his new views, and Wilson's December 1915 preparedness message to Congress was, in the words of his official biographer, "generously though not enthusiastically received." The week following the message, Representative Clyde H. Tavenner, an old Bryan follower, delivered a detailed and elaborately documented speech exposing the ties between the Navy League and the private munitions industry. Tavenner, who was a longstanding advocate of taking the profits out of war and preparation for war, now declared his belief "that if this Republic is in danger, it is danger not from the peoples beyond the seas, but from a clique of men within this country who would tax the people until their backs break, simply that they might make profit supplying battleships, armor and guns." Tavenner tried to make it clear that he opposed the Navy League, not because it advocated preparedness, but because it advocated a kind of preparedness in which the government and people of the United States were defrauded by selfish interests. "In tracing the business connections of the men behind the Navy League one cannot avoid being impressed," he asserted, "by the number of instances in recent years in which those identified with the steel and armor making concerns find their way into the official life of the Navy Department, the Department of Justice, and even the Department of State." Though President Wilson disassociated his concept of preparedness from that espoused by the Navy League and big business, Tavenner's attack on its business and financial affiliations hit the preparedness movement in its most vulnerable spot. The theme of his speech was much repeated on the floor of Congress, and his printed remarks were widely circulated by peace groups.

What impelled Wilson to change his ideas on the country's defense needs has never been satisfactorily explained by his biographers. Preparedness was not after all a single issue without implications for a much stronger American stand with respect to the European war. In all likelihood, it could be expected to carry the nation further away from its historic isolationist and antimilitarist traditions. Thus the President's about-face was all-important. Domestic political considerations were obviously a factor, and Wilson was also probably influenced by an aroused public opinion after the *Lusitania* crisis. It is difficult to believe, however, that the stern and calm President, so determined and strong-willed throughout his career, and so adept at building public support for his own policies—even as he distrusted the motives of his opponents—would have surrendered so easily to the preparedness advocates unless he was prepared to go further and adopt as well the essence of their beliefs on foreign policy.

What Arthur Link calls the "confusions and crises" in Wilson's thinking and policies in the early months of 1916 seemed to indicate that the President was troubled by his new role as an advocate of both peace and preparedness. The reception in the Middle West to his speaking tour in behalf of preparedness in January and February 1916 revealed considerable sympathy for the President personally, but also much concern lest preparedness lead to militarism. William Jennings Bryan, no longer a part of the President's official family, in an angry editorial in the February issue of his *Commoner*, charged that if Wilson's words meant anything at all, they indicated that the "preparedness for which he asks is not for the purpose of preventing future wars, BUT IS FOR USE IN THE PRESENT WAR, if he thinks it necessary."

Even though he accepted leadership in the drive for greater military preparedness, Wilson still refused to be stampeded into war. To mitigate the danger of submarines attacking merchantmen without prior warning—a necessary tactic if the submarines were to avoid retaliatory action from armed ships—Wilson seriously considered a request to the Allies that they should refrain from placing defensive guns on their vessels. But he refused to yield his dominance in foreign affairs and accede to the demands in Congress—climaxed in January 1916 by the Gore and McLenmore resolutions—that Americans be urged to stay off, or forbidden to travel on, any armed ships. Wilson's moral rigidity over the issue of neutral rights and the submarine weakened the Congress' belief in his adherence to a strict neutrality and heightened the intensity of his own personal dilemma concerning the war. The whole problem, which was becoming more serious in 1916, was illustrated in an incident that Joseph Tumulty, Wilson's personal secretary, later recalled and which Link, for example, accepts as authentic. In a talk to Tumulty at the peak of the crisis in United States–Mexican relations, Wilson revealed the depths of his desire for peace:

> It is not a difficult thing for a president to declare war, especially against a weak and defenseless nation like Mexico. . . . But this has never been in my thoughts for a single moment. The thing that daunts me and holds me back is the aftermath of war, with all its tears and tragedies. . . . I will not resort to war against Mexico until I have exhausted every means to keep out of this mess. I know they will call me a coward and quitter, but that will not disturb me. Time, the great solvent, will, I am sure, vindicate this policy of humanity and forbearance.

Divided in his own mind between his hope of peace and his public position urging a stronger Army and Navy, Wilson waged his extraordinary 1916 campaign for re-election. In speaking for arms, he used the language of the pacifist Progressives, but he also marched at the head of the preparedness parades, and he permitted his party to hail him as the President who "kept us out of war." At the same time, despite the threat of renewed German submarine warfare, Wilson tried to remain neutral and, in fact, grew more and more impatient over Allied interference with American trade. There was no real possibility, of course, that the United States would challenge the essentials of the British and French positions in the war. However much his Anglophile

Republican critics applauded a more aggressive American diplomacy, it remained true that they had even less desire than the President to enforce anti-British policies.

It was hardly naval weakness or unpreparedness, as the American people were led to suppose, that prevented a stronger American foreign policy in respect to the belligerent powers. Rather it was the fact that the United States could not insist on its rights as a neutral against *both* the Allies and the Central Powers. Open United States naval action against Germany's violations of American rights would have been inconsistent with Wilson's efforts to preserve peace, and a similar strong stand against the Allies was unthinkable. Thus the American public continued to suffer from the misleading notion that the nation was unable to maintain its rights on the high seas, never understanding how awkward such a vigorous assertion of American rights would have been in terms both of Wilson's official neutrality and the increasingly pro-Allied and prowar views of his critics.

Preparedness by itself was, indeed, largely a false issue. If America had been willing to adhere to an isolationist neutrality, as the more pacifist political leaders like Bryan and La Follette urged, there was little or no danger of war. Only if the American people, following the lead of the Administration after May 1915, were no longer content to remain "impartial in thought as well as action" was preparedness justified—not for defense, but for an eventual intervention in the war. It was for the latter reason that Herbert Croly, editor of *The New Republic,* urged support of the Administration's preparedness program. Although it violated America's historic traditions, Croly believed that preparedness was necessary because of Wilson's decision that there was a threat of war. "The usual explanation that the United States is preparing only for defense, which is a policy on which all good citizens can agree, merely begs the question," Croly asserted, because in the case of a large nation like the United States, "no sharp line can be drawn between defensive and agressive armament." Much more frank than most of the nationalistic Progressives, Croly admitted that "there is a very real probability that the new Army and Navy will be used chiefly for positive and for aggressive as opposed to merely defensive purposes."

Although increased preparedness, obviously aimed at Germany, was hardly compatible with a strict and impartial neutrality, the American people hoped that it might somehow avert United States entrance into the war. Moreover, only the most radical pacifists and socialists were willing to disavow the President and take their case directly to the public in demonstrations against preparedness and war. Most of the liberal pacifists and antimilitarists—people like Jane Addams, Lillian Wald, Paul U. Kellogg, Oswald Garrison Villard, Rabbi Stephen S. Wise, and the Reverend John Hayes Holmes, who were all leaders in the crusade for social justice—tried to trust and support Wilson throughout his presidency. In reality, they had few alternatives, and some, moreover, enjoyed the seductive appeal of direct access to the White House and a personal correspondence and friendship with the President. Thus Fred Howe, the Cleveland Progressive and Wilson's Commissioner of Immigration, clung to the conviction that it was not the President but selfish business and economic interests that were pushing the preparedness program. And William E. Dodd, the historian and future Wilson biographer, expressed the belief that the President had been forced to march in the preparedness parades. Likening the more vociferous preparedness advocates to the German militarists of Bismarck's time, Dodd reluctantly concluded that the President had become convinced by their propaganda.

So strong was liberal confidence in the President's sincerity that, even as late as the end of February 1917, after he had broken off diplomatic relations with Germany, a delegation of the American Union Against Militarism, a leading pacifist organization, came away from an hour's talk in the White House still hopeful of peace. But, if the President solicited the pacifists' good faith and understanding, it was nonetheless true that he ignored their grievances and program.

For American entrance into the war, the American people were indeed unprepared until those final, fateful steps along the road to war in February and March of 1917. But the nagging question still remains of whether a stronger and earlier American effort at military preparedness might have deterred Germany from the decision, on January 31, 1917, to renew its submarine warfare. Here it is important to point out that the American electorate, short of an actual declaration of war, would probably not have approved an American Army large enough to affect the course of the fighting in Europe. The American Navy was already formidable, but again it is most doubtful that the people would have accepted in 1915 or 1916 the kind of unneutral use to which American naval units were put by the Franklin D. Roosevelt Administration before World War II. What Germany really feared after 1914 was United States economic aid to the Allies. A greater American military effort could not have increased such aid; indeed actual belligerency might even have decreased it by concentrating war production on the United States's own needs. It was America's economic power accordingly, rather than its military preparedness, or the lack thereof, that largely determined Germany's decision to resume all-out submarine warfare on the high seas.

From the German point of view, America's ever-increasing trade and financial support to the Allies was in itself a hostile, unneutral act. Since the United States would not curb a wartime trade on which its own prosperity had come to depend, the German naval experts were able to convince their government that it had little to lose by unleashing the submarines for total warfare against all Allied and American shipping across the Atlantic. *"The United States,"* they argued in May 1916, *"can scarcely engage in more hostile activities than she has already done up to this time."* The German army, its leaders believed, could win the war on the Western Front before the United States could get a sizable expeditionary force to France. Meanwhile, by holding Germany to strict account for the consequences of its submarine warfare, Wilson had lost the initiative in the matter of peace or war. Whenever Germany decided that its national interest dictated a challenge to America's position in respect to trade on the high seas, hostilities would become almost inevitable. Field Marshal Paul von Hindenburgh, speaking for the German high command in the spring of 1917, summed up the delicate situation: "We are counting on the possibility of war with the United States, and have made all preparations to meet it. *Things cannot be worse than they now are.* The war must be brought to an end by the use of all means as soon as possible."

Already in 1916, at least a year before the final decision for war, it was apparent to the President and his inner circle of advisers that, if America was indeed to stay out of the struggle, it would have to use the great prestige of its neutral position and power to bring the belligerents to the conference table—whether or not each side was, in fact, willing to negotiate a peace short of victory. Colonel Edward M. House, the President's personal diplomatic emissary to the belligerents, was convinced that war with Germany was inevitable. Although Wilson, unlike House, was not ready as yet to join the Allies in order to force the issue of America mediating the war, he clearly understood how precarious the popular hopes of an American isolationist and neutralist peace really were. World peacemaking, on the other hand, offered an escape, a last chance for Wilson to avert the final testing of his own ambiguous and contradictory diplomacy.

To prod the Allies and to further his diplomatic efforts, Wilson in May 1916 delivered a significant address to the newly founded League to Enforce Peace, the first major internationalist organization in the United States. In a speech that Harley Notter has called "the most important pronouncement on American policy since 1823," Wilson explained what he believed were the causes of war in which "our own rights as a Nation, the liberties, the privileges, and the property of our people have been profoundly affected." Not only did the American people desire to see the war concluded, but the United States, as much as the nations at war, was concerned to secure a peace that would be permanent and "part of the common interest of mankind. . . . So sincerely do we believe in these things," the President concluded, "that I am sure that I speak the mind and wish of the people of America when I say that the United States is willing to become a partner in any feasible association of nations formed in order to realize these objects and make them secure against violation."

More attractive than the old idea of an association of nations was the new concept now made explicit by the League to Enforce Peace. A peace enforced by American arms in cooperation with the Allies offered a solution to the conflicting views of the pacifists and preparedness advocates. A disciplined and calculated preparation for war, plus the inexorable process of the war itself, could become the pathway to an enduring peace, enforced by the collective will of the victor nations. *The New Republic* asserted in its comments on his speech:

> Mr. Wilson has broken with the tradition of American isolation in the only way which offers any hope to men. Not only has he

broken with isolation, he has ended the pernicious doctrine of neutrality, and has declared that in the future we cannot be neutral between the aggressor and the victim. That is one of the greatest advances ever made in the development of international morality. . . . Our offer to join in a guaranty of the world's peace opens up the possibility of a quick and moderate peace.

Until his own far-from-certain re-election was assured, Wilson remained hampered in his ambitious plans. But by mid-November of 1916 the situation appeared favorable. The war in Europe was at a stalemate, while Germany intimated it might soon be forced to regain its freedom of action with respect to the submarine. It seemed apparent, therefore, as Wilson told House, that "the submarine situation would not permit of delay and it was worth while to try mediation before breaking off with Germany." At home Wilson realized that he would now be under increased pressure from Congress and the country to heed the pacifist pleas for American mediation. In December he sent out his so-called peace notes requesting the belligerents to state their war aims. Since neither side offered satisfactory replies, Wilson was spared the embarrassing possibility that Germany, rather than the Allies, might have accepted American mediation. Then on January 22, 1917, Wilson spelled out his own terms. It must, the President declared, "be peace without victory," a peace founded on an equality of rights among nations and upon "the principle that governments derive all their just powers from the consent of the governed. . . ."

Wilson's climactic appeal for peace came too late. Germany's considered decision to resume submarine warfare was announced on January 31, effective the next day, and on February 3 the United States broke off diplomatic relations. In March the Russian revolution overthrew the czarist government and brought into power the provisional Kerensky regime, dedicated hopefully to democratic ideals and the continuance of the war against Germany. Strangely, if the outbreak in Russia, which strengthened Wilson's idealistic arguments for entering the war, had come a month or two earlier, the German government, looking expectantly to Russia's military collapse, might have foregone its resumption of the submarine attacks on the Atlantic, and the United States might never have had to enter the war. By the same token, if Wilson could have foreseen the heavy casualties of the American Expeditionary Forces in 1918, he might have chosen to postpone America's Armageddon.

As it was, the varied pieces in the Wilsonian foreign policy now gradually fell into place. The inner contradictions of peace and war, preparedness and neutrality, isolation and intervention, were all reconciled in the concept of a crusade for peace and democracy with the goal of a league of nations to make good the terms of the postwar settlement. In place of a limited peace, "a peace without victory," mediated with the help of a neutral United States and continuing the European balance of power, American belligerency implied total victory and a war to the utopian end of a new democratic and international association of the world's nations. In behalf of such a lofty ideal, Wilson could ask the people of the United States and the Allies to fight in what, in his own mind, was essentially a holy war—an unprecedented kind of secular crusade for the future of all mankind.

CHAPTER 16

Apotheosis in War

PROGRESSIVISM and war were not unrelated, and the era of Theodore Roosevelt and Woodrow Wilson saw almost as much attention devoted to foreign as to domestic policy. War also defined the chronological limits generally ascribed to the main phase of Progressivism. Thus Theodore Roosevelt became President three years after the war with Spain, and Woodrow Wilson was by 1917 a war President.

The usual historical view that the first world war killed the Progressive movement has been questioned in recent years by a number of historians. Social reform and liberal political ventures, it has been pointed out, attracted considerable popular interest and support even in the conservative 1920's and revived again with full strength in the era of the Depression and the New Deal. On the other hand, it seems clear that the war marked an abrupt decline in the liberal as distinct from the nationalistic side of Progressivism. Civil liberties and the right of dissent were suppressed for individuals and organizations alike, not only during the war, but in the Red Scare of 1919. Moreover, much of this antiliberal feeling lingered on in the twenties in the Ku Klux Klan and other censorious, superpatriotic organizations. Measured in terms of the ensuing conservative climate of opinion, dearth of advanced social reforms, and reality of reactionary politics, the heritage of the world war left Progressivism in the United States and social democracy in Europe weaker than either had been in 1914. Yet our historical knowledge of its dismal aftermath could not stand revealed at the time to the great majority of the citizenry who viewed America's participation in the war in a "frenzy of idealism and self-sacrifice." It was in this latter sense that the great struggle marked, as Richard Hofstadter observed, "the apotheosis as well as the liquidation of the Progressive spirit."

Instructive for American Progressives, beset by conflicting emotions in regard to the war, was the intellectual temper and example of social democracy in Europe before 1914. Increasingly in the years immediately preceding the war, the pursuit of power politics by the major European countries had encouraged a nationalistic and expansionist mood among the people. At the same time, a psychology of fear and suspicion spread over international relations and influenced popular feeling. Even such traditional liberal strongholds as the international socialist movement and the cosmopolitan community of literary figures and scholars were affected. Moreover, business interests, hitherto engaged in the relatively free trade of the Century of Peace, now drew closer to the national state and accepted the neo-mercantilism of the twentieth century. Indeed, almost everywhere liberal and progressive ideals endured only at the price of their subordination to the insatiable demands of the respective selfish interests of the great powers.

In Germany militarism gradually spread from the army to industrial life, and even the academic community and the Social Democrats became a part of the state socialism fastened on the German empire by Bismarck's leadership. By 1900 a bargain was sealed between agrarian interests and large landowners, each desiring a protective tariff, and the military–industrial groups pushing for naval construction and expanded export markets. Nationalized liberals, now more and more the advocates of military, naval, and colonial expansion, no longer contested the leadership of the German military machine. Even those men considered the true representatives of democratic liberalism—Max Weber and Theodor Barth, for example—hoped by supporting a navy and an imperialistic policy to break down the privileges of the old conservative agrarians. And among German intellectuals generally there was a revolt against interest politics and a desire to support "the national cause."

In England the Conservative or Union party, in power during the Boer War, was repudiated three years later by the voters. In theory the Liberals, upon returning to office in 1905, should have been able to resist the new nationalistic trends. In adherence to its historic antimilitarism and anti-imperialism, the Liberal party might have cut naval appropriations and still satisfied most of the popular demands for welfare measures. In practice, however, the Liberals in the famous Lloyd George budget of 1909 adopted new taxes and began the road to eventual national bankruptcy via the twin means of social reform and armaments. In foreign policy especially, there remained little to distinguish between the new Liberal Imperialists and the Conservatives. For the former, Lloyd George, forsaking his Boer War pacifism and early efforts at German rapprochement, "came forward in opposition to Germany as the mouthpiece of British patriotism and imperialism." Moreover, it was not lost upon the prowar Conservatives that, if the European crisis broke, the British masses would accept with better grace a declaration of war by the government and party identified with the social reforms and welfare program of 1909. Thus there was a cult of continuity in English diplomacy and politics not unlike that of imperial Germany before the great war.

After the assassination of the Austrian Archduke Franz Ferdinand at Sarajevo on June 28, 1914, Europe moved steadily, if gradually, over the next two months toward a general war. The intricate system of alliances, ententes, and treaties supposed to ensure peace worked instead for war as each nation's political position hardened to prevent the flexibility and compromise essential to diplomacy. In the midst of this breakdown of the old concert of Europe, nongovernmental agencies also failed to fulfill the idealistic aspirations of their founders. At Brussels, Belgium, at the end of July, separate groups of socialists and peace leaders met in last-ditch efforts to avert the war. Realizing full well the futility now of their cause, and unable to gain from President Wilson some proffer of American mediation, the respective delegates bade each other farewell and returned home.

The European war effectively destroyed the old liberal and radical hopes of international solidarity in the cause of peace and socialism. American peace groups were disposed at first to place full blame for the war on Old World militarism. Later, out of sympathy with the war aims of the Allies, some of the organizations discontinued their financial support and cooperation with the few friends of peace left on the Continent. Even the American Socialist party severed connections with the European movement and largely gave up the effort to bring the war in Europe to a quick, negotiated settlement. Meanwhile, apart from a few intransigent individuals like Bertrand Russell in England and Romain Rolland in France, the intellectuals in Europe offered their talents to the war effort. Not content like the masses to accept the stand "my country right or wrong," they contrived their complex and tortured rationalizations to justify each nation's position. Thus they urged national unity over the needs of mankind, the heroic spirit over the materialism of the bourgeoisie, and war as a spiritual renewal and agent of the apocalypse. More perceptive was the poignant comment of the British Foreign Secretary, Sir Edward Grey, one of the central figures in the decision for war who also understood its tragic import. "The lamps are going out all over Europe," Grey remarked; "we shall not see them lit again in our lifetime."

Most disheartening was the failure of the European socialist and labor movements to hold fast to peace. Instead, when war came, the expected dissident elements in each country went the way of the intellectuals, the churches, and the peace organizations and stood with the governments that had gone to war. At the several congresses of the Second International in the 1900's, the assembled Socialist delegates had repeated their opposition to all capitalistic wars. Now, except for a scattering of independent radicals, the Socialists supported their respective national causes. "We do not imagine for a moment," the editors of the *International Socialist Review* wrote in 1914, "that a single German Socialist actually wanted War any more than we believed the English, French, and Belgian comrades wanted War. Just the same . . . in spite of the strong anti-military sentiment of the French Socialists, in spite of the anti-war propaganda of the English movement, above all, in spite of the 4,500,000 voting Social Democrats in Germany, we find the working classes of Europe flying at each other's throats."

Though puzzling to American Socialists, it seems clear in retrospect that the increasingly middle-class, evolutionary nature of the Socialist movement on both sides of the Atlantic forecast the nationalistic and patriotic position taken by the various radical and laborite parties in Europe in 1914. In Germany the Social Democrats, considered the hope of world socialism, were actually without real political influence at home. Revisionism along more moderate, nonrevolutionary lines reinforced national as opposed to class tendencies and made party members "more obedient than bold." This trend was already made explicit when, in a sensational speech in the Reichstag on April 25, 1907, on the eve of the Second Hague Conference, the Socialist deputy Gustav Noske labeled a "bourgeois illusion" the notion of automatic Socialist support for disarmament. Socialists would fight for Germany, he said. "We have always demanded an armed nation. . . ."

Although American Socialists cooperated with peace groups to try to keep the United States neutral, some held the peace societies in low esteem. On the left wing the IWW, though refusing to sanction the war, took no specific action against American involvement. A few of the more conservative Socialists like W. J. Ghent, in line with their own later support for Wilson's war message, also defended their European colleagues who backed the war. In most of the European countries, the old pacifism of the Socialist parties was compromised by the fact that they formed a responsible political opposition with much of their strength in the trade unions which, in turn, were generally prowar. But the American Socialist party, weak in numbers and influence because it had no such close relationship with the government and organized labor, was able to adhere more easily to its doctrinaire, Marxist opposition to all capitalist wars. Perhaps, too, as David Shannon points out, American Socialists, "if they had known what was to happen to them during the conflict," would have taken a less clear-cut stand against America's entrance into the war.

In America, as in the social democracy of Europe, the more nationalistic elements within the Progressive movement gradually gained predominance over liberal pacifist opinion. Almost lost to view accordingly, in the midst of President Wilson's narrow 1916 electoral victory on a platform of peace and Progressivism, was the way in which the American public mind was being prepared for war. Among many of the more nationalistic and bellicose American Progressives, a vital center of intellectual influence was *The New Republic* under Herbert Croly's editorial direction. Croly, long an admirer of European ideas of state socialism in their American context of nationalism and democracy, believed in 1916 that the United States needed "the tonic of a serious moral adventure." He complained of the "real danger of national disintegration" under an American democracy in which the average citizen selfishly put "having his own way" ahead of the obligation for some form of "national service."

Continually weighing the claims on America of a policy of peace or war and the merits of Wilson's versus Roosevelt's stand on foreign policy, Croly and *The New Republic* attempted to unite a romantic national idealism with a realistic Progressivism. This same duality characterized the articles which John Dewey, America's senior philosopher and leading pragmatist, published mostly in the pages of *The New Republic* during the war years. Originally critical of German idealist philosophy for the way in which it had hardened into a narrow nationalistic justification of imperial war aims, Dewey by 1917 moved steadily to a position favoring American entrance into the war on the side of the Allies. And, though he warned against the suppression of dissenting opinions, he also castigated old pacifist friends for their failure to recognize the "immense impetus to reorganization afforded by this war."

As a pragmatist and instrumentalist, Dewey pointed out that war could not be dissociated from the ends that it sought to achieve. Thus he found the customary pacifist objection to all use of force absurd and based on a lack of understanding of the function of a political state. What was objectionable was not the use of force itself, but the unwise or ineffective use of force. It "all depends," said Dewey, "upon the efficient adaptation of means to ends." His major concern with regard to censorship in wartime, for example, was not that free speech might be lost permanently but rather that inept attempts on the part of the government to censor thought and speech would hamper effective United States military participation and interfere with the solidarity of the war effort. "Here, I repeat," Dewey declared, "is the real danger in that policy of 'Hush, don't think, only feel and act' to which every forward step in the conscription of thought commits us."

To counteract what he considered as the pacifists' muddled thinking, and to help overcome American apathy regarding the war, Dewey called for more attention to the means of its prosecution. Instead of creating a war motivation by appeals to patriotic hysteria, Dewey stressed the need for a practical "businesslike psychology" that would perceive the ends to be accomplished and make an "effective selection and orderly arrangement of means for their execution." American national intelligence seemed to lie in the direction of the practical; and a realistic, businesslike attitude, he felt, should be emphasized along with the Wilsonian liberal note of "an underlying national idealism."

In attempting to find an answer to the age-old question "What Are We Fighting For?" Dewey explored the progressive social possibilities of the war. The more extensive use of science for communal purposes and the formation of large political groups indicated that the world would be better organized, though not necessarily organized for a better world. Old conceptions of private property, however, had been killed by the war's emphasis on "the public aspect of every social enterprise." And these changes, Dewey believed,

could no longer be dismissed by labeling them "state socialism." On the other hand, the state capitalism or socialism of a
few super states would not lead to a true democratic federation of nations. Finally, in his assessment of social changes
that might result from the war, Dewey noted that "conscription has brought home to the countries which have in the past
been the home of the individualistic tradition the supremacy
of public need over private possession."

For Dewey, Croly, and many of the Progressives, a major
justification of the war was the new sense of national purpose
that it engendered. With its demands for social control and
economic planning, war solved, or seemed to solve, Walter
Lippmann's old concern over drift versus mastery. Hopefully
the sense of community achieved in wartime might serve as a
prelude, not only to further domestic progress and reforms,
but also to a new international order. Even more significant
therefore than the sublimation of the New Freedom within
the New Nationalism at home was their possible extension
abroad under the aegis of the President's missionary diplomacy.

American world leadership via Wilson's concepts of a
"peace without victory" and a war "for peace and democracy"
suggested the hope of transferring the ideals of the New
Freedom to an international stage. A democratic equality and
self-determination among nations, lowered tariffs and trade
barriers, substantial disarmament, and the end of secret treaties together offered an essentially nineteenth-century liberal
version of international relations—a blueprint for a New
Freedom in world affairs. Excepting only the more modern
concept of a league of nations to enforce the peace, the ideas
asserted in Wilson's Fourteen Points were admirably suited to
serve as a replica abroad for the kind of traditional liberal
program fast being abandoned at home. Eric Goldman is
probably correct accordingly in his contention that the adop-

tion of Wilson's idealistic peace program would have proven disappointing to many of his more Progressive followers. The root of the trouble was not that Wilson's policies were later rejected at the Paris Peace Conference, but that those policies were already hopelessly out of date. The President, in other words, was trying to recast the world in a nineteenth-century liberal mold which, if realized, would have been anathema to many of his Progressive supporters in the United States. For their peace of mind it was well that Wilson did not win his fight for the Fourteen Points and also that he lost the backing of those liberal idealists who had been most attracted by the original promise of the New Freedom.

Both Wilson and Dewey had insisted on the primacy of America's idealistic war aims. The United States, entering upon the war without the conditions of its participation determined in advance, would have to use what means it could, Dewey decided, to see that its ideals were "forced upon our allies, however unwilling they may be, rather than [be] covered up by the debris of war." The folly, and indeed impossibility, of imposing this position upon the forum of power politics remained to be demonstrated later at the Paris Peace Conference and before the United States Senate when the President fought for the Treaty of Versailles. Wilsonian idealism unfortunately included much self-righteous dogmatism. And certainly it was idealism run wild for Wilson to hope that the New Freedom could be refashioned into some kind of new world order. The unhappy thought lingers that more modest goals might have succeeded. Idealism and internationalism might have been better served if America had remained neutral in 1917 as the more pacifist and isolationist among the Progressives had hoped. In a world still amuck after 1918, the United States, as the last great neutral power, could have been a strong force for peace and genuine international order.

Meanwhile the Progressives' conduct of the war, as it developed after April 1917, seems in retrospect to have been as calculating as their espousal of the New Nationalism over the New Freedom. Once they had recovered from the shock of America's actual entrance into the European conflict, the old reform leaders again sought to promote their favorite programs. Although they had been in a number of instances formerly pacifists, many of the reformers, to their own surprise, as Allen Davis has shown, "came to view the war despite its horror and its dangers, as a climax and culmination of their movement for social justice in America."

Much of the economic planning vital to the war effort was reformist only by accident, but the social workers, along with businessmen, intellectuals, and Progressives in general, were caught up in the excitement of wartime Washington. Money was suddenly available, and for those on the inside there was the charm of being "a big shot," or what Harold Stearns later called the "Timidity and the Seductions of Office or Career." Progressives applauded the weakening of laissez faire carried out by the government's mobilization of industry and agriculture and its operation of the railroads. Still more they welcomed the war's encouragement of better labor standards, social insurance, improved urban housing, women's rights, jobs for Negroes, morals legislation, and prohibition of alcoholic beverages. Yet, as Davis demonstrates, "the progressives deluded themselves. They were the victims of their own confidence and enthusiasm, for the social reforms of the war years were caused more by the emergency situation than by a reform consensus. Quickly after the war, the Wilson Administration abandoned public housing and social insurance. . . . The gains for labor and the Negro proved ephemeral. . . . By 1920 there was little left from wartime social reform except prohibition, immigration restriction and racist hysteria."

More realistic, therefore, than the social reformers' visions of a reconstructed liberal America was the impetus that the war gave to a stronger paternalism and nationalism. Wartime government–business relations did little to disturb the essentials of capitalism or the soaring profit rates accompanying improved industrial production. Entrepreneurs like Bernard Baruch, head of the War Industries Board, and Daniel Willard, in charge of transportation, understood the importance of reconciling the interests of government and business. The kind of cooperation urged in the prewar years by the National Civic Federation now received, in the stress of hostilities, the accolade of Progressive sanction and support. Wartime regulations, marked by production quotas and price fixing, were carried out with the advice and consent of American industry. Moreover, governmental control of prices and markets tended to encourage the larger producers and manufacturers as distinct from the small businessmen. Industry also reaped the benefits of a wartime suspension of the antitrust acts, while labor's cooperation was secured by higher wages and patriotic restraints on strikes and work stoppages. The mobilization and disciplined control of the nation's labor force was further abetted by the threat of military conscription for nondeferred workers under the Selective Service Act of May 1917.

In view of its strong support among Progressives and businessmen, protest over the illiberal aspects of the war was left to a curious combination of radical intellectuals and old-fashioned conservatives. Among Wilson's supporters a few Jeffersonian Democrats like Frederic C. Howe, author of *Why War,* and William E. Dodd, the historian, protested against the economic interests behind the war and the danger that, as Dodd wrote, "the President would be compelled to adopt the very programme which Bismarck had employed in the building of imperialist Germany."

To a radical like Randolph Bourne, John Dewey's former disciple and most trenchant wartime critic, it was the intellectuals with their delusive hopes of change and reforms who were responsible for the war. At the same time, they failed to recognize clearly enough that the illiberalism, of which they complained, was part of the very nature of war. The discipline and organization needed to gain a military victory was hardly compatible with the ideals of a voluntary community or social democracy. Dewey's pragmatism, the philosophy that he relied on "almost as our American religion," no longer seemed to work. It is "inspiring enough," Bourne wrote, "for a society at peace, prosperous and with a fund of progressive good-will. . . . It is a scientific method applied to 'uplift.' " But he emphasized: "What concerns us here is the relative ease with which the pragmatist intellectuals, with Professor Dewey at the head, have moved out their philosophy, bag and baggage, from education to war." "Willing war," Bourne concluded, "means willing all the evils that are organically bound up with it."

Bourne's memorable phrase "War is the health of the state" was echoed by economists as radical as Thorstein Veblen and as conservative as Thomas Nixon Carver. Veblen, in his *Imperial Germany and the Industrial Revolution,* in noting the subserviency of the German community to the dynastic aims of the Hohenzollerns, observed that "chief of the agencies that have kept the submissive allegiance of the German people to the State intact is, of course, successful warfare, seconded by the disciplinary effects of warlike preparation and indoctrination with warlike arrogance and ambitions." This spirit was also carried over into peace, but what was a justifiable military discipline in war became a servile organization in peacetime. The Germans made duty their goal and ideal. Yet duty, Veblen pointed out, "of course, comprises the exercise of arbitrary command on the part of the superior as well as the obedience of the inferior. . . ."

Like Veblen, Thomas Nixon Carver, professor of economics at Harvard, in a wartime article entitled "Are We in Danger of Becoming Prussianized?" noted the German boasts of efficiency and organization. These, however, were not just German characteristics but an integral part of the process of war, which was a compulsory business from beginning to end. Indeed, the basic distinction in government was between a voluntary and compulsory process, and it therefore makes "more difference to the soldier," Carver asserted, "whether he volunteers or is drafted than whether he is drafted by a democracy, a republic, or a constitutional monarchy, either of the liberal or illiberal sort." The effective use of compulsory power required centralization:

> Already, in our war, along with the increased use of governmental authority has come a corresponding centralization of power. Centralization, carried to its logical and efficient extreme, results in Caesarism, Bonapartism, bureaucracy, Prussianism. However democratic the authoritarian may think that he is, or pretend to be, the very nature of his programme carries him logically and unavoidably toward that centralization of power which the world now calls Prussianism.

Carver complained that socialism, in contrast to liberalism or democracy, tended toward Prussianism, and he decried the way democracy was juggled about in wartime and used to justify compulsion. "Nothing," he wrote, "can be more democratic than a voluntary agreement. . . ." He admitted, however, that a compulsory system was probably necessary for the army in wartime even though voluntary arrangements were better for industry. Alarmed at what he felt were the symp-

toms of decline among liberal democratic nations at the hands
of militant strong ones, Carver, like Dewey, saw as a solution
the adoption of a system of voluntary community discipline to
take the place of compulsion by the state.

World War I, verging upon the later climax of the New
Deal and World War II, immensely stimulated the role of the
government as against the individual citizen. The federal controls demanded by Progressives in the 1900's as a part of a
program of reform were achieved after 1917 in connection
with a war economy. Regulation in the sense of trying to restore a competitive individualism now frankly yielded to regulation to achieve economic integration and greater industrial
efficiency. The war made partners of government and business, and the individual caught up in the rising tide of nationalism and patriotism could offer only feeble protest. Because
the new role of the state was subjected to less criticism in wartime, the Progressives and reformers could indulge themselves in the illusion of success and power. War offered the
supreme example of the classless national state, with country
above party and all particular or individual loyalties. Thus the
Progressive exhortations of sacrifice and duty, of social justice
at home, were easily translated into a crusade to make democracy and peace, and indeed all desired values, open to the rest
of the world.

In arguing the case for a more positive national state and
government, American Progressives, like the social democrats
in Europe, confused ends and means and were reduced finally to accepting war as the best way to institute social change
and reform. From their original revolt against corporate
power and the old formalistic absolutisms in thought, the
Progressives now had turned to the new Leviathan of the
modern warfare state. It was ironic, perhaps, that the final example of European social democracy to American Progressivism should have been this common experience of a world

war. But the war, it must be remembered, merely exaggerated the nationalism and statism already implicit in both American Progressivism and European social democracy. Thus the irony of Progressivism swallowed up in the fact of war was a paradox only for the more naïve and uninitiated children of America's past.

Bibliographical Essay

THE following bibliography includes the references on which I have relied most, as well as those secondary works deemed useful to the student who wishes to go further in his reading. It also locates sources not already specified in the text or generally familiar to scholars. I have not attempted, however, to duplicate the bibliography on *The Progressive Era and the Great War, 1896–1920,* compiled by Arthur S. Link and William M. Leary, Jr. (New York, 1969). This convenient and comprehensive work lists a wide range of books and articles arranged by subject.

The scholarly literature of the Progessive period is evaluated for the student in George E. Mowry, *The Progressive Era, 1900–1920: The Reform Persuasion,* American Historical Association Pamphlet Series (Washington, 1972) and in John D. Buenker, "The Progressive Era: A Search for a Synthesis," *Mid-America,* LI (July, 1969), 175–193.

Books available in paperback are marked with an asterisk (*) following the title.

CHAPTER 1   *Europe and America*

Useful for placing the Progressive Era within the context of United States history are such interpretive studies as Samuel P. Hays, *The Response to Industrialism, 1885–1914* * (Chicago, 1957); Ray Ginger, *The Age of Excess: The United States from 1877 to 1914* * (New York, 1965); Robert H. Wiebe, *The Search for Order, 1877–1920* * (New York, 1967); and Bernard A. Weisberger, *The New Industrial Society* * (New York, 1969).

George E. Mowry, "Social Democracy, 1900–1918," in C. Vann Woodward (ed.), *The Comparative Approach to American History* * (New York, 1968) is a suggestive essay that relates Progressivism to European developments. Robert Kelley adopts a similar comparative method for an earlier period in his book *The Transatlantic Persuasion: The Liberal–Democratic Mind in the Age of Gladstone* (New York, 1969). The European political and intellectual background is set forth in Carlton J. H. Hayes, *A Generation of Materialism, 1871–1900* * (New York, 1941) and Oron J. Hale, *The Great Illusion, 1900–1914* * (New York, 1971).

General works by Progressive historians, which provide contemporary appraisals, include Charles A. Beard's pioneer textbook, *Contemporary American History* (New York, 1914); Frederick Jackson Turner's essays, collected in *The Frontier in American History* * (New York, 1920); and Benjamin Parke De Witt, *The Progressive Movement,* * first published in 1915 and now reprinted with an introduction by Arthur Mann (Seattle, Wash., 1968).

David W. Noble, *The Paradox of Progressive Thought* (Minneapolis, Minn., 1958); Thomas L. Hartshorne, *The Distorted Image: Changing Conceptions of the American Character Since Turner* (Cleveland, Ohio, 1968); and Richard Hofstadter, *The Progressive Historians: Turner, Beard, Parrington* * (New York, 1968) offer interesting interpretations of the historiography of the period by intellectual historians. Sidney Fine, *Laissez Faire and the General-Welfare State* * (Ann Arbor, Mich., 1956) and Arthur A. Ekirch, Jr., *The Decline of American Liberalism* * (New York, 1955) take differing views of Progressivism in its relationship to liberal reform.

George Harvey is quoted from "The Editor's Diary," *North Ameri-*

can Review, CLXXXIII (October 19, 1906), 824, and Jane Addams from her *Newer Ideals of Peace* (New York, 1907), pp. 88, 123.

CHAPTER 2 *Insurgent Intellectuals*

The standard intellectual histories of the United States all devote considerable attention to Progressivist ideologies. Merle Curti, *The Growth of American Thought* (3rd ed.; New York, 1964) and Ralph H. Gabriel, *The Course of American Democratic Thought* (2nd ed.; New York, 1956) are classic general accounts. Of the works more specifically related to the Progressive Era, John Chamberlain's *Farewell to Reform* * (New York, 1932) is still a fascinating overview of thinkers and doers. Henry S. Commager, *The American Mind* * (New Haven, 1950) is good on literature and political thought; Eric F. Goldman, *Rendezvous with Destiny* * (New York, 1952) on politics and reform; and Morton White, *Social Thought in America* * (New York, 1949) on the philosophy of the major academic thinkers of the period. Merle Curti, *The Social Ideas of American Educators* * (New York, 1935) includes helpful chapters on James and Dewey. David W. Noble, *The Progressive Mind, 1890–1917* * (Chicago, 1970) is a brief topical interpretation of the period.

Jacques Barzun's *Darwin, Marx, Wagner: Critique of a Heritage* * (Boston, 1941) offers an interpretive study of the European intellectual background. Richard Hofstadter, *Social Darwinism in American Thought* * (rev. ed.; Boston, 1955) is the best account of its subject and the source of the quotation from Kropotkin. Also useful and broader in scope are the essays in Stow Persons (ed.), *Evolutionary Thought in America* (New Haven, 1950). The anthology *Darwin,* * edited by Philip Appleman (New York, 1970) includes selections from Darwin's writings as well as contemporary and scholarly summaries of his influence on science and social thought. Charles F. Thwing's *The American and the German University* (New York, 1928) is basic but should be supplemented by Jurgen Herbst, *The German Historical School in American Scholarship* (Ithaca, N.Y., 1965) and Richard T. Ely's memoir, *Ground Under Our Feet* (New York, 1938).

Special studies which I found helpful include Daniel M. Fox's Introduction to Simon N. Patten, *The New Basis of Civilization* (Cambridge, Mass., 1968); Frank D. Graham, "Ethnic and National Factors in the American Economic Ethic," in David F. Bowers (ed.), *Foreign Influences in American Life* * (Princeton, 1944); Sidney Fine, "Richard T. Ely, Forerunner of Progressivism, 1880–1901," *Mississippi Valley Historical Review*, XXXVII (March, 1951), 599–624; Benjamin G. Rader, *The Academic Mind and Reform: The Influence of Richard T. Ely in American Life* (Lexington, Ky., 1966).

The Ely quotations are from his memoir and his article "Fraternalism *vs.* Paternalism in Government," *Century*, LV (March, 1898), 780–784. The Patten quotation is from his *The New Basis of Civilization* (New York, 1907), pp. 25–26.

CHAPTER 3   *Populists and Socialists*

John D. Hicks, *The Populist Revolt* * (Minneapolis, Minn., 1931), the basic political history of the movement, and Norman Pollack, *The Populist Response to Industrial America* * (Cambridge, Mass., 1962), a brief interpretation, are favorable accounts, while Richard Hofstadter, *The Age of Reform from Bryan to F.D.R.* * (New York, 1955) illustrates recent criticism of the agrarians. Charles A. Barker, *Henry George* (New York, 1955); Paola E. Coletta, *William Jennings Bryan: Political Evangelist, 1860–1908* (Lincoln, Neb., 1964); and Arthur E. Morgan, *Edward Bellamy* (New York, 1944) are useful biographies of transitional figures.

Socialism in its varied manifestations, including European antecedents, is discussed at length by the contributors to Donald D. Egbert and Stow Persons (eds.), *Socialism and American Life* (2 vols.; Princeton, 1952). R. Laurence Moore, *European Socialists and the American Promised Land* (New York, 1970) is an excellent study of changing attitudes toward America. Howard H. Quint, *The Forging of American Socialism* * (Columbia, S.C., 1953) is especially good in relating Socialism to such other reform movements as Populism, Bellamy Nationalism, and the Social Gospel. Ira A. Kipnis, *The American Socialist Movement, 1897–1912* * (New York, 1952) and David A. Shannon, *The Socialist Party of America: A History* * (New York, 1955) cover the factionalism and political history of the party from differing points of view. See also James Gilbert, *Designing the Industrial State: The Intellectual Pursuit of Collectivism in America, 1880–1940* (Chicago, 1972).

For the British Fabians see George Bernard Shaw (ed.), *Fabian Essays in Socialism* (London, 1889); Henry Pelling (ed.), *The Challenge of Socialism* (London, 1954); and Pelling, *America and the British Left* (London, 1956).

Periodical sources include: Hamlin Garland and B. O. Flower in the *Arena*, III (January, 1891), 159, and VIII (July, 1893), 260; Eugene Debs, *Independent*, LII (August 23, 1900), 2018; O. G. Villard, *Nation*, LXXX (April 27, 1905), 324–325; editorial, *Independent*, LV (August 27, 1903), 2067–2068; W. J. Bryan, *Century*, LXXI (April, 1906), 856–859; R. H. Hoxie, *Journal of Political Economy*, XIX (October, 1911), 623–624; S. P. Orth, *World's Work*, XXIV (August, 1912), 459.

Edmond Kelly is quoted from his books *Government or Human Evolution* (New York, 1900–1901), II, 1–2, and *Twentieth Century Socialism* (New York, 1910), p. 3. H. D. Lloyd's comment on Socialism is from Caro Lloyd, *Henry Demarest Lloyd* (New York, 1912), I, 295; Theodore Roosevelt's from his *Letters,* edited by Elting E. Morison and John M. Blum (Cambridge, Mass., 1951–1954), IV, 1113; and Morris Hillquit's from his *Socialism in Theory and Practice* (New York, 1909), p. 193.

CHAPTER 4 *Urban Evangelists*

On the Social Gospel and Christian Socialism, Aaron I. Abell, *The Urban Impact on American Protestantism, 1865–1900* (Cambridge, Mass., 1943); Charles H. Hopkins, *The Rise of the Social Gospel in American Protestantism, 1865–1915* * (New Haven, 1940); and Henry F. May, *Protestant Churches and Industrial America* * (New York, 1949) are authoritative works. Also helpful are the biographical studies by Jacob H. Dorn, *Washington Gladden: Prophet of the Social Gospel* (Columbus, Ohio, 1967) and Vernon P. Bodein, *The Social Gospel of Walter Rauschenbusch* (New Haven, 1944). The Catholic affirmation of social reform without socialism is developed in Aaron I. Abell, *American Catholicism and Social Action: A Search for Social Justice, 1865–1950* * (Garden City, N.Y., 1960).

Trends in American literature are evaluated in terms of their social significance in Alfred Kazin, *On Native Grounds: An Interpretation of Modern American Prose Literature* * (New York, 1942); Grant C. Knight, *The Strenuous Age in American Literature* (Chapel Hill, N.C., 1954); Frederic C. Jaher, *Doubters and Dissenters: Cataclysmic Thought in America, 1865–1918* (New York, 1964); and John G. Cawelti, *Apostles of the Self-Made Man* * (Chicago, 1965). Louis Filler, *Crusaders for American Liberalism* * (New York, 1939) is still the best full account of the muckrakers, but also useful are the excellent anthology by Arthur and Lila Weinberg, *The Muckrakers* * (New York, 1961) and the brief studies of David M. Chalmers, *The Social and Political Ideas of the Muckrakers* * (New York, 1964) and Stanley K. Schultz, "The Morality of Politics: The Muckrakers' Vision of Democracy," *Journal of American History*, LII (December, 1965), 527–547.

Josiah Strong's remark is from his book *The Twentieth Century City* (New York, 1898), p. 121.

CHAPTER 5   *The Crusade for Social Justice*

Harold U. Faulkner, *The Quest for Social Justice, 1898–1914* * (New York, 1931) remains the most comprehensive book on Progressive social reforms. Its coverage has been extended recently by a number of more specialized studies. On poverty the best work is Robert H. Bremner, *From the Depths: The Discovery of Poverty in the United States* * (New York, 1956). Bremner's more general *American Philanthropy* * (Chicago, 1960) provides a helpful interpretation and synthesis. Allen F. Davis, *Spearheads for Reform: The Social Settlements and the Progressive Movement, 1890–1914* * (New York, 1967) is the most scholarly study, but the earlier account of Arthur C. Holden, *The Settlement Idea: A Vision of Social Justice* (New York, 1922) contains useful material.

Roy Lubove has written three important books related to the field of social work: *The Progressives and the Slums: Tenement House*

Reform in New York City, 1890–1917 (Pittsburgh, 1962); *The Professional Altruist: The Emergence of Social Work as a Career, 1880–1930* * (Cambridge, Mass., 1965); and *The Struggle for Social Security, 1900–1935* (Cambridge, Mass., 1968). Walter I. Trattner, *Crusade for the Children: A History of the National Child Labor Committee and Child Labor Reform in America* (Chicago, 1970) is a well-documented account. Clarke A. Chambers, *Seedtime of Reform: American Social Service and Social Action, 1918–1933* * (Minneapolis, Minn., 1963) carries the story of social justice beyond the Progressive Era to the New Deal.

For the leading social reformers there are a number of memoirs and biographies. Of their own books, Jane Addams's writings are the best known. See especially *Twenty Years at Hull-House* * (New York, 1910). Her *Newer Ideals of Peace,* cited in Chapter 1, is the source of her comment on urban life. Arthur Mann, "British Social Thought and American Reformers of the Progressive Era," *Mississippi Valley Historical Review,* XLII (March, 1956), 672–692, establishes the influence of English ideas on American reformers.

Lawrence A. Cremin, *The Transformation of the School: Progressivism in American Education, 1876–1957* * (New York, 1961) is the authoritative work on its subject. The transformation of education in an industrial society is also discussed in Raymond E. Callahan, *Education and the Cult of Efficiency* * (Chicago, 1962); Merle Curti and Roderick Nash, *Philanthropy in the Shaping of American Higher Education* (New Brunswick, N.J., 1965); Richard Hofstadter and Walter P. Metzger, *The Development of Academic Freedom* * (New York, 1955); Joel H. Spring, *Education and the Rise of the Corporate State* * (Boston, 1972); and Laurence R. Veysey, *The Emergence of the American University* * (Chicago, 1965).

Prejudice against the immigrant is analyzed in detail in John W. Higham, *Strangers in the Land: Patterns of American Nativism, 1860–1925* * (New Brunswick, N.J., 1955), and against a broader background in Oscar Handlin, *Race and Nationality in American Life* * (Boston, 1957), and E. Digby Baltzell, *The Protestant Establishment: Aristocracy & Caste in America* * (New York, 1964).

The particular problems of the South regarding the relationship of race and education to social justice are well treated in Louis R. Harlan, *Separate and Unequal: Public School Campaigns and Racism in* *the Southern Seaboard States, 1901–1915* * (Chapel Hill, N.C., 1958) and in Henry Allen Bullock, *A History of Negro Education in the South from 1619 to the Present* * (Cambridge, Mass., 1967). See also the more general accounts by John Hope Franklin, *From Slavery to Freedom: A History of American Negroes* * (New York, 1947); August Meier, *Negro Thought in America, 1880–1915: Racial Ideologies in the Age of Booker T. Washington* * (Ann Arbor, Mich. 1963); Dewey W. Grantham, Jr., "The Progressive Movement and the Negro," *South Atlantic Quarterly*, LIV (October, 1955), 461–477. Gilbert Osofsky, "Progressivism and the Negro: New York, 1900–1915," *American Quarterly*, XVI (Summer, 1964), 153–168; and Seth M. Scheiner, *Negro Mecca: A History of the Negro in New York City, 1865–1920* * (New York, 1965) are informative local studies which transcend the New York area.

CHAPTER 6   *Forces of Urban Liberalism*

A broad general background is provided in Lewis Mumford, *The City in History* * (New York, 1961). For the United States, more specific material may be found in Constance M. Green, *American Cities in the Growth of the Nation* * (New York, 1957) and in Morton G. and Lucia White, *The Intellectual Versus the City: From Thomas Jefferson to Frank Lloyd Wright* * (Cambridge, Mass., 1962). R. G. Tugwell and E. C. Banfield, "Governmental Planning at Mid Century," *Journal of Politics*, XIII (May, 1953), 133–163, is a thoughtful overview.

Comprehensive period studies include Blake McKelvey, *The Urbanization of America, 1860–1915* (New Brunswick, N.J., 1963) and Arthur M. Schlesinger, *The Rise of the City, 1878–1898* * (New York, 1933). Faulkner, *The Quest for Social Justice*, cited in Chapter 5, includes urban problems, as do Russel B. Nye, *Midwestern Progressive Politics* * (East Lansing, Mich., 1951) and Hoyt L. Warner, *Progressivism in Ohio, 1897–1917* (Columbus, Ohio, 1964), both good regional studies.

Oscar Handlin, *The Uprooted* * (Boston, 1951) interprets the immigrant's role in urban reform. J. Joseph Huthmacher, "Urban Liberalism and the Age of Reform," *Mississippi Valley Historical Review*, XLIX (September, 1962), 231–241, overstates his case and provides little documentation for the thesis that urban labor and immigrants, rather than middle-class reformers, were the major influence upon Progressivism. I find Roy Lubove, "The Twentieth Century City: The Progressive as Municpal Reformer," *Mid-America*, XLI (October, 1959), 195–209, more convincing than Wayne E. Fuller, "The Rural Roots of the Progressive Leaders," *Agricultural History*, XLII (January, 1968), 1–13.

The views of the earlier mugwump liberal reformers are covered in John G. Sproat, *The Best Men: Liberal Reformers in the Gilded Age* * (New York, 1968). James Weinstein, *The Corporate Ideal in the Liberal State, 1900–1918* * (Boston, 1968) has a good chapter on the business interest in better city government. Also excellent are Samuel P. Hays, "The Politics of Reform in Municipal Government in the Progressive Era," *Pacific Northwest Quarterly*, LV (October, 1964), 157–169; Richard Skolnik, "Civic Group Progressivism in New York City," *New York History*, LI (July, 1970), 411–439; James B. Crooks, *Politics and Progress: The Rise of Urban Progressivism in Baltimore, 1895–1911* (Baton Rouge, La., 1968).

On the status-revolution thesis, see especially Hofstadter, *The Age of Reform*, cited in Chapter 3; Alfred D. Chandler, Jr., "The Origins of Progressive Leadership," Appendix III, vol. VIII, pp. 1462–1465, of Morison and Blum (eds.), *The Letters of Theodore Roosevelt*, cited in Chapter 3; and George E. Mowry, *The California Progressives* * (Berkeley, Calif., 1951). Examples of a recent criticism and defense of the thesis are Jack Tager, "Progressives, Conservatives and the Theory of the Status Revolution," *Mid-America*, XLVIII (July, 1966), 162–175, and Bonnie R. Fox, "The Philadelphia Progressives: A Test of the Hofstadter–Hays Theses," *Pennsylvania History*, XXXIV (October, 1967), 372–394.

Contemporary opinion is quoted from: Charles B. Spahr, *An Essay on the Present Distribution of Wealth* (New York, 1896); L. S. Rowe, *American Journal of Sociology*, XI (July, 1905), 75–84; Frederic C. Howe, *The City the Hope of Democracy* * (New York, 1905), pp. 7, 86, 114; J. Allen Smith, *The Spirit of American Government* (New York, 1907), p. 355; Tom L. Johnson, *My Story* (New York, 1911), p. xxxv; Albert Shaw, *Municipal Government in Great Britain* (New York, 1895), pp. 1–2, 7–8, 18–19; Shaw, *Municipal Government* *in Continental Europe* (New York, 1895), pp. 291, 323; Howe, *The British City: The Beginnings of Democracy* (New York, 1907), p. xi; Howe, *The Modern City and Its Problems* (New York, 1915), p. 4. See also Howe, *European Cities at Work* (New York, 1913).

Lincoln Steffens, *The Shame of the Cities* * (New York, 1904) and *The Autobiography of Lincoln Steffens* * (New York, 1931) are classics well worth reading, as is Howe's *The Confessions of a Reformer* * (New York, 1925).

CHAPTER 7   *The States as Laboratories of Reform*

The Progressives' concern with efficiency and organization in government regulation and reform is discussed in Hofstadter's *Age of Reform,* cited in Chapter 6, which gives as much attention to these questions as it does to status. Samuel Haber, *Efficiency and Uplift: Scientific Management in the Progressive Era, 1890–1920* * (Chicago, 1964) is an important study. Paul P. Van Riper, *History of the United States Civil Service* (Evanston, Ill., 1958) and Marver H. Bernstein, *Regulating Business by Independent Commission* * (Princeton, 1955) are standard references. Also useful is Stephen E. Ambrose (ed.), *Institutions in Modern America* (Baltimore, 1967), from whom I quote at the end of the chapter. Weinstein, *The Corporate Ideal in the Liberal State,* cited in Chapter 6, is a series of case studies showing the influence of the business ethos on Progressivism.

Superior studies of individual states include: Mowry, *The California Progressives* and Warner, *Progressivism in Ohio,* both cited in Chapter 6; Richard M. Abrams, *Conservatism in a Progressive Era: Massachusetts Politics, 1900–1912* (Cambridge, Mass., 1964); Winston A. Flint, *The Progressive Movement in Vermont* (Washington, D.C., 1941); Ransom E. Noble, Jr., *New Jersey Progressivism Before Wilson* (Princeton, 1946); Robert F. Wesser, *Charles Evans Hughes: Politics and Reform in New York, 1905–1910* (Ithaca, N.Y., 1967); Robert S. Maxwell, *La Follette and the Rise of the Progressives in Wisconsin* (Madison, Wis., 1956).

On the Wisconsin Idea, see Merle Curti and Vernon Carstensen, *The University of Wisconsin* (2 vols.; Madison, Wis., 1949) and the contemporary books by Frederic C. Howe, *Wisconsin: An Experiment in Democracy* (New York, 1912) and Charles McCarthy, *The Wisconsin Idea* (New York, 1912). Ransom E. Noble, Jr., "Henry George and the Progressive Movement," *American Journal of Economics and Sociology*, VIII (April, 1949), 259–269, shows George's influence upon reformers in Oregon, Ohio, and New Jersey.

Valuable broader studies that devote attention to the states include Faulkner, *The Quest for Social Justice*, cited in Chapter 6; George E. Mowry, *The Era of Theodore Roosevelt, 1900–1912* * (New York, 1958); Nye, *Midwestern Progressive Politics*, cited in Chapter 6; C. Vann Woodward, *Origins of the New South, 1877–1913* * (Baton Rouge, La., 1951); Arthur S. Link, "The Progressive Movement in the South, 1870–1914," *North Carolina Historical Review*, XXIII (April, 1946), 172–195; Hugh C. Bailey, *Liberalism in the New South: Southern Social Reformers and the Progressive Movement* (Coral Gables, Fla., 1969); Daniel Levine, *Varieties of Reform Thought* * (Madison, Wis., 1964). De Witt's contemporary work, *The Progressive Movement*, cited in Chapter 1, is also useful.

Labor developments are traced in Gerald N. Grob, *Workers and Utopia: A Study of Ideological Conflict in the American Labor Movement, 1865–1900* * (Evanston, Ill., 1961); Philip Taft, *The A.F. of L. in the Time of Gompers* (New York, 1957); Marc Karson, *American Labor Unions and Politics, 1900–1918* (Carbondale, Ill., 1958); Irwin Yellowitz, *Labor and the Progressive Movement in New York State, 1897–1916* (Ithaca, N.Y., 1965). Milton J. Nadworny, *Scientific Management and the Unions, 1900–1932: A Historical Analysis* (Cambridge, Mass., 1955) and Milton Derber, "The Idea of Industrial Democracy in America, 1898–1915," *Labor History*, VII (Fall, 1966), 259–286, discuss special aspects of labor's role. Philip S. Foner, *History of the Labor Movement in the United States*, * vols. III and IV (New York, 1964–1965) offers a radical critique of both the A.F. of L. and the IWW.

Woman's rights, including the suffrage, are covered in Eleanor Flexner, *Century of Struggle: The Woman's Rights Movement in the United States* * (Cambridge, Mass., 1959) and Aileen S. Kraditor, *The Ideas of the Woman Suffrage Movement, 1890–1920* * (New York, 1965).

On the question of direct democracy versus administrative control, I have drawn upon sources quoted in Chapter 8 of my *The Amer-*

ican Democratic Tradition: A History * (New York, 1963). See also the
revisionist articles by John D. Buenker, "Progressivism in Practice:
New York State and the Federal Income Tax Amendment," *New
York Historical Society Quarterly,* LII (April, 1968), 139–160; "The
Urban Political Machine and the Seventeenth Amendment," *Journal
of American History,* LVI (September, 1969), 305–322.

The citations of liberal complaint over censorious reforms are
from: Albert B. Hart, *National Ideals Historically Traced* (New York,
1907), p. 82; Brand Whitlock, *Forty Years of It* (New York, 1914), p.
303; Allan Nevins (ed.), *The Letters and Journal of Brand Whitlock* (New
York, 1936), I, 97–100, 168; Albert Jay Nock, *Memoirs of a Superflu-
ous Man* * (New York, 1943), pp. 117–120.

Important secondary works include: James H. Timberlake, *Prohibition and the Progressive Movement, 1900–1920* * (Cambridge, Mass.,
1963); William L. O'Neill, *Divorce in the Progressive Era* * (New
Haven, 1967); and Nathan G. Hale, Jr., *Freud and the Americans: The
Beginnings of Psychoanalysis in the United States, 1876–1917* (New York,
1971). The interesting, though tendentious, articles of James R.
McGovern, "The American Woman's Pre-World War I Freedom in
Manners and Morals," *Journal of American History,* LV (September,
1968), 315–333, and John C. Burnham, "The Progressive Era Revolution in American Attitudes toward Sex," *Journal of American History,* LIX (March, 1973), 885–908, show an increasing liberalization,
especially after 1910, but hardly a revolution in the Progressives' attitudes toward sex until, at least, the World War I period.

CHAPTER 8   *T.R.: The Leader of the Band*

The highly critical view of Theodore Roosevelt by his earlier
scholarly biographers has been modified in recent years. In that first
group is Henry F. Pringle, *Theodore Roosevelt: A Biography* * (New
York, 1931), from which I have taken the remarks by Henry Adams
and Secretary John D. Long. Other older works, equally harsh in
their portraits of T.R., which remain valuable studies of the galaxy
of Progressives are Matthew Josephson, *The President Makers* (New
York, 1940) and Daniel Aaron, *Men of Good Hope: A Story of American*

Progressives * (New York, 1951). Additional comments on T.R. are from: Donald Richberg, *Tents of the Mighty* (New York, 1930), p. 34; Walter Lippmann, *A Preface to Politics* * (New York, 1913), p. 98; Ross E. Paulson, *Radicalism and Reform: The Vrooman Family and American Social Thought* (Lexington, Ky., 1968), p. 17.

A basic work, useful throughout, is George E. Mowry, *The Era of Theodore Roosevelt,* cited in Chapter 7. William H. Harbaugh, *Power and Responsibility: The Life and Times of Theodore Roosevelt* * (New York, 1961), the most authoritative biography, interprets T.R. as a forerunner of the modern welfare state. John M. Blum's excellent brief account, *The Republican Roosevelt* * (Cambridge, Mass., 1954), emphasizes his contribution as a politician and administrator. G. Wallace Chessman, *Theodore Roosevelt and the Politics of Power* * (Boston, 1969) is another short study, somewhat broader in scope than Blum's book. Morton Keller (ed.), *Theodore Roosevelt: A Profile* * (New York, 1967) is a useful collection of familiar essays. Seth M. Scheiner, "President Theodore Roosevelt and the Negro, 1901–1908," *Journal of Negro History,* XLVII (July, 1962), 169–182, is a good summary.

In addition to Roosevelt's messages to Congress, I have used his *Letters,* cited in Chapter 3, especially I, 600; III, 8; V, 351; VI, 1401; VII, 185; VIII, 1253; his articles including *Century,* LIX (January, 1900), 471; *Outlook,* XCI (March 27, 1909), 662–664; *ibid.,* XCIV (April 30, 1910), 988; and his book *Foes of Our Own Household* (New York, 1917), pp. 85, 92. See also Harbaugh's convenient anthology, *The Writings of Theodore Roosevelt* * (Indianapolis, Ind., 1967).

CHAPTER 9 *The Uses of Public Power*

The competition of public and private power as a legacy of Progressivism is analyzed by Grant McConnell, *Private Power and American Democracy* * (New York, 1966). The influence of conservative business interests upon Progressive legislation and economic thought is the subject of Gabriel Kolko, *The Triumph of Conservatism* * (Glencoe, Ill., 1963) and Robert H. Wiebe, *Businessmen and Reform* * (Cambridge, Mass., 1962). My quotation from Wiebe is from his more recent book, *The Search for Order,* cited in Chapter 1. Harold U.

Faulkner, *The Decline of Laissez Faire, 1897–1917* * (New York, 1951) offers a more traditional view of the significance of Progressive reforms.

Mark Sullivan, *Our Times: The United States, 1900–1925*, vol. II, *America Finding Herself* * (New York, 1927) is filled with useful data concerning T.R. and the trusts. Other sources quoted include: Roscoe Pound, "Common Law and Legislation," *Harvard Law Review*, XXI (April, 1908), 384; John Bates Clark, *The Control of the Trusts* (New York, 1901), p. 16; Clark, "The Real Dangers of the Trusts," *Century*, LXVIII (October, 1904), 956–957; Rudolf Roesler, "Attitude of German People and Government Towards Trusts," *Annals of the American Academy of Political and Social Science*, XLII (July, 1912), 182. George W. Perkins's unpublished address, *The Modern Corporation*, is in the Columbia University Library.

The discussion of conservation as part of the Progressive movement draws upon my book *Man and Nature in America* * (New York, 1963). Valuable secondary authorities offering different interpretations of the significance of conservation are Samuel P. Hays, *Conservation and the Gospel of Efficiency: The Progressive Conservation Movement, 1890–1920* * (Cambridge, Mass., 1959); J. L. Bates, "Fulfilling American Democracy: The Conservation Movement, 1907–1921," *Mississippi Valley Historical Review*, XLIV (June, 1957), 29–57; Erich W. Zimmermann, *World Resources and Industries* (New York, 1933). Gifford Pinchot, *The Fight for Conservation* * (New York, 1910) and Charles R. Van Hise, *The Conservation of Natural Resources in the United States* (New York, 1910) are the two most important and influential contemporary books. See also Harold T. Pinkett, *Gifford Pinchot: Private and Public Forester* (Urbana, Ill., 1970).

CHAPTER 10   *The Solemn Referendum*

The roles of the two major protagonists in the 1912 election are studied in detail in George E. Mowry, *Theodore Roosevelt and the Progressive Movement* * (Madison, Wis., 1946) and Arthur S. Link,

Wilson: The Road to the White House * (Princeton, 1947). Link, *Woodrow Wilson and the Progressive Era, 1910–1917* * (New York, 1954); John M. Blum, *The Republican Roosevelt,* cited in Chapter 8; and Blum, *Woodrow Wilson and the Politics of Morality* * (Boston, 1956) provide excellent brief interpretations from which I have quoted. Taft and La Follette may be followed in Kenneth W. Hechler, *Insurgency: Personalities and Politics of the Taft Era* (New York, 1940) and Nye, *Midwestern Progressive Politics,* cited in Chapter 7. Ray Ginger, *The Bending Cross: A Biography of Eugene Victor Debs* * (New Brunswick, N.J., 1949) is a good personal portrait.

Herbert Croly's important intellectual contribution via *The Promise of American Life* * (New York, 1909) is analyzed thoroughly by Charles Forcey, *The Crossroads of Liberalism: Croly, Weyl, Lippmann and the Progressive Era, 1900–1925* * (New York, 1961) and more briefly in Eric F. Goldman's *Rendezvous with Destiny,* cited in Chapter 2. The quoted review of the *Promise* is from the *Political Science Quarterly,* XXV (December, 1910), 688. Roosevelt's letter to Amos Pinchot, August 18, 1908, and Pinchot's letter of September 1, 1910, commenting on the Osawatomie speech, are both in the Amos Pinchot Collection in the Library of Congress.

Elihu Root's criticism of the recall of judges is in *The Independent,* LXXII (April 4, 1912), 704–707. T.R. replied in his address at Philadelphia on April 10, 1912. Donald R. Richberg's comment on T.R.'s defeat is quoted from his book *My Hero: The Indiscreet Memoirs of an Eventful but Unheroic Life* (New York, 1954), p. 51; Norman Hapgood's from his *The Advancing Hour* (New York, 1920), p. 71. The *Nation* critique is from the issue of September 5, 1913.

Wilson's intellectual development may be traced through his articles and speeches, especially: "Politics," *Atlantic Monthly,* C (November, 1907), 635–646; *The New Freedom* * (New York, 1913); E. David Cronon (ed.), *The Political Thought of Woodrow Wilson* * (Indianapolis, Ind., 1965); John W. Davidson (ed.), *A Crossroads of Freedom: The 1912 Campaign Speeches of Woodrow Wilson* (New Haven, 1956). William Diamond, *The Economic Thought of Woodrow Wilson* (Baltimore, 1943) is broader than its title. Ely's criticism of his former student is from his memoir, *Ground Under Our Feet,* cited in Chapter 2.

CHAPTER 11   *Hands Across the Seas*

The close relationship of reform ideals at home to expansion abroad is the theme of the influential article by William E. Leuchtenburg, "Progressivism and Imperialism," *Mississippi Valley Historical Review*, XXXIX (December, 1952), 483–504. Also important in developing aspects of this thesis is Robert E. Osgood, *Ideals and Self-Interest in America's Foreign Relations* * (Chicago, 1953). Charles A. Beard, *The Idea of National Interest* * (New York, 1934) and *The Open Door at Home* (New York, 1934); Walter La Feber, *The New Empire: An Interpretation of American Expansion, 1860–1898* * (Ithaca, N.Y., 1963); and William A. Williams, *The Roots of the Modern American Empire* * (New York, 1969) stress the economic forces in American expansion. Albert K. Weinberg, *Manifest Destiny: A Study of Nationalist Expansionism in American History* * (Baltimore, 1935) is a classic work. Useful, though more limited in scope, is David Healy, *US Expansionism: The Imperialist Urge in the 1890s* (Madison, Wis., 1970).

In contrast to the Beardians is the emphasis on diplomacy and ideology in Ernest R. May, *Imperial Democracy: The Emergence of America as a Great Power* * (New York, 1961); May, *American Imperialism: A Speculative Essay* (New York, 1968); and Julius W. Pratt, *Expansionists of 1898* * (Baltimore, 1936). Transatlantic cross currents in intellectual history are explored by Richard H. Heindel, *The American Impact on Great Britain, 1898–1914* (Philadelphia, 1940) and Bradford Perkins, *The Great Rapprochement: England and the United States, 1895–1914* (New York, 1968). Useful general accounts are Foster Rhea Dulles, *America's Rise to World Power, 1898–1954* * (New York, 1955) and Arthur A. Ekirch, Jr., *Ideas, Ideals, and American Diplomacy* * (New York, 1966).

On anti-imperialism see the articles by Fred H. Harrington, "The Anti-Imperialist Movement in the United States, 1898–1900," *Mississippi Valley Historical Review*, XXII (September, 1935), 211–230; and "Literary Aspects of American Anti-Imperialism, 1898–1902," *New England Quarterly*, X (December, 1937), 650–667; as well as the recent studies by Robert L. Beisner, *Twelve Against Empire: The Anti-Imperialists, 1898–1900* * (New York, 1968) and E. Berkeley Tompkins,

Anti-Imperialism in the United States: The Great Debate, 1890–1920 * (Philadelphia, 1970). For the equivocal attitude toward imperialism on the part of American and British radicals, see Howard H. Quint, "American Socialists and the Spanish-American War," *American Quarterly*, X (Summer, 1958), 131–141; Henry Pelling, *The Origins of the Labour Party, 1880–1900* (Oxford, 1954); and G. D. H. Cole, *The Second International, 1889–1914*, vol. III, part 1, *A History of Socialist Thought* (London, 1956).

Howard K. Beale, *Theodore Roosevelt and the Rise of America to World Power* * (Baltimore, 1956) is the most important biographical study of the imperialist mind. Also helpful are Claude G. Bowers, *Beveridge and the Progressive Era* (Boston, 1932); Arthur F. Beringause, *Brooks Adams* (New York, 1955); Henry D. Cater, *Henry Adams and His Friends* (Boston, 1947); and David H. Burton, *Theodore Roosevelt: Confident Imperialist* (Philadelphia, 1968). Leuchtenburg's thesis is modified, but not refuted, in the studies by Padraic C. Kennedy, "La Follette's Imperialist Flirtation," *Pacific Historical Review*, XXIX (May, 1960), 131–144; Barton J. Bernstein and Franklin A. Lieb, "Progressive Republican Senators and American Imperialism, 1898–1916: A Reappraisal," *Mid-America*, L (July, 1968), 163–205.

Original material is quoted from: Edward Dicey, *Nineteenth Century*, XLIV (September, 1898), 487–501; W. J. Ghent, *Independent*, LII (June 14, 1900), 1439–1442; W. A. Peffer, *North American Review*, CLXXI (August, 1900), 246–258; Franklin Pierce, *Federal Usurpation* (New York, 1908), p. 152; H. O. Mahin (ed.), *The Editor and His People: Editorials by William Allen White* (New York, 1924), pp. 304–306; Theodore Roosevelt, *Independent*, LI (December 21, 1899), 3401–3405; and Roosevelt, *Letters*, cited previously, I, 763–764; IV, 1174.

CHAPTER 12 *The New Navalism and Incipient Militarism*

Harold and Margaret Sprout, *The Rise of American Naval Power* * (Princeton, 1939) and George T. Davis, *A Navy Second to None* (New

York, 1940) cover fully the development of American naval policy. On Mahan consult also W. E. Livezey, *Mahan on Sea Power* (Norman, Okla., 1947); W. D. Puleston, *Mahan* (New Haven, 1939); and Mahan's collected articles in *The Interest of America in Sea Power* (Boston, 1911).

C. Vann Woodward, "The Age of Reinterpretation," *American Historical Review,* LXVI (October, 1960), 1–19; and Walter Millis, *Arms and Men: A Study in American Military History* * (New York, 1956) offer penetrating comments on American military policy. Alfred Vagts, *A History of Militarism* * (New York, 1937), the standard work, devotes little attention to the United States. Secretary Root's role is assessed in Richard W. Leopold, *Elihu Root and the Conservative Tradition* * (Boston, 1954) and, less favorably, in my article "The Idea of a Citizen Army," *Military Affairs,* XVII (Spring, 1953), 30–36. Additional source material is taken from my book *The Civilian and the Military* * (New York, 1956).

CHAPTER 13   *The Paradox of Peace*

Merle Curti, *Peace or War: The American Struggle, 1636–1936* (New York, 1936) is still the best overall history of the American peace movement. Sondra R. Herman, *Eleven Against War: Studies in American Internationalist Thought, 1898–1921* * (Stanford, Calif., 1969) analyzes the interest in world cooperation through case studies of prominent American intellectuals. Somewhat broader in scope is Warren F. Kuehl, *Seeking World Order: The United States and International Organization to 1920* (Nashville, Tenn., 1969). Calvin D. Davis, *The United States and the First Hague Conference* (Ithaca, N.Y., 1962) points out well the paradox of the great powers preparing for war while talking peace.

The conservative, quasi-official nature of the growing peace movement of the early 1900's is described in Barbara S. Kraft, "Peacemaking in the Progressive Era: A Prestigious and Proper Calling," *Maryland Historian,* I (Fall, 1970), 121–144, and in more comprehensive detail in C. Roland Marchand, *The American Peace Movement and Social Reform, 1898–1918* (Princeton, 1972). Ira V.

Brown, *Lyman Abbott Christian Evolutionist: A Study in Religious Liberalism* (Cambridge, Mass., 1953) delineates Abbott's equivocal advocacy of peace. Lloyd C. Gardner, "American Foreign Policy, 1900–1921: A Second Look at the Realist Critique of American Diplomacy," in Barton J. Bernstein (ed.), *Towards a New Past* * (New York, 1968), argues that the Progressives' espousal of international arbitration was recognition of the need for world peace if America's expanding trade was to prosper.

For the Taft and Wilson views on peace and arbitration, see Henry F. Pringle, *The Life and Times of William Howard Taft* (2 vols.; New York, 1939) and Harley Notter, *The Origins of the Foreign Policy of Woodrow Wilson* (Baltimore, 1937).

CHAPTER 14 *Woodrow Wilson*

The basic work is Link, *Woodrow Wilson and the Progressive Era*, cited in Chapter 10. See also Link, *Woodrow Wilson: The New Freedom* * (Princeton, 1956). An older general account is Frederic L. Paxson, *Pre-War Years, 1913–1917* (Boston, 1936). My interpretation has benefited from the incisive article by Melvin I. Urofsky, "Wilson, Brandeis and the Trust Issue, 1912–1914," *Mid-America*, XLIX (January, 1967), 3–28. Urofsky's comment on the significance of the FTC is from his book *Big Steel and the Wilson Administration: A Study in Business–Government Relations* (Columbus, Ohio, 1969). See also Martin J. Sklar, "Woodrow Wilson and the Political Economy of Modern United States Liberalism," reprinted from *Studies on the Left* (1960) in *A New History of Leviathan* *, edited by Ronald Radosh and Murray N. Rothbard (New York, 1972).

Wilson's views on public administration and leadership in a democracy are developed in his articles "The Study of Administration," *Political Science Quarterly*, II (June, 1887), 197–222; "Character of Democracy in the United States," *Atlantic Monthly*, LXIV (November, 1889), 577–588; "Democracy and Efficiency," *ibid.*, LXXXVII (March, 1901), 289–299.

On the race question there are brief summaries in Link, as cited above, and in Kathleen L. Wolgemuth, "Woodrow Wilson and Federal Segregation," *Journal of Negro History,* XLIV (April, 1959), 158–173. The best treatment of the attitude of Negro leaders and of Villard's role, with a thorough use of the latter's letters to and from Wilson, is in Charles F. Kellogg, *NAACP: A History of the National Association for the Advancement of Colored People,* vol. I, 1909–1920 (Baltimore, 1967). See also Villard's article "The President and the Segregation at Washington," *North American Review,* CXCVIII (December, 1913), 800–807.

CHAPTER 15 *Troubled Neutrality*

For Wilson's foreign policy the most authoritative work is Arthur S. Link's biography, *Wilson: The Struggle for Neutrality, 1914–1915; Wilson: Confusions and Crises, 1915–1916;* and *Wilson: Campaigns for Progressivism and Peace, 1916–1917* (3 vols.; Princeton, 1960–1965). Link, *Woodrow Wilson and the Progressive Era,* cited previously, offers a briefer treatment. In my own interpretation I have also been guided by Ernest R. May, *The World War and American Isolation, 1914–1917 ** (Cambridge, Mass., 1959). The older work by Walter Millis, *Road to War: America, 1914–1917* (Boston, 1935), strongly anti-Wilson, provides a full account of popular feelings. Paul Birdsall, "Neutrality and Economic Pressures, 1914–1917," *Science and Society,* III (Spring, 1939), 217–228, is a convincing analysis of the way American wartime trade influenced the thinking of the German navalists and statesmen.

The views of the American preparedness advocates and their opponents are drawn from my *The Civilian and the Military,* cited in Chapter 12. Millis, *Arms and Men,* also cited therein, provides additional background information. Herbert Croly, "The Effect on American Institutions of a Powerful Military and Naval Establishment," *Annals of the American Academy of Political and Social Science,* LXVI (July, 1916), 157–172, sums up his opinions on preparedness. The story of Wilson's private confession of his desire for peace is told in Joseph P. Tumulty, *Woodrow Wilson As I Know Him* (Garden City, N.Y., 1925), p. 158.

Charles Hirschfeld, "Nationalist Progressivism and World

War I," *Mid-America,* XLV (July, 1963), 139–156, is a key article. A different view that stresses the Progressives' opposition to preparedness is John M. Cooper, Jr., "Progressivism and American Foreign Policy: A Reconsideration," *Mid-America,* LI (October, 1969), 260–277. Other more specialized accounts include: Chase C. Mooney and Martha E. Layman, "Some Phases of the Compulsory Military Training Movement, 1914–1920," *Mississippi Valley Historical Review,* XXXVIII (March, 1952), 633–656; George G. Herring, Jr., "James Hay and the Preparedness Controversy, 1915–1916," *Journal of Southern History,* XXX (November, 1964), 383–404; Charles Chatfield, "World War I and the Liberal Pacifist in the United States," *American Historical Review,* LXXV (December, 1970), 1920–1937; Christopher Lasch, *The American Liberals and the Russian Revolution* * (New York, 1962).

CHAPTER 16   *Apotheosis in War*

Hofstadter's discussion of Progressivism and war is from his *Age of Reform,* cited previously. Henry F. May, *The End of American Innocence: A Study of the First Years of Our Own Time, 1912–1917* * (New York, 1959) argues that disillusionment was already widespread before the war. Harry N. Scheiber, *The Wilson Administration and Civil Liberties, 1917–1921* * (Ithaca, N.Y., 1960) is an excellent brief survey and strong indictment.

The background of Europe on the eve of the great war is the subject of a voluminous literature. Barbara W. Tuchman, *The Proud Tower: A Portrait of the World Before the War, 1890–1914* * (New York, 1966) is a brilliant impressionistic work and the source of the quotations from Grey and Noske. A valuable specialized account of German thought is Fritz K. Ringer, *The Decline of the German Mandarins: The German Academic Community, 1890–1933* (Cambridge, Mass., 1969). For Great Britain see: George Dangerfield, *The Strange Death of Liberal England* * (New York, 1935); Samuel J. Hurwitz, *State Intervention in Great Britain: A Study of Economic Control and Social Response, 1914–1919* (New York, 1949); Henry Pelling, *Modern Britain, 1885–1955* * (London, 1960); Bernard Semmel, *Imperialism and Social*

Reform: English Social–Imperial Thought, 1895–1914 * (Cambridge, Mass., 1960). Elie Halevy, *The Rule of Democracy, 1905–1914* (first published in France and England, 1932, 1934; New York, 1952), II, 427, is author of the comment on Lloyd George.

The Socialists' stand in Europe and America is summarized in Merle Fainsod, *International Socialism and the World War* * (Cambridge, Mass., 1935) and Shannon, *The Socialist Party of America,* cited in Chapter 3. James Weinstein, *The Decline of Socialism in America, 1912–1925* * (New York, 1967) denies that it was the war that killed the party. See also his essay, "War as Fulfillment," in *The Corporate Ideal in the Liberal State,* cited in Chapter 6.

Most of John Dewey's wartime essays are conveniently collected in the second volume of his *Character and Events,* edited by Joseph Ratner (New York, 1929). For brief critical studies of Dewey's wartime views, see Ekirch, *The Decline of American Liberalism,* cited in Chapter 1, and Alan Cywar, "John Dewey in World War I: Patriotism and International Progressivism," *American Quarterly,* XXI (Fall, 1969), 578–594.

The best study of the Progressives' support of the war is Hirschfeld, "Nationalist Progressivism and World War I," cited in Chapter 15. Also useful are Christopher Lasch, *The New Radicalism in America, 1889–1963* * (New York, 1965) and Charles Forcey, *Crossroads of Liberalism,* cited in Chapter 10. Walter I. Trattner, "Progressivism and World War I: A Reappraisal," *Mid-America,* XLIV (July, 1963), 131–145, finds relatively few important examples to support his attack on the thesis that the Progressives were prowar. Allen F. Davis, "Welfare, Reform and World War I," *American Quarterly,* XIX (Fall, 1967), 516–533, is a convincing refutation of the Progressives' hope of reform being advanced by the war. N. Gordon Levin, Jr., *Woodrow Wilson and World Politics: America's Response to War and Revolution* * (New York, 1968) is a detailed account of the long-range purposes of Wilson's foreign policy.

Comments that I have used criticizing aspects of the war are taken from: Harold Stearns, *Liberalism in America* (New York, 1919), pp. 102–103; William E. Dodd, *Woodrow Wilson and His Work* (Garden City, N.Y., 1920), pp. 177–178; T. N. Carver, *Military Historian and Economist,* III (April, 1918), 112–127. Randolph Bourne's essays are accessible in the anthologies: *War and the Intellectuals: Essays, 1915–1919,** edited by Carl Resek (New York, 1964); *The World of Randolph Bourne,** edited by Lillian Schlissel (New York, 1965).

Index